A PRESCRIPTION FOR MURDER

The Chicago Series on Sexuality,
History, and Society

Edited by John C. Fout

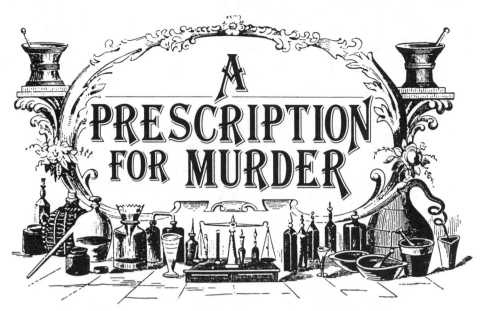

A PRESCRIPTION FOR MURDER

THE VICTORIAN SERIAL KILLINGS OF Dr. Thomas Neill Cream

ANGUS McLAREN

The University of Chicago Press
Chicago and London

The University of Chicago Press, Chicago 60637
The University of Chicago Press, Ltd., London
© 1993 by The University of Chicago
All rights reserved. Published 1993
Paperback edition 1995
Printed in the United States of America

02 01 00 99 98 97 96 95   5 4 3 2

ISBN 0-226-56067-8 (cloth)
ISBN 0-226-56068-6 (paper)

Library of Congress Cataloging-in-Publication Data

McLaren, Angus.
    A prescription for murder : the Victorian serial killings of Dr.
Thomas Neill Cream / Angus McLaren.
        p. cm. — (The Chicago series on sexuality, history, and society)
    Includes bibliographical references and index.
    1. Serial murders—England—London—Case studies. 2. Prostitutes—
England—London—Crimes against—Case studies. 3. Sex role—
England—London—History—19th century. 4. Cream, Thomas Neill,
1850–1892. 5. Murderers—England—London—Biography.
6. Physicians—England—London—Biography. I. Title. II. Series.
HV6535.G6L6564   1993
364.1′523′0942165—dc20   92-20219
                                                                  CIP

CONTENTS

ACKNOWLEDGMENTS

"He sounds like the most geographically energetic of villains." Such was the guarded response made many years ago by an English acquaintance after hearing my brief account of the killer whose career I was trying to trace. Her words have floated back into my memory as I begin to tote up all the help provided by friends and colleagues scattered around the world.

I have many people to thank and only hope I have not forgotten anyone. The book began as a talk delivered in 1981 to the Women and Power Conference at the University of Toronto, where I was given initial encouragement by Mary O'Brien, Sheila Rowbotham, and Ruth Roach Pierson. Although they may well have forgotten by now, Judy Walkowitz in New York, John Beattie in Toronto, and John Gillis at Rutgers over meals and in informal conversations all generously shared with me their insights and findings.

A first draft of the manuscript was read and valuable critiques delivered by Arlene Tigar McLaren in Vancouver, by Brian Dippie on his way to Texas, by Anita Clair Fellman in Virginia, by John McLaren in Victoria, and by Kathy Mezei on Hornby Island. Andrée Lévesque arranged for me to give lectures at McGill University, which allowed time for research in Montreal. Catherine Crawford in Essex and Barbara Brookes in New Zealand sent along useful citations. John Fout, whom I first met in Madrid and who is the editor of the series in which this book appears, was from the start enthusiastically support-

Acknowledgments

ive. Douglas Mitchell and Jennie Lightner in Chicago made the publication process a pleasure.

For efficient assistance I would like to thank the staffs of the interlibrary loan office at the University of Victoria, the Law Library and Woodward Medical Library at the University of British Columbia, the Archives of McGill University, the Wellcome Institute for the History of Medicine, the British Library, the British Library Newspaper Repository at Colindale, and the Public Record Office. At the University of Victoria June Bull and Karen McIvor were at hand to force my computer to disgorge material it had eaten; Colette Hogue and Barbara Coldwell acted as able research assistants. Research trips to England were made possible by the timely support of the Social Sciences and Humanities Research Council of Canada and the University of Victoria.

The thought has crossed my mind that there might have been something in the transient life of this study's central character that attracted my attention. I too live a curiously peripatetic existence. Although the waters between Vancouver Island and the British Columbia mainland are among the most beautiful in the world, I hate to think of how many times I have crossed them. I owe a special debt of gratitude to Brian, Donna, Blake, and Scott Dippie for the generous hospitality they have shown their star boarder. The fact that such a life is not only bearable but actually rewarding is due to Arlene and Jesse.

DRAMATIS PERSONAE

Thomas Neill Cream	Doctor of medicine; 1850–92

The Victims

Flora Eliza Brooks	Marries Cream 11 September 1876; dies 12 August 1877
Kate Gardener	Patient; dies 8 May 1879
Mary Anne Faulkner	Patient; dies 23 August 1880
Ellen Stack	Patient; dies December 1880
Daniel Stott	Patient; dies 14 June 1881
Ellen Donworth	Prostitute; dies 13 October 1891
Matilda Clover	Prostitute; dies 20 October 1891
Emma Shrivell	Prostitute; dies 12 April 1892
Alice Marsh	Prostitute; dies 12 April 1892

The Witnesses

Elizabeth May	Prostitute
Eliza Masters	Prostitute
Lou Harvey	Prostitute

Dramatis Personae

The Police

George Comley	Constable, Lambeth
William Eversfield	Constable, Lambeth
George Harvey	Inspector, Lambeth
John Haynes	Secret agent
Frederick Jarvis	Inspector, C.I.D.
Patrick McIntyre	Sergeant, Special Branch
John Tunbridge	Inspector, C.I.D.
Alfred Ward	Sergeant, Lambeth

INTRODUCTION

In the session papers of the Old Bailey there are strong
facts. Housebreaking is a strong fact; robbery is a strong
fact; and murder is a *mighty* strong fact: but is great praise
due to the historians of these strong facts? No, Sir.

James Boswell, *The Life of Samuel Johnson* (1791)

Murder trials light up the years and give a more precise
sense of period than the reigns of monarchs or the terms
of office of presidents.

Richard Cobb, *A Second Identity* (1969)

The most terrifying aspect of strychnine poisoning is that although
the convulsions are terrible, you do not lose consciousness; in fact, the
mental faculties are largely unimpaired until death ensues. You know
you are dying. The first symptoms are feelings of apprehension and
terror followed by muscle stiffness, twitching of the face, and finally
tetanic convulsions of the entire body. The body relaxes, and then the
spasms strike again. You have a sense of being suffocated. Indeed,
death is actually caused by anoxia—lack of oxygen due to contraction
of the lungs. All the muscles go rigid, and the face and lips turn blue.
Death occurs in one to three hours, the face fixed in a macabre grin
and the body arched in hyperextension.[1] Such ghoulish deaths unfortunately figure centrally in the following study.

Most of my work in the past decade or so has concerned the history of birth, not death. In unearthing the wide variety of fertility control tactics women employed in previous centuries, I was led to conclude that women were not, as some historians have argued, passive victims of biology. There was evidence that they turned to all kinds of herbal and mechanical means to limit births. My approach to history, which stressed the centrality of women's agency, paralleled that of scholars who showed that Victorian prostitutes, as desperate as many of them were, did have some margins of maneuver and often made a "rational" choice in taking to the streets.[2] Given such preoccupations I was understandably struck when, in researching the history of abortion in late-nineteenth-century London, I stumbled upon the case of Thomas Neill Cream, a serial murderer who wielded strychnine as a weapon when preying upon both prostitutes and women seeking to end their pregnancies.

Cream's victims included at least three women in North America and a further four in England. And yet I had never heard of him. But along with countless others I was aware of the many books, plays, and films devoted to the career of Jack the Ripper, who in the same years carried out fewer murders. Why was this? One obvious reason is that the very fact that the Ripper was not identified has never ceased to tantalize the speculative and has led author after author to spin out their own interpretations of his infamous deeds and sordid motives. A second and related reason is that since the Ripper character is a sort of blank slate we can attribute to him the most horrific appetites without having to trouble ourselves with the question of where they came from. In other words, this fixation on the psyche of the mysterious murderer, as understandable as it is, has inevitably resulted in our slighting the culture which produced him. In contrast the dossiers assembled by the authorities when tracking down and trying Cream promised, if carefully employed, to open a window, both into the mind of a murderer and into a remarkable range of intimate aspects of the Victorian age which we would otherwise miss.

But could the Cream affair, a shocking case study, be successfully exploited—that is, capture the flavor of both late Victorian street life and the cultural preoccupations of the age—without itself becoming "exploitative" in unconsciously pandering to prurient interests in sex and violence? The demand for murder mysteries, itself a product of the nineteenth century, has meant that most popular books about real crimes have been unsatisfyingly sensationalized accounts of infamous villains.[3] Serious social historians who have turned to the history of crime to answer "big" questions about changing economic relations dismiss as juvenile the fixation on acts of individualistic violence. The academic who employs criminal records to understand the past, they argue, is best advised to focus primarily on forms of "social crime"—food riots, poaching, and smuggling, for example—which, in revealing the ways in which the disenfranchised masses protested against the laws of the propertied, chronicle otherwise hidden class conflicts.[4]

Do such social histories of crime offer any guidance in understanding homicide? As instructive as many of them are, some often come close to romanticizing the outlaw. If we turn from property crimes to crimes of violence, and in particular to crimes committed by men against women, the assertion that the criminal is in some sense a rebel against the anonymous forces of the law and accordingly deserves our consideration, if not sympathy, rings hollow. Indeed, one's first hunch is that the subject of this study, a serial murderer who killed "deviant" women—prostitutes and those seeking abortions—is likely best understood not so much as an "outlaw" as an "oversocialized" individual who saw himself simply carrying out sentences that society at large leveled against rebellious females.

Accordingly there exists no single study on which I could model this book. Although far more men murder women than women murder men, we do not have any serious historical overview of this phenomenon. Ironically enough, we do have such works as *Victorian Murderesses* that chronicle the far less common case of women having recourse to murderous violence against men.[5] That such studies exist is perhaps not altogether surprising. While we assume misogyny, we have to be taught by murderesses that women harbor deep grievances against men with whom they live. And just as the labor historian must find some obvious satisfaction in producing an account that legitimates the activities of a Robin Hood–like poacher or smuggler, so too the feminist historian is likely to be drawn to cases of desperate women driven in self-defense to murder. Such psychological rewards are not available to those who write about men who murder women.

The investigation of men murdering women appears to promise no surprises; some may have shied away from the topic for the very reason that its study threatens to reinforce the stereotypical view of the aggressive male and the victimized female. In chronicling the grisly career of a serial murderer, one can in fact easily fall into the trap of simply assembling evidence of women carelessly "taking chances" and thereby falling into the clutches of a shrewd villain. This is the very sort of material that fueled the nineteenth-century moralist's message that the women who did not follow respectable norms of behavior were in some way responsible for their own victimization.[6] Left out of these accounts was the acknowledgment that neither the murderer nor his victims acted completely "freely"; he was not particularly bright, and they were not especially gullible. The actions of both were determined largely by the society that produced them. The murderer in this study was, as we shall see, only able to prey on the sorts of women whom the larger community, in depriving them of security, respect, and safe options, had already placed in jeopardy.

What do we mean by "serial murderer?" The term was coined relatively recently to describe the individual who over a period of time coldly tracks down and kills victim after victim, as opposed to the "mass murderer," who in one bloody outburst kills two or more victims. The serial murderer is almost by definition a white male who kills white females.[7] He usually kills women, current researchers tell us, because he views them as sinful. Such murderers take the fact that their victims accept their offers of friendship as a sign of their guilt.[8] The psychological profile drawn of the twentieth-century sex murderer—a man with a distant, punitive father and close but cloying mother, vain, sensitive, attracted to pornography and cruelty, rational but emotionally dead, outwardly conventional but inwardly enraged— sounds a good deal like Cream.[9] But that still does not tell us very much. There are many such men, but they do not all become killers. The preoccupation with the question of psychological motivation and the slighting of social context continues to be the most glaring weakness of studies of serial murder.[10] "What we need," an expert in the field has pointed out, "are accounts of the victims, their changing environments, and the police attitudes that decide on the priorities in cases of murder or suspicious disappearance. We need to study the complex ecology that links 'predator' and 'prey.'"[11] Our study, in investigating the significance of sexual tensions in the late nineteenth century, provides just such an overview.

The use of the term "prey" can, however, be misleading. That women in past ages led constrained lives and were often the victims of the unbridled power of males has become a commonplace. But historical accounts which portray women only as victims, and thereby deprive them of individuality, at worst are patronizing and at best provide no more than a partial view of gender relations. The most creative scholars in women's history have successfully demonstrated that by recognizing the margins of maneuver available to even the most humble women and the variety of ways in which they tried to fashion their lives, a fuller and more believable picture of male-female relationships can be obtained.[12] A careful reading of the evidence shows that, although the police and the courts chose to present the women in the following murder case simply as victims, these women in fact played crucial roles in tracking down and convicting the killer.

The first part of this study provides a narrative account of the murders, the tracking down of the suspect, and his trial and execution. The murderous activities chronicled in part 1, though horrific, are in part 2 shown to be a product of their epoch. The central argument of this analytical portion of the book is that an investigation of the linkages of crime and respectability casts a lurid light upon many aspects of late-nineteenth-century society that might otherwise escape detection. Historically, the serial killer appears to have emerged in the nineteenth century. Why? Why were doctors associated, at least in the public mind, with such crimes? Were changing patterns of violence and sexual activity linked? Why did the sending of blackmail letters, elicited by new sexual sensitivities, erupt in the 1880s? What was it about the relations of doctor and patient, client and prostitute, police and suspect, male and female that seemed to suggest that they were all going through similar transformations at the turn of the century? A close examination of one murderer and his subsequent trial, by helping to recast the way in which we view the last decades of the nineteenth century, provides some unexpected answers.

PART ONE: THE CRIMES

Where lewdness leads to murder, and ends in hanging, the disease and medicine go together.

Saturday Review (1858)

1

THE TIME AND PLACE

London is the epitome of our times, and the Rome of
today.

R. W. Emerson, *English Traits* (1856)

The mention of nineteenth-century, working-class London immediately conjures up the images of the bustling streets and crowded rookeries of the eastern parishes—Stepney, Shoreditch, and Whitechapel. Nineteenth-century social investigators were, and twentieth-century social historians still are, attracted by East London's colorful history—the tragic fate of its impoverished Huguenot silk weavers in the early 1800s, the waves of Jewish and East European immigrants it greeted in the last decades of the century, its political radicalism and, last but not least, the notoriety created in 1888 by Jack the Ripper's horrific murders.[1] In contrast, the flat lands of South London are commonly represented as both topographically and culturally insignificant. But dingy, nineteenth-century Lambeth, little more than a stone's throw across the river from the glittering spires of Westminster, offers a particularly striking portrayal of the ways in which a working-class community accommodated itself to the social disruptions wrought by the nineteenth century.

The lowlands on the south bank of the Thames were—as names like Lower Marsh Street still indicate—long susceptible to flooding.[2] In the early 1800s the area known as Lambeth Marsh and St. George's

Thomas Neill Cream's London. From Walter Besant, *The Thames* (London: A. & C. Black, 1903).

Fields was dotted with orchards, nurseries, ponds, and ditches. The cheapness of real estate—much of it held by the archbishop of Canterbury—prompted many charitable institutions, including Bethlehem Hospital (or "Bedlam"), the School for the Indigent Blind, the Fishmonger's Almshouses, and the Magdalen Hospital, to build there. Some potteries and timber yards were in operation, but there was otherwise little local industry. Until the 1830s the Thames fishermen found few competitors for space on the Lambeth riverbank and were only gradually driven out by the growth of wharves and warehouses, lumberyards and varnish factories.

The extension of the South Western Railway from Nine Elms into Lambeth in 1848 dramatically changed what had been a sleepy backwater parish. The Waterloo Bridge, built between 1811 and 1817, had already laid the basis for Lambeth's subservient role as the southern approach to the metropolis. The construction of Waterloo Station on the site of what had once been a pleasure garden at the bridge's southern end permitted the disgorging into Lambeth each morning of thousands of commuters who then made their way over the river and into the city. "Over the remainder of the century Waterloo grew into a hideous labyrinth of wooden sheds covering odd groups of platforms with a locomotive depot in their midst."[3]

Gangs of navvies spent much of the later 1800s tearing down Lambeth's modest homes and cottages to prepare tunnels and cuttings for the approaches to Waterloo Station and to the Hungerford Railway Bridge, which took trains straight in to Charing Cross. In their wake there was little of architectural interest aside from viaducts and gasworks left to attract the eye. The major charitable institutions moved to more distant suburbs. The remaining housing stocks deteriorated. Streets like Lambeth Walk and Union Street were very rough, the ironically named Paradise Street being one of the poorest in the parish. A workhouse was established on Chester Street and a police court and poorhouse on Renfrew Road. Lambeth, a country backwater in the late eighteenth century, had declined by the mid-nineteenth century into an urban slum.

Waterloo Station and its neighbor, the red brick Royal Hospital for Children founded in 1816, were the most imposing buildings in the community. York Road, a street of eating houses and small hotels harboring unemployed actors and prostitutes, led west from the station parallel to the Thames, to St. Thomas's Hospital. Founded in 1552 the hospital, enclosing nine acres with eight pavilions, was newly rebuilt in 1871 and protected from flooding by the Albert Embankment. Lambeth Palace Road led further along the river from

St. Thomas's to Lambeth Palace, London residence of the archbishop of Canterbury, acknowledged as the only picturesque site on the south bank.[4]

The destruction of old Lambeth by the coming of the railway led to significant population shifts.[5] Between 1845 and 1848 over seven hundred homes were destroyed.[6] Whatever middle-class breadwinners the parish once sheltered retreated further south to neighborhoods like Clapham, Stockwell, or Brixton and made their way each morning into the city by omnibus and later, tram. But they were replaced by impoverished newcomers moving into Lambeth who had in turn been driven out of more prosperous neighborhoods north of the river. The poor of Chelsea, whose cottages were demolished to make way for more substantial middle-class housing, flooded into the district.[7]

Lambeth increased in population, but its cheap terraced housing, thrown together in the early 1800s, and its warren of narrow streets decayed as the century progressed.[8] The growth of Waterloo Station and the network of lines and cuttings leading to it exacerbated the housing crisis. Large families paid high rents—higher per square foot than those paid in the West End—for the most sordid accommodations.[9] Unscrupulous landlords rented out damp cellars and subdivided two-room tenements. The homes found in Gun Street, where up to ten people lived in two rooms, were not necessarily the worst.[10] In 1876 a woman was charged with letting out to a family with five children and two sewing machines one room which had not been disinfected after smallpox.[11]

Lambeth's streets smelled of fish shops, jam factories, and hop yards—the smells of the slum.[12] Charles Booth, who studied the area in the 1890s, described its narrow streets and damp courts as harboring "poverty, dirt and sin." The sidewalks were clogged with swarms of "dirty and often sore-eyed" children hovered over by mothers in filthy trailing skirts and shawls.[13] The Women's University Settlement workers claimed to have uncovered evidence of high levels of degeneration and feeblemindedness in the parish; there was no doubt that physical ill health was widespread. "How," asked one sympathetic observer, "does a Lambeth working man's wife with four children manage on a pound a week?"[14] Bread, margarine, and tea had to form the basis of most meals. Meat sold in Lambeth Walk on Sunday was not fit for sale on Monday. Milk was adulterated or, if purchased by the tin, devoid of vitamins. Children died in great numbers of diarrhea and measles. Lambeth's infant mortality rate was 205 per 1,000 whereas it was 167 per 1,000 for the whole of London; the parish's overall mortality rate was 27.7 per 1,000 as compared to 19.3 for the metropolis.[15] Because of the sense of shame conjured up in the working-class household by a pauper's funeral, burial insurance was always paid, even when other sacrifices had to be made. Weddings and christenings were far less important.

Sixty-three Lambeth women who in the autumn of 1891 gave birth to babies were attended by a young obstetric clerk who had just begun his studies at St. Thomas's; his name was Somerset Maugham. Years later he recalled the experiences that provided the basis of his first novel, *Liza of Lambeth* (1897).

> The messenger led you through the dark and silent streets of Lambeth, up stinking alleys and into sinister courts where the police hesitated to penetrate, but where your black bag protected you from harm. You were taken to grim houses, on each floor of which a couple of families lived, and shown into a stuffy room, ill-lit with a paraffin lamp, in which two or three women, the midwife, the mother, the "lady as lives on the floor below" were standing round the bed on which the patient lay.[16]

Such wives and mothers, engaged in an endless battle against dirt, disease, and vermin, were likely to have lost their looks by the age of thirty.

Philanthropists could think of no easy way to improve such abject living conditions; simple giving, the Charity Organization Society primly warned, was not the answer because in Lambeth it resulted in a "deplorable . . . spirit of expectancy."[17] Nevertheless, the Salvation Army opened a soup kitchen off Blackfriars Road.[18] Church missions complete with brass bands sought to make converts and arouse backsliders.[19] The lecturers of the Social Democratic Federation preached the need for revolution.[20] All were disappointed at the apathy they encountered. Socialists, settlement workers, and missionaries put it down to Lambeth's lack of social cohesion. The parish could boast of few successful clubs or societies. Drinking and betting, to the dismay of middle-class observers, appeared to be the most popular pastimes of the common laborer.

The notion that Lambeth did not have a solid core of respectable working-class households was not a figment of the middle-class imagination. The engineering firms that in the early 1800s had taken advantage of the cheap land and easy access to river transport to establish themselves along the Thames, in the latter half of the century found it more profitable to move on to the north of England.[21] The breweries and vinegar makers, the potteries and the great gasworks provided regular work, but much of the population remained underemployed and transient. The local builders, clothiers, furriers, and hatters needed few skilled workers. The mass of the male laboring population was unskilled and accordingly poorly paid. Railway workers and navvies were, of course, much in evidence. The station in turn drew hoards of cabmen who, for a five shilling license fee, could describe themselves as "self-employed." In reality, there were far too many competitors in the trade; the cabmen who made their home in the area west of Blackfriars Road lived in endemic poverty.[22]

Ironically, the coming of the railway increased rather than diminished the demand for horse-drawn vehicles. In addition to the laborers burned at the gasworks, cut by chisels, maimed by pottery machinery, or crushed on the docks, St. Thomas's continued to receive a steady stream of pedestrians bitten by horses or run over by vans. Lighter loads were pushed by handcarts. Lambeth was home to many of London's costermongers—known for their easy-come, easy-go view of life—who were self-recruited from what was close to a hereditary caste. Some traded in the area's two largest markets at New-Cut Lambeth and Lambeth Walk. Most costers retailed across London—in addition to fruits and vegetables—meat and fish, drapery and haberdashery, iron- and tinware, furniture and upholstery, crockery and glass, fine goods and ornaments, books and papers, flowers and roots, photographs and paraffin. Lambeth did not have as many European immigrants as Whitechapel, but by the 1890s Russian and Polish Jews added to the number of the parish's force of casual laborers. And finally there were the hoards of working children who, by pushing carts, selling newspapers, delivering milk, and performing a host of other small jobs, added their mite to the family income.

Charles Booth characterized South London as "invertebrate."[23] By this he meant that the area had little in the way of secure industrial employment. Its workers depended largely on wages earned across the river, many having to walk miles to work. The Westminster, Waterloo, and Blackfriars Bridges were so clogged with pedestrians, cabs, and costers moving north in the morning and south at night that it was next to impossible to move against this tide of humanity.[24]

Lambeth was a tough district, though perhaps not as bad as Whitechapel. Cecil Chapman, who was appointed a police court magistrate in the mid-1890s, recalled that the district was "notorious for the number of charges for drunkenness on Monday mornings." Chapman initially found it as difficult to communicate with the police as with their prisoners.

> It was very usual for a policeman to tell me of a woman charged with drunkenness that when he first saw her she was "laying upon the pavement." I always murmured "lying you mean," but generally without effect, unless it was to create some confusion as to the prisoner having spoken falsely.[25]

Daily reports of fights in the streets and overturned costers' carts filled the columns of the local newspapers. The intercession of the police, whose duties necessarily included the harassment of unlicensed cabmen and itinerant traders, was rarely sought; "the hatred of a costermonger to a 'peeler,'" reported Henry Mayhew, "is intense."[26] Frederick Porter Wensley ruefully remembered years later that as a fresh-faced, twenty-three-year-old constable transferred into "L Division" (Lambeth) in 1887 he made the mistake of trying single-handedly to break up a street fight. The combatants proved true to the "Lambeth Code" in uniting against the bobby and throwing him through a plate glass window.[27] That locals were used to such disturbances was made plain to a middle-class observer when he asked a woman why, hearing a cry for help in the streets, she failed to respond. "'Lor' love yer, sir!' was the reply, 'if we was to get out o' bed every time we 'eard murder shouted in this 'ouse we'd be 'oppin in and out all night.'"[28] Women were not immune from this world of violence. In April 1892 a man in the York Road stabbed his wife and daughter before taking his own life with a razor. A more typical case of wife abuse took place a week later when a drunken laborer returned home at 2:00 A.M., insisting that his wife get up and prepare dinner. When she was slow in responding, he threw her in her night clothes into the street and assaulted both her and Police Constable 250L, who intervened.[29] On Sunday, the busiest day in the streets, middle-class observers were shocked to see the number of women hurrying home from market, their aprons full of provisions, who sported faces bruised or blackened as a result of a Saturday night bout of drunkenness.

What gaiety there was in Lambeth was found largely in its pubs and music halls. In some areas there were forty to fifty drinking establishments within a quarter-mile radius. Moreover, Lambeth could pride itself on being the home of the musical hall. Charles Morton's Canterbury Music Hall, which opened in 1849 in Royal Street, was England's first. In 1891 for as little as four pence one could see everything from ventriloquists to Lockhart's Elephants. Gatti's Music Hall, at 214 Westminster Bridge Road, was built in 1862. South of Waterloo

Station stood Victoria Hall, once a great theater but in decline for most of the nineteenth century. Tragedy struck in 1858 when a false fire alarm resulted in a crush causing fifteen deaths. The Vic was closed in 1871 and was taken for a time by the Salvation Army. By the end of the century it was used for "penny science lectures, cheap opera, and concerts."[30] The Vic in the 1890s enjoyed a doubtful reputation as a theater where the crowd drank ginger beer, munched cracked nuts, and threw oranges and apples at unsuccessful acts. Cheap melodramas with titles like *Innocent or Guilty, Charlie Wagg, or the Mysteries of London,* and *The Hand of Death* were standard fare.

The adventuresome could cross the bridges to sample the shows put on in the music halls between Piccadilly and the Strand. The Strand was London's most theatrical street, boasting the Savoy, Terry's, and the Tivoli on its south side and the Adelphi, Vaudeville, the Gaiety, and the Olympic on the north. The six arc lights set up outside the Gaiety in August 1878 introduced the English public to electric lighting.[31] Gatti's Royal Adelaide was just off the Strand on Villiers Street, and there was also a string of Gatti Tea Shops that flourished until the advent of Lyons' Tea Shops in the mid-1890s. The more affluent might visit a first-class music hall like the St. James Hall at Piccadilly to see the *Jockey's Clog Dance,* the *Darkies' Courtship,* and *Dietz's New Tyrolian Dance* or the Oxford Theater at St. Giles Circus, where in the 1890s Vesta Tilley and Dan Leno topped the bill and the young Marie Lloyd made her name as much by the high kicks that revealed her amber silk drawers as by her coy rendition of "Oh, Mister Porter." The Oxford, opened in 1861 by Charles Morton where Tottenham Court Road meets Oxford Street, was opulently rebuilt in 1892. More exotic shows such as *Rivalli, the Fire-Proof Prince* and *Paula, the Reptile Conqueror* were found at the Royal Aquarium. The Alhambra and the Empire were best known for their "promenades," the open parading of prostitutes during the intervals, which Mrs. Ormiston Chant and her followers (dubbed by the press "Prudes on the Prowl") sought to end.[32]

Those who could not afford the price of a music hall ticket could always find some entertainment in the streets of Lambeth—a funeral, a fire, an epileptic fit, or coronet playing. According to Mayhew the public inevitably gave a few pennies to the musician who was either talented or severely handicapped.[33] Bobbies spent much of their time asking street buskers and organ grinders to move along. Readers of *Lloyd's Weekly* were informed in April 1892 that three Frenchmen who were slow to understand that they and their performing bears were obstructing a public thoroughfare found themselves in Lambeth Court. "The bears were placed in the dock with the defendants," reported the press. "The animals displayed a restless desire to go on with their performance."[34]

The artists, actors, musicians, and agents who staffed London's halls and theaters were but one more colorful segment of Lambeth's transient population. South of the river the cheap lodgings found in sordid Stamford Street served as the home base for music hall agents and artists. "Misery Junction" was the name out-of-work actors gave Stamford Street and the adjoining area around Waterloo Station "noisy with omnibuses, trams, cabs and heavy vans."[35] The pursuit of a life on the stage had its particular risks. John Gardiner and Louis Goldstein ran the Theatrical and Music Hall World at 165 Stamford Street where, the press revealed, unwary young women in search of music instruction were both defrauded and sexually assaulted.[36]

The theaters and music halls in turn attracted many prostitutes; the risqué referred to the district as "Whoreterloo."[37] The eighteenth-century pleasure ground through which the approaches to Waterloo Bridge were carved had been appropriately dubbed "Cupid's Garden."[38] In St. George's Field a "Magdalen Hospital" was established as early as 1758. It had, a benefactor claimed, "restored a great number of unfortunate young women to their afflicted parents and friends, to honest industry, to virtue and happiness."[39] Although the hospital was later moved to Streatham, prostitution remained a very visible aspect of late-nineteenth-century Lambeth street life. "Prostitutes of the Waterloo Road," reported the *Weekly Dispatch* of 1840, "used rough music and hot pokers to resist attempts by the policemen and respectable inhabitants to suppress their trade."[40] All of this took place just a few minutes' walk from the House of Commons.

Thomas Hood's 1844 poem, "The Bridge of Sighs," crystallized the middle-class notion of Waterloo Bridge, linking sordid Lambeth with opulent Westminster, as being the most likely edifice in London from which repentant prostitutes seeking a watery grave would leap.

> Alas! for the rarity
> Of Christian charity
> Under the sun!
> Oh! it was pitiful!
> Near the whole city full,
> Home she had none!
> Picture it—think of it,
> Dissolute man![41]

Despite his poem's maudlin excesses, Hood usefully reminded his readers that the bridge's nine austere arches of Cornish granite drew the inhabitants of the slums south of the river and those of the heart of respectable London into a surprisingly close proximity.

Of the female trades plied in the most impoverished parts of South London, streetwalking obviously held an important place. The few jobs available to women—as domestics, as fur pullers, or as operatives in jam, pickle, or sweet factories—hardly provided appealing alternatives. Moreover, it was to be expected that prostitutes, using cabmen to make contacts, would be found in the neighborhood of a major railway station and of the nearby pubs and music halls. The prostitutes formed an integral part of the shifting community of cabmen, costers, and unemployed actors finding housing in the same cheap hotels and sordid rooming houses. And just as the costermongers lived in the shabby tenements of Lambeth but picked up their wares in Convent Garden and Billingsgate and then sought their trade across London, so too the Lambeth prostitutes spread their net wide. Booth described the women of one such Lambeth street. "In the foreground is Stamford Street, still much frequented by a rather low, though not by many degrees the lowest class of prostitutes, whose clients seek them here, but who, if ambitious, extend the field of their operations as far as Piccadilly Circus."[42] When the pickings in Lambeth were slim, the women "on the game" would in the early evening make their way via Waterloo Bridge to the music halls and pubs of Piccadilly, the Strand, and Fleet Street seeking custom. Hours later, as the journalist James Greenwood, accompanied by a constable with a "bull's-eye" lamp discovered on a wet night in the mid-1870s, streams of young women, their narrow shoulders draped in thin shawls, could be encountered tramping back across the bridge to South London. At one or two in the morning one was astounded by

> the amazing number of wretched girls and women who come hurrying from the Strand side of the bridge, and, with an aspect exactly as opposite to "gay" as black is to white, making haste, through the rain which had saturated their flimsy skirts and covered the pavement with a thick paste of mud, cruelly cold to ill-shod feet, towards the miserable "lodgings" in the poorer neighbourhoods of Lambeth and Blackfriars which were dignified with the name of home.[43]

Greenwood, true to the convention of portraying the abject nature of prostitutes' lives, contrasted the "drooping feathers and festoons of rainbow ribbon with which their hats were trimmed" to their "pinched and haggard faces." But many returned singing a song—in 1891 it would undoubtedly have been "Ta-ra-ra-boom-de-ay," which Miss Lottie Collins had made wildly popular—in anticipation of the steaming coffee sold for a penny and the noisy companionship found at a snug stall at the Lambeth side of the bridge. The lucky might have met a generous client. The unlucky might have found death.

2

THE MURDERS

My homicidal maniac is of a peculiar kind. I shall have to invent a new classification for him, and call him a zoopha-gous (life-eating) maniac; what he desires is to absorb as many lives as he can, and has laid himself out to achieve it in a cumulative way.

Bram Stoker, *Dracula* (1897)

On the rainy evening of Tuesday, 6 October 1891, a Lambeth prosti-tute by the name of Eliza Masters, who had made her way into the city, encountered a client at Ludgate Circus, just west of St. Paul's cathedral.[1] He wore a dark mackintosh and a flat-topped felt hat. The pair first went to a pub and then back across the river to her lodgings in South London at 9 Orient Buildings, Hercules Road, just off Lam-beth Road. The well-dressed man told Masters he once had been a medical student at nearby St. Thomas's Hospital and had recently re-turned from North America to finalize an inheritance. He showed her pictures of his mother and brother. He was mustachioed, balding, and heavily built, but Masters was most struck by his squint, accentu-ated rather than attenuated by his gold-rimmed spectacles.

After a time Eliza Masters and her companion left her room at the Orient Buildings and made for the tawdry splendor of Gatti's Music Hall a few streets away behind Waterloo Station on the left side of Westminster Bridge Road. There at the bar they met and had a drink with Elizabeth May, a friend of Masters', who also lodged in the Orient Buildings. All three ended the evening by returning by hansom cab to Ludgate Circus, where they had a last drink at the King Lud Public House. The man said he had not yet settled in London but was staying at Anderton's Hotel in Fleet Street. Before the little party broke up at Ludgate Hill, he promised Masters, once he had found lodgings, to write to arrange another meeting.

On the morning of Friday, October 9, Eliza Masters received the man's note saying he would come to see her that afternoon between three and five and asking her not to be as cross as she was at their first meeting. He also made the unusual request that his letter be kept and returned to him. It was postmarked Lambeth. May and Masters, obviously relishing the idea of another night out with the free-spending gentleman, waited that afternoon by the window looking into the street for their visitor. But he no sooner appeared than his eye was caught by yet another prostitute that he began to follow. Masters and May knew her as a neighbor, though not by name. The young woman was wearing a hat over her long dark brown hair and a white apron with shoulder straps, and was carrying a basket. Overcome by either curiosity or rivalry, the two women put on their hats and followed the couple to a house at 27 Lambeth Road, a few steps from the Masons' Arms pub. The smiling woman stopped at the door, and she and the man went in. Neither reappeared; after having lingered on in the street for a half hour, Masters and May returned disappointed to Hercules Road. Weeks later Elizabeth May passed the man, but he did not notice her. Eliza Masters, as instructed, dutifully kept his letter for a month or so more, but eventually destroyed it.[2]

Ellen Donworth, a nineteen-year-old prostitute, lived a few streets over from Masters and May at 8 Duke Street, off Commercial Road. According to her father, a laborer, "She was a prudent girl at the time she left home." But she had soon grown tired of working at Vauxhall labeling bottles and took to a life on the streets. On 13 October Ellen received a letter and told Annie Clements, a charwoman living in the same building, that she was going out between six and seven in the evening to meet a gentleman at the York Hotel on the Waterloo Road.[3] She said she expected to hear from him on a regular basis. After having dinner with Ernest Linnell, the soldier with whom she lived, and a drink with a friend at the Lord Hill Public House, she went off to her rendezvous.[4]

At about seven o'clock Constance Linfield noticed her friend "Nellie" and a stranger with a peculiar look in his eye emerge from a darkened court.[5] A few minutes later James Styles, a costermonger standing at the entrance to the Wellington Public House, saw Donworth, now alone, supporting herself with some difficulty, as though drunk, against a wall in Morpeth Place next to the Artisan's Dining-Room and Coffee House. Suddenly she fell face-down into the street. "Someone has given me a drink. Take me home," she begged.[6] Styles picked her up and with the assistance of a man called Adams helped the young woman, now writhing in pain, back to Duke Street. Her landlady at first took her trembling and twitching for signs of excessive drinking. But in between her bouts of agonizing convulsions Ellen Donworth was able to mumble, "A tall gentleman with cross eyes, a silk hat, and bushy whiskers gave me a drink twice out of a bottle with white stuff in it." Little attention was initially paid to her ravings.

Linnell was fetched from the Canterbury Public House at eight thirty. By the time John Johnson, one of Dr. Lowe's assistants from the South Lambeth Medical Institute, arrived at Duke Street Ellen Donworth was undergoing spasmodic convulsions that were so violent that several people had difficulty holding her down. Johnson recognized them as tetanic convulsions that could only be caused by a poison like strychnine. The police were called. Between her attacks Donworth told Inspector George Harvey of L Division that she had received two letters from a tall, cross-eyed man who, when they had met earlier that evening, had requested their return. She repeated her statement that he had given her "stuff" and begged, "Let me die at home, don't leave me, doctor."[7] At nine o'clock she was rushed to St. Thomas's. She was dead before she arrived. The postmortem carried out on 15 October by Thomas Herbert revealed in her stomach's contents large amounts of strychnine.[8]

A week later, on October 20, Matilda Clover, the twenty-seven-year-old pockmarked, brown-eyed young woman with slightly projecting front teeth whom Masters and May had followed with her male friend to 27 Lambeth Road, suffered an equally agonizing death. Clover had often shared her two rooms on the second floor with a man known as "Fred," the father of her two-year-old child, but four weeks earlier they had quarreled and he had decamped. Once he left she was distraught but had to go out more often at night to make ends meet.[9] Clover, recollected a servant in the house, "was in the habit of bringing men to 27; it is four doors from the Masons' Arms." Although the landlady feigned ignorance, it appeared that other women who had lodged in the house had also worked the streets.

"Clover was very much given to drink," her landlady reported, "and just before the 20th she had been drinking very heavily. She had about eleven shillings worth of brandy in one day about eight days before she died."[10] "She gave way to drink," concurred an acquaintance; "her eyes were very red and swollen when she had been drinking."[11] Drink was blamed by many middle-class observers for leading women into prostitution, but one sympathetic investigator who actually questioned women like Clover concluded that the "life" led to drink, not the other way around. "We could not go out if we didn't drink," he was told. "We must drink, and that is how we get a taste for it."[12]

As was the custom among the poor, Matilda Clover had purchased the right to rudimentary medical services by paying a few pennies a week to a society that retained for its members a physician. For the previous fortnight she had been seeking treatment for her alcoholism from Dr. Robert Graham, her "club doctor." On 19 October, Graham prescribed a bromide of potassium to counter the ravages caused by her bouts of drinking.[13]

The same day that Matilda Clover saw Dr. Graham, Lucy Rose, a newly employed twenty-one-year-old servant at 27 Lambeth Road, found a letter in Clover's room that read:

> Miss Clover, meet me outside the Canterbury at 7:30 if you can come clean and sober. Do you remember the night I bought you your boots? You were so drunk that you could not speak to me. Please bring this paper and envelope with you.
>
> Yours,
>
> Fred[14]

On the evening of 20 October Matilda Clover left 27 Lambeth Road for the Canterbury Music Hall. Coming up Westminster Bridge Road, the Canterbury was on Clover's right under the railway bridge leading to Waterloo Station and about two hundred yards from Gatti's Music Hall. Clover returned home that night with a male companion. Lucy Rose let them in and in the glow of the small paraffin light in the hall noticed the man's broad frame, heavy moustache, and tall silk hat. Clover went out to fetch two Bass ales while her caller made up some pills for her. When the man finally left, Clover called out, "Goodnight, Fred." An hour later, some time before ten, Clover left the house again, asking Lucy Rose to listen for her child. Mrs. Vowles, the landlady, went upstairs to her own room to await her husband, a cabman who seldom returned before midnight. The house fell silent. No one knew exactly when Clover returned, but toward three in the morning Mrs. Vowles and Lucy Rose were awakened by her screams from the second floor. They found her stretched across her bed writhing in agony, her back arched and head jammed between the bedstead and the wall. Between spasms she whimpered, "That man Fred has poisoned me . . . He gave me some pills." [15]

Matilda Clover's fits went on for the rest of the night. She said she felt that something was stuck in her throat and she was being suffocated. She was given tea and milk but could keep nothing down. At one point, bathed in perspiration, she said she thought she was going to die and asked to see her baby. Mrs. Vowles sent for Dr. Graham; he did not come. Not until seven o'clock in the morning did Francis Coppin, the unqualified assistant of Dr. McCarthy, appear. Lucy Rose told Coppin about the pills, but he attributed Clover's twitches, vomiting, and convulsions to alcoholic poisoning, provided some medicine, and, despite her shrieks of agony, quickly left. The medicine only made Clover worse. Her face turned black, and Coppin was sent for again. He did not come. Lucy Rose, although terrified, stayed on alone with Clover until a final convulsion ended her frightful struggle at about nine that morning. [16]

Matilda Clover's uncle, Robert Taylor, a Southwark brass finisher who came by that morning, was shocked to hear that his niece was dead. He thought it was strange for "a young girl like that to go off so suddenly" but accepted the story that she had died of drink. [17] At noon Dr. Graham—who did not examine Clover but simply had her symptoms described to him by Mrs. Vowles—signed a death certificate stating that "to the best of my knowledge and belief the cause of her [Clover's] death was, primarily, delirium tremens; secondly syncope." [18] No autopsy was carried out; on 27 October Matilda Clover was buried, another presumed victim of alcoholism, in a pauper's grave, number 22154, in Tooting Cemetery. "Just before her death she was wearing a brand new pair of boots." Lucy Rose later recalled that the boots had been purchased at Lilley's on Westminster Bridge Road. "They were pawned the day after her death." [19] Matilda Clover's baby was placed up for adoption in the local workhouse. [20]

Mrs. Vowles, Matilda Clover's landlady, considered the death a tragedy that touched her in a special way. "Her rooms were not let again for months after her death . . . My rooms used not to be long empty, but since her death I have not let so well. I don't remember how long it was after her death before a lodger came; it was a long time." [21]

The day after Matilda Clover's death the killer struck again. A little after midnight on 22 October, outside St. James Hall just off Piccadilly, a man dressed in a black suit and overcoat came up to a prostitute known as Lou Harvey, touched her on the shoulder, and asked her to go with him. They had eyed each other earlier in the evening at the Alhambra Theater, where unescorted young women promenaded under a sky blue dome and arches of Moorish fretwork. The man spoke with an accent and joked that Lou should return to America with him. They did not go to her lodgings in St. John's Wood but stayed the night at the Palace Hotel on Garrick Street. The next morning Lou Harvey was pleased to hear that the gentleman, who said he was a doctor at St. Thomas's Hospital, wanted to see her again, though she was a bit taken aback by his saying that he would bring her some pills to improve her complexion.

They met the next night as arranged on the Thames Embankment near Charing Cross and went for a drink. At the Northumberland Public House the man bought Lou Harvey a glass of wine and she asked if she should take the pills first. "No, not till afterwards," he replied. Harvey then said she would like some roses that a woman was selling in the pub. "Yes, certainly; you shall have your wish," replied the doctor, who bought the flowers and led Harvey back to the darkened Embankment.

In the lamplight the doctor took two pills from his waistcoat pocket and gave them to Lou Harvey along with some figs that she was to eat. She was reluctant to swallow the capsules, but he was insistent. Finally satisfied that she had taken them, he suddenly announced he could not accompany her, as planned, to the Oxford Music Hall; he had to return to St. Thomas's Hospital. He gave her five shillings for cab fare and a ticket to the performance, promised to meet her at 11:00 P.M., and walked quickly away toward Westminster Bridge.[22] He must have imagined that they would never meet again, but fate dictated otherwise.

St. John's Wood, where Lou Harvey had a temporary abode, enjoyed in the late nineteenth century the dubious distinction of being a neighborhood in which wealthy London men kept their mistresses. In 1888 Prince George (the future George V) wrote in his diary that it was there that he had shared with Prince Eddy, his elder brother, a young woman's favors. "She is," he privately confided, "a ripper."[23] The vacuous Prince Eddy, named in 1890 the duke of Clarence, was not to enjoy such pleasures for long. In January of 1892 he suddenly came down with influenza and died within a few days.

The winter was unusually severe. As late as April 1892 snowstorms hit the south coast knocking down telegraph poles that blocked the

London-to-Chatham rail line. The grieving prince of Wales and his family took up residence in the south of France. Prince George, shocked by the death of his brother and himself recovering from typhoid, was put under the care of Dr. Broadbent, an eminent heart specialist.[24] In the popular press the number of column inches devoted by journalists to the sojourns of the royal family in continental health spas was only rivaled by those devoted to the most sensational of London slum murders.

A few hundred feet up Lambeth Road from where Matilda Clover died lies St. George's Circus. Waterloo Road and Blackfriars Road radiate out from it, leading one back either northwest or due north to the Thames. The last major street before the river is dreary Stamford Street, which runs parallel to the south bank of the Thames between the Waterloo and Blackfriars Bridges. "Stamford Street," sniffed a contemporary chronicler, "is one of the ugliest and most sordid streets in London. It is full of dirty so-called hotels and disreputable apartment houses, and is the headquarters of theatrical and music hall agents."[25] At 118 Stamford Street, in the spring of 1892—six months after Clover's death—lived two young women, Alice Marsh, twenty-one, and Emma Shrivell, eighteen, who had recently come up to London from Brighton.

Their landlady, Charlotte Vogt, accepted unblinkingly their assertion that they were actresses waiting for a theatrical engagement.[26] Without having read George Bernard Shaw, she no doubt shared the view that there were some women who were "actresses in a highly technical sense of that word."[27] Mary Eden Matthews, an acquaintance of Alice and Emma's, later recalled that they had lived in London two years before. She did not know precisely how they made their living, but she could make a good guess. Their families had little with which to assist them. The father of Alice Marsh (whose real name was Burgess) was dead, and her mother's second husband was a paperhanger named Waller. Emma Shrivell was also from a broken home. Her mother, who had been a midwife, was dead; her father, Henry Washer, made a modest living as a fish hawker. Emma's most prosperous relative was an uncle who kept the Star Tavern in Brighton. Alice and Emma worked for a time in a biscuit factory but finally decided to try their luck in London. Emma told her aunt that she had pawned her possessions to go up to the city; she did not say she and Alice were going there to work the streets.[28]

The two young women appeared to have given some thought to taking a businesslike approach to their new life. They had slips of paper made up that read:

Miss Marsh and Miss Shrivell
118 Stamford St.
Please ring middle bell.[29]

They had separate rooms on the second floor where, in April 1892, they entertained a new friend known as "Fred," a thickset, balding man with glasses who claimed to be a doctor. On the night of 11 April he shared with them a dinner of beer and canned salmon and gave each of them three long pills. He left at about two in the morning.

At two thirty Mrs. Vogt was awakened by screams. She found Alice in her nightshirt in the hallway foaming at the mouth and Emma writhing in great pain in her room crying for Alice. "Do you think we are poisoned?" Shrivell asked her landlady and described the visitor. When Mrs. Vogt marveled that they had been so foolish as to take medicine from someone they did not know, Emma Shrivell made the pathetic reply, "He is not a stranger; he is a doctor."[30]

Both women's bodies twitched uncontrollably. Mrs. Vogt gave them an emetic of mustard and water and sent her husband for help. The police arrived and rushed the women to St. Thomas's. Alice Marsh died on the way. Emma Shrivell was given chloroform by Mr. Wyman, the house surgeon, but it only delayed matters; she died six hours later.[31] At the inquest convened on 14 April by George Wyatt, the East Surrey coroner, suspicions were raised that the tinned salmon had caused ptomaine poisoning; this was soon discounted. Dr. Thomas Stevenson concluded on 5 May that death had been caused by strychnine poisoning.[32]

In the fall and winter of 1888 the energies of the metropolitan police had been focused on tracking down Jack the Ripper. Now in late 1891 and the spring of 1892 the poisonings of Donworth, Marsh, and Shrivell provided stark evidence that another London serial killer was on the loose. The Lambeth police were used to dealing with blatant acts of street violence; they were poorly prepared to counter a campaign of random murders.

3

THE POLICE

The criminal is the type of the strong man in unfavorable
surroundings, the strong man made sick.

F. W. Nietzsche, *The Twilight of the Idols* (1889)

Night duty for Lambeth constables ended at 6:00 A.M. At about
2:00 A.M., in the cold morning of 12 April 1892, Police Constable
George Comley, 211L, while on his beat saw a man let out of
118 Stamford Street by a young woman whom he later identified as
Emma Shrivell. Comley did not think such comings and goings at this
early hour especially unusual. "There are several houses there where
prostitutes live. It was not an extraordinary thing for me to watch a
man coming out of a special house." In the pale light of the street
lamp all he noticed of the man walking "smartly" away toward York
Road were his glasses, moustache, and dark overcoat.[1] Forty minutes
later Comley was jolted from his reveries by a speeding horse-drawn
cab that clattered to a halt in Stamford Street. Police Constable William Eversfield, 194L, leapt out and entered 118. Comley followed,
and the two officers found the dying forms of Alice Marsh and Emma
Shrivell. Eversfield recognized that the emetic of mustard and water
provided by Mrs. Vogt had proven futile, and the constables rushed
the women to nearby St. Thomas's Hospital by cab, Comley riding on
the outside. Emma Shrivell, who lingered until 8:00 A.M., made a
statement; Alice Marsh was dead before she reached the hospital.[2] In

their rooms the police found an empty salmon tin of an unusual brand; in the fireplace were the remains of a burned postcard canceling a meeting arranged for 11 April—the signature was missing.[3]

The women's convulsions suggested to Dr. Wyman, the house physician at St. Thomas's, the ingestion of strychnine, but there lingered the suspicion that perhaps ptomaine poisoning might have been caused by the tinned salmon. Dr. Thomas Stevenson, lecturer on medical jurisprudence at Guy's Hospital, began the women's postmortem examination on 16 April, looking for evidence of poison by color, alkaloid, and taste tests. All provided positive evidence of the presence in the stomach of strychnine, Stevenson recognizing by taste the "distinct, peculiar metallic bitterness" of the alkaloid. He found six and three-quarter grains of strychnine in Alice Marsh's viscera and over three grains in Emma Shrivell's. One-twelfth of a grain was the maximum medically allowable dosage; one grain was considered fatal.[4]

Before Stevenson's postmortem was completed, Dr. Joseph Harper of Barnstaple on 26 April received a letter from a "W. H. Murray" offering, in exchange for £1500, to destroy the evidence proving that Harper's son Walter, an intern at St. Thomas's Hospital, had poisoned Alice Marsh and Emma Shrivell.[5] Although the letter only referred overtly to the deaths of Marsh and Shrivell, it also inexplicably contained "three enclosures of Ellen Donworth's death and the cutting from *Lloyd's Weekly News*." Harper showed the letter to his solicitor and waited for his son's return from London before determining whether he should, as "Murray" had instructed, make contact through the personal column of the *Daily Chronicle*. On 5 May George Percival Wyatt, the deputy coroner of East Surrey in charge of the Stamford Street inquest, received a similar letter from "Wm. H. Murray" asserting that proof of Harper's guilt would be provided through the intermediary of George Clarke, detective, of 20 Cockspur Street, Charing Cross.[6] But the police's attempts to contact "Murray" through the detective agency proved futile. When the autopsy on Alice Marsh and Emma Shrivell was completed on 5 May, all the police knew for certain was that they were dealing with both a poisoner and a blackmailer. But were they one and the same person?

Following Ellen Donworth's death the previous October the authorities had also uncovered some curious letters. On 19 October Wyatt, deputy coroner for East Surrey in charge of the Donworth inquest (and in 1892 of those of Marsh and Shrivell), received a letter signed "A. O'Brien, detective" which claimed that the author could name the murderer of Ellen Donworth, "alias Ellen Linnell," "provided your Government is willing to pay me £300,000 for my services."[7] A second letter was received on 6 November by Frederick Smith of W. H. Smith and Son, booksellers on the Strand, from an "H. Bayne" asserting that the author had proof that Smith was responsible for Ellen Donworth's death.[8] Enclosed was a letter that "Bayne" claimed Donworth, also known as Linnell, had earlier been sent.

> Miss Ellen Linnell,
>
>   I wrote and warned you once before that Frederick Smith of W. H. Smith & Son, was going to poison you, and I am writing now to say that if you take any of the medicine he gave you for the purposes of bringing on your courses you will die. I saw Frederick Smith prepare the medicine he gave you, and I saw him put enough strychnine in the medicine he gave you to kill a horse. If you take any of it you will die.
>
>   H.M.B.[9]

The police were notified of the letters but could make little of them. What sort of crank would make a ludicrous demand for £300,000? What could link the murder of a prostitute by poisoning with the provision of a woman with medicine for the purposes of bringing on her courses? Why would any sane person choose to accuse Frederick Smith, a well-known, recently elected member of Parliament, of either murdering an impoverished Lambeth prostitute or aborting her fetus? What did "Bayne" want?

"Bayne" promised that he would be able to save Smith from his fate. Smith was instructed to signal his agreement to follow instructions by pasting a paper on one of the windows of the Strand shop stating "Mr. Fred Smith wishes to see Mr. Bayne, the barrister, at once."[10] At the request of the police the notice was posted and a watch kept, but "Bayne" never renewed contact. On 16 November Horace Smith, the magistrate of Clerkenwell Police Court, also received a letter. This time the author claimed to have evidence that Frederick Smith had murdered Ellen Donworth and implored the police to act immediately. But once again, nothing came of it.[11]

Matilda Clover's death on 20 October, having been attributed to alcoholism, was not reported to the police. But they did learn that someone was also trying to collect blackmail money based on the claim that she had been murdered. On 30 November 1891, Dr. William Broadbent, a distinguished doctor attached to St. Mary's Hospital, received a letter that began, "Miss Clover, who until a short time ago lived at 27 Lambeth Road, S.E., died at the above address on 20th October (last month) through being poisoned with strychnine." The writer—an "M. Malone"—claimed to have information implicating Broadbent in the crime that he would give to either the doctor or the police in return for £2500.[12] Broadbent was to signal his agreement to pay by placing an advertisement in the *Daily Chronicle* asking Malone to call. The advertisement was placed: "Personal—M. Malone. Call or send this morning to arrange as in your letter of 28 ult. B."[13] The police lay in wait at Broadbent's house in Portland Square, but no one came.

Finally, an equally bizarre letter was sent in December to the Countess Russell at the Savoy Hotel which accused her husband of Matilda Clover's murder.[14] It stated that the writer was "in a position to obtain Lady R's divorce, more than that, in possession of unfortunate information that would hang her husband as he had poisoned a woman named Clover of 27 South Lambeth Road."[15] George Rich, the Countess Russell's coachman, found that no one at 27 South Lambeth Road had ever heard of Clover and handed the letter over to Scotland Yard.

The police put these letters down to the work of one or more lunatics. In the Russell letter Scotland Yard noted that the would-be blackmailers had gotten the address wrong, mistaking South Lambeth Road with Lambeth Road. But what was of even greater significance in the police's dismissal of the seriousness of such letters was their belief that Clover had not been murdered; they believed that, like so many of her sisters, she had simply dropped dead from drink.

But why, then, were Frederick Smith, Dr. Broadbent, and the Countess Russell sent such letters? The police concluded that some deranged individual who knew of Clover's unfortunate end was simply trying to turn it to the purposes of harassing prominent members of the establishment. The Countess Russell was no doubt victimized because her name was very much in the news due to the complicated divorce proceedings in which she and her husband were currently embroiled. The Russells had married in February 1890 but separated by mutual consent in May 1891. In November, Countess Russell filed for a judicial separation based on cruelty "including unnatural criminal offenses with a third party," that is, homosexuality. The charges were not substantiated, but the countess—viewed by many as a fortune hunter—persisted in broadcasting them, even in popular papers like the *Hawk*. In a further attempt to harass her husband, she filed for restitution of conjugal rights, knowing that he would refuse and thereby make himself liable to the charge of desertion.[16] Frederick Smith, having recently inherited both his father's bookselling empire and his seat in the House of Commons, was much in the news.[17] Broadbent, an eminent physician who was known to be attending Prince George for typhoid fever at Marlborough House, was also in the public eye and accordingly another likely target of poison pen letters.[18] Since nothing came of these demands, they were soon forgotten. In any event, as far as the police were concerned, the Clover correspondence was simply a clumsy attempt at blackmail whose charges that a homicide had been committed should not be taken seriously. Scotland Yard lost the Russell letter and failed to inform the Lambeth police of the contents of the Broadbent letter. No inquiries were made at 27 Lambeth Road. The idea of ordering the exhumation of Clover's body to see if there was any basis to the claim that she had been murdered was not entertained.[19]

But the police were not inactive. They interviewed chemists to determine who had made recent purchases of strychnine.[20] A likely suspect who was quickly targeted was a forty-five-year-old jeweler's traveler by the name of William Slater. A tall man with drooping shoulders and a straggly beard, Slater's injured eye gave him a peculiar appearance. At the time of Ellen Donworth's death he was already under remand for an apparent attack on another woman, so Inspector George Harvey of L Division took some of the witnesses in the Donworth tragedy to see if they could recognize him.[21] Most did not, but Constance Linfield, Ellen Donworth's friend, identified Slater as having been in Ellen's company. Moreover, the *Morning Advertiser* reported on 4 November 1891 that nux vomica (the form in which strychnine was usually sold by chemists) and morphia had been found at Slater's home on the Caledonia Road. But on 16 November, in the midst of the Slater investigation, Horace Smith, the magistrate at Clerkenwell, received the already-mentioned Bayne letter saying that there was enough evidence to hang Frederick Smith for the Ellen Donworth murder along with another copy of the note signed H.M.B. that warned Donworth that Smith was going to poison her.[22]

Slater was ultimately not accused of the Ellen Donworth murder but was handed over to the Clerkenwell Police Court, where he faced the charge of allegedly having administered poison to Annie Bowden. They had met on 26 October and gone to a public house. There Slater had spoken of suicide and supposedly put something in Bowden's beer. On these slim grounds he was tried at the Central Criminal Courts on 16 December. The jury quickly found him not guilty, and Lord Chief Justice Coleridge declared that it had been ridiculous for the Treasury to have pursued the case.[23] But the following April when Alice Marsh and Emma Shrivell, like Ellen Donworth before them, were found to have been murdered with strychnine, the police launched a manhunt for Slater in the Kings Cross area.[24]

The police also made inquiries about Joe Simpson, a wealthy stock-broker who had apparently attempted to "rescue" Emma Shrivell from her life on the streets. By 21 April they were convinced that he was not involved in her murder.[25]

A third suspect was a man named Clifton who the *South London Chronicle* of 16 April 1892 reported had eaten with Alice Marsh and Emma Shrivell the night of their death. At the hospital Shrivell said she "felt unwell after eating the salmon" and then was given pills by "Clifton."[26] In the women's rooms the police found a letter on note-paper from the Prince of Wales Hotel, Chatham, dated 10 April signed by George Clifton saying that he would come to tea on the 11th.[27]

In May 1892 the police added to their list of suspects the name of Thomas Neill, an American doctor living in Lambeth. Neill was an acquaintance of John Haynes, an ex-detective, and of Sergeant Patrick McIntyre, a police officer connected with Scotland Yard. If it had not been for his deep-set, crossed eyes that required him to wear glasses, the heavily built, square-shouldered Neill might have been taken for a policeman himself. He was about forty-five years of age and balding, but sported a thick, dark ginger moustache. It was at William Armstead's photographic studio at 129 Westminster Bridge Road, where Neill went in April to have his picture taken, that he met Haynes, who in March had taken up lodgings with the Armsteads. The two men, who had both spent some years in the United States, quickly became quite close, seeing each other almost every day, dining out and going to the music halls together. Neill was very chatty and in the context of the press reports of the Stamford Street murders told Haynes that he knew of three other prostitutes who had been poisoned—Ellen Donworth, Matilda Clover, and Lou Harvey. The murder of Donworth had created a sensation, but Haynes asked for more details concerning the two other deaths. Neill not only obliged by pointing out the houses where Clover and Harvey had lived, but pressed Haynes to confirm his assertions.

After making his inquiries, Haynes was not sure if he was dealing with a simple spinner of tales or a lunatic. Neither Matilda Clover nor Lou Harvey had been reported murdered. Haynes was told at 27 Lambeth Road that Matilda Clover had died of drink. Neill said Lou Harvey, who supposedly had dropped dead between the Oxford Music Hall and the London Pavilion, had lived at 55 Townsend Road, St. John's Wood; the people there informed Haynes they had never heard of such a woman.[28] But by May Haynes was impressed by evidence of Neill's increased nervousness. On one occasion when they were riding at the top of an omnibus near Charing Cross they heard the newspaper boys shouting "Arrest in Stamford Street Case." Neill was clearly agitated, got off, and bought all the papers only to find that the reports concerned another case, not that of the Alice Marsh and Emma Shrivell murders.[29]

Coincidentally, on the evening of 12 May, Neill was observed by the police closely watching the women entering the Canterbury Music Hall on the Westminster Bridge Road. He struck Constable Comley as very much resembling the individual whom he had witnessed leaving 118 Stamford Street shortly before the bodies of Alice Marsh and Emma Shrivell were found. Comley had, from 16 April, been detailed to a plainclothes detachment with the special duty of looking for the Stamford Street suspect. Comley alerted Sergeant Alfred Ward, who agreed that Neill "was watching women very narrowly indeed." That night Ward and Comley followed Neill and the prostitute he picked up along St. George's Road toward the Elephant and Castle to the woman's home at 24 Elliott's Row, and then Neill alone back to his own lodgings on Lambeth Palace Road at 1.30 A.M. Full-time police shadowing of Neill was begun in the following days.[30]

Haynes, as a professional, soon noticed the surveillance and asked Neill if there were any reason why he should be shadowed. Neill at first claimed there was none but later said he was being mistaken for Walter Harper, a fellow lodger at 103 Lambeth Palace Road, who was responsible for the deaths of Alice Marsh and Emma Shrivell. On 15 May, Haynes, while dining with Neill at the Café de Paris in Ludgate Hill, took down Neill's accusation against Harper. The young Harper, claimed Neill, had "criminal intercourse" with three women at Mutton's Hotel, Brighton. One had become "enceinte" and died as a result of an abortion Harper performed on her. The other two then blackmailed him. Haynes's rough notes read:

> W.J.H. got girl at Mutton's, at Brighton in trouble some time back; procured abortion for her. Stamford Street girls aware of this. H. visiting them, they threatened him, blackmail, victims. W.J.H. weeks before tried to purchase strychnine, telling him [Neill] of his trouble, asking what he could do under the circumstances, be well to get rid of them, &c.[31]

Neill also showed Haynes a small book in which he said were the initials of the women poisoned by Harper and the dates of their deaths. He further claimed that he not only had refused to provide his fellow lodger with strychnine but had sent the Stamford street women the anonymous letter warning that Harper was going to poison them. Haynes later presented himself as alarmed at such revelations.

> I said the matter was so grave that I should have to report it to the authorities. He said it would be very foolish of you to do so. There is more money to be made out of the matter if you come with me to Barnstaple to see Dr. Harper's father and tell him that I have sufficient evidence to hang the son for the murder of those girls, and the older Harper would pay any sum sooner than have the odium of the murder on his family.[32]

Whether any of this was true or not, the unemployed Haynes appeared to view his stumbling upon Neill as a piece of luck. He may initially have entertained the idea—which he later attributed solely to Neill—that money could be made from the affair by blackmailing Harper. But once he realized that the police were on to Neill, he saw as his only safe course that of handing over his information with the hopes that something would come of it—perhaps employment by Scotland Yard or the Home Office.

Haynes's contact at Scotland Yard was Patrick McIntyre, a police sergeant with the Criminal Investigation Department whom he had known for some years. Both men had been involved in the Home Office's clandestine investigation of terrorist activities in London and the arrival of suspicious individuals from America.[33] Like Haynes, McIntyre had struck up an acquaintance with Neill at the end of April at Armstead's. McIntyre told Neill he was impressed with his knowledge of the rash of recent London poisonings, including the Kings Cross case. "Yes," replied Neill, "I have followed the matter closely in the *British Medical Journal.* Being a medical man, I take an interest in matters of this kind."[34] But McIntyre in the meantime was alerted to Neill's curious behavior by Haynes, who took the sergeant to the Townsend Road house where Lou Harvey had supposedly lived.

On 19 May, McIntyre, after reporting these developments to Inspector George Harvey and Chief Inspector Mulvaney of the Lambeth Division, met Neill at the Pheasant Public House in Lambeth Palace Road. Neill, according to McIntyre, complained that a "rip," or prostitute, in the Westminster Bridge Road had told him she had been sent by the police, who suspected him of the Stamford Street murders, to spy on him.[35] This was the first time that Neill mentioned the affair to McIntyre. When McIntyre questioned him again on 24 May, Neill produced a letter that he said had been given to him by a detective called Murray, a man about forty-two years of age, five foot nine inches tall, wearing a full black beard. The letter, which had passed through the post, warned Alice Marsh and Emma Shrivell to beware of Dr. Harper or he would do to them what he had done to Lou Harvey and Matilda Clover.[36] But Dr. Harper, as McIntyre discovered, had given up his lodgings on Lambeth Palace Road on 4 May and left London.

Neill seemed to McIntyre to know a surprising amount about the deaths of Donworth, Marsh, and Shrivell. But he also made mysterious references to the murders of Matilda Clover and Lou Harvey. The police had never heard of Harvey, and Clover was on record simply as a wretched prostitute who the previous autumn had died of drink. Could Matilda Clover's death have been a poisoning that the authorities had missed? And given the fact that prostitutes often changed their names, was it possible that "Lou Harvey" had been murdered and buried as someone else?

Alfred Ward, the police sergeant who with Constable Comley had tracked Neill on the night of 12 May, had already begun the process of solving this puzzle. Following the Marsh and Shrivell murders he had been sent by Inspector George Harvey of L Division to "make inquiries of prostitutes." Ward was carrying out interviews on 26 April concerning Ellen Donworth's death "among that class of women" when Mrs. Robertson, the landlady at 88 Lambeth Road, mentioned that her new maid, Lucy Rose, could tell him something about another prostitute who had died mysteriously about the same time as Ellen Donworth. The next day Lucy Rose described Matilda Clover's last agonizing hours.[37] The symptoms described and reported by Ward led Inspector Harvey to speak to Lucy Rose himself and then to check her recollections with those of her old employer, Mrs. Vowles, at 27 Lambeth Road.

By 28 April Scotland Yard was of the opinion, on the basis of Lucy Rose's description of both Matilda Clover and her friend "Fred," that Clover's death was linked to the murders of Donworth, Marsh, and Shrivell.[38] Each appeared to have been poisoned; each knew a man called "Fred." Alice Marsh and Emma Shrivell's "Fred" resembled in description the dark gentleman seen with Ellen Donworth. Unfortunately, Matilda Clover's "Fred"—described by her landlady as a slight, fair young man with blue eyes—was nothing like the gentleman to whom Lucy Rose had heard Clover call out, "Goodnight, Fred." Frederick Smith, who had been accused in the anonymous letter of Ellen Donworth's death, was, of course, also known as "Fred," but the police dismissed the idea that an eminent businessman and politician could be involved in such a sordid case. Given that the murders had taken place close to the Thames and had been separated by considerable lengths of time—two in October and two in April—Scotland Yard thought it likely that "Fred" was a seafaring man. Orders were issued for the docks and ships to be watched for suspicious characters.[39]

Dr. Henry, the Lambeth detachment's divisional surgeon, when given an account of Matilda Clover's symptoms as described by Lucy Rose and Mrs. Vowles, concluded that they sounded very much like the symptoms of strychnine poisoning. On these grounds Inspector Harvey sought an order from the Home Secretary for the exhumation of Clover's body.[40] Neill said that he welcomed this investigation. He told his landlady's daughter, Emily Sleaper, that he knew that Clover's body was to be exhumed because he had informed Haynes of her poisoning and Haynes in turn had alerted Scotland Yard. What he did not know was that the police had spoken to Lucy Rose.[41]

Matilda Clover's body was exhumed on 6 May. Fourteen coffins had to be taken out of the paupers' grave before hers could be removed. Dr. Thomas Stevenson undertook the autopsy.[42] The grave was dry and the body remarkably well preserved. Stevenson spent three weeks carrying out the complicated process of shredding the internal organs, dissolving them in methylated spirit, and boiling, cooling, and filtering the residue. He found that six months after her death Matilda Clover's viscera still contained about one-sixteenth of a grain of strychnine. Probably about as much again had been vomited up. The residue was bitter to the taste—nineteenth-century forensic scientists obviously needed a strong stomach—and appeared purple when color-tested. A frog injected with the fluid found in the corpse's stomach, liver, brain, and chest died within a matter of minutes in the throes of the characteristic symptoms of strychnine poisoning—tetanic convulsions.[43] The autopsy left no doubt in Stevenson's mind that Clover had been poisoned.[44]

One puzzle had been solved; a host of questions remained. How had Neill known of Matilda Clover's murder before anyone else? Who was Neill? Who was "Fred?" And who and where was Lou Harvey?

THE SUSPECT

When a doctor goes wrong he is the first of criminals. He
has nerve and he has knowledge.

Arthur Conan Doyle, "The Speckled Band" (1891)

On the warm summer night of 17 May 1892 Violet Beverley, a plucky
Lambeth prostitute, brought back to her rooms at 3 North Street,
Kennington, a man who called himself Thomas Neill. After having
sex he told her he was a representative of a New York firm of druggists and showed her his sample of pills. He then specially prepared
for her an "American drink." Perhaps the pills aroused her suspicions; she refused to sample it. Undeterred, on 18 May Neill visited
Beverley again, "having connection twice with her," in the words of
the plainclothes constables who followed and later interrogated the
young woman.[1]

The conclusion drawn by the police from their investigations was
that Neill was "an extremely sensual person, but he makes no effort
to conceal his identity, and we are of the opinion that he is not the
man we are seeking known as Fred."[2] Neill did carry a pill case, but it
had been determined that he was a bona fide representative of the
Harvey Company of Saratoga, New York. Superintendent Braman
did add to the report the notation that Neill was most certainly a
blackmailer. "Dr. Neal [sic] has acted in a most suspicious manner and
his connection with the man Hayes [sic] goes to show he is the author
of his statement re Dr. Harper."[3]

On 26 May, Inspector Tunbridge of Scotland Yard's Criminal Investigation Department was instructed to assume the direction of the South Lambeth poisonings cases. Inevitably a certain amount of friction occurred between the divisional officers and those of the C.I.D, but Tunbridge received a full report from Superintendent Braman of Lambeth.[4] Despite the conclusions drawn in the 23 May report, Neill was still the best suspect the police had. Tunbridge accordingly interviewed him and with other police officers slowly began to put together a portrait of the man Braman called a "strange customer."

Inspector John McCarthy was sent to Brighton to see if there was any truth to the story that Neill had told Haynes of abortions and blackmail leading to murder. All that McCarthy succeeded in confirming was the fact that Emma Shrivell's sister, Nelly Washer, had indeed worked at Mutton's. On his return to London McCarthy went to Somerset House, where he searched in vain for a notice of the death of Lou Harvey.[5] But McCarthy did establish that what Tunbridge had been told by Neill of his trips to and from England was correct. On 18 June Scotland Yard dispatched Inspector Frederick Smith Jarvis to the United States to determine just what sort of life Neill had led there.[6] By late July a remarkable picture had emerged.

Thomas Neill was born in Glasgow on 27 May 1850, the eldest son of William Cream and Mary Elder. He had been baptized Thomas Neill Cream, the name by which he will be called hereafter. William Cream immigrated with his family to Canada in 1854, where he became manager of Gilmour and Company, a major Quebec shipbuilding and lumber firm located in Wolfe's Cove.[7] Thomas followed in his father's footsteps. He attended the company school, taught at Chalmer's Sunday School, and began an apprenticeship in the shipbuilding firm of Baldwin and Company. But William Cream's success in establishing himself as a lumber merchant allowed his eldest son to set his sights higher.

In October 1872 Thomas Neill Cream entered McGill College in Montreal, where he spent four academic years studying medicine, returning to Quebec City each summer to work for his father. McGill's faculty of medicine, established in 1829 with the support of wealthy benefactors, was well on its way to becoming one of the best on the continent. That its students were studying spermatorrhea and syphilis testified to the nineteenth-century physician's expanding role as moral arbiter. Completing a thesis on the effects of chloroform, Cream was one of thirty-four young men on 31 March 1876 to receive his medical degree at crowded graduation ceremonies in William Molson Hall. The prophetic title of the address given to the graduating class in medicine was, "The Evils of Malpractice in the Medical Profession."[8]

Dr. Craik, professor of chemistry at McGill, recalled that Cream was "rather wild and fond of ostentatious displays of clothing and jewelry."[9] Having won the reputation of being a "fast and extravagant liver," he was strongly suspected of having set fire to his rooms at 106 Mansfield Street in April 1876 in order to collect on the insurance.[10] At about that same time, he met and seduced Flora Eliza Brooks, daughter of Lyman Henry Brooks, owner of the main hotel in Waterloo, a small town located in the eastern townships some seventy miles south of Quebec City.[11] The couple were soon engaged, but on 9 September 1876 Flora fell ill and her physician, Dr. Phelan, informed her father that she had recently been surgically aborted. Cream was dragged back to Waterloo by the enraged Brooks and, at a private ceremony in the hotel, forced at gunpoint to marry Flora.[12] It was largely a matter of form. After a marriage contract was drawn up by a notary, Cream was allowed to leave the next day to continue his medical studies in England.[13]

When Cream arrived in London in late September or early October of 1876, the country was enjoying a sudden burst of fine weather that increased the crowds assembled to protest the Bulgarian atrocities.[14] But Cream could not have been ignorant of the fact that London had its own atrocities. Dr. Albert James Bernays, professor of chemistry at St. Thomas's Hospital, where Cream was studying, had been an expert witness in a sensational poisoning that the press referred to as the "Vauxhall Strychnine Case."[15] It was a sordid affair in which Silas Barlow, a bigamous railwayman, had been accused of poisoning his common-law wife, Ellen Sloper, with the strychnine contained in Battle's Vermin Killer. The first doctor to see Sloper had attributed her convulsions to epilepsy; it was only the discovery of the rat poison that led to a postmortem examination and ultimately in December to Barlow's execution at Horsemonger Lane. The *British Medical Journal's* complaint that the lack of uniformity in the inquest law meant that violent deaths by poisoning often went uninvestigated must have given Cream food for thought.

On 7 October 1876, Mr. Francis Mason delivered the inaugural address at St. Thomas's, referring briefly to the previous year's vivisection bill in tracing the noble calling of medicine back to Galen and Hippocrates.[16] Cream attended lectures at St. Thomas's Hospital until 1878, also serving as a temporary obstetric clerk. It was a fascinating time to be involved in issues pertaining to gender and medicine. Lister, the pioneering proponent of antisepsis, was consulting surgeon at the nearby General Lying-In Hospital on York Road. At St. Thomas's itself Florence Nightingale had established in 1871 her

Nightingale School for Nurses.[17] Medical degrees were about to be offered to women in Dublin but not at the University of London, where the issue was debated in May 1877 and defeated 142–29. A majority of English medical men still obviously looked askance at competition from women.[18]

Few could be unaware that women were seeking to gain greater control over their lives in other ways. In March 1877 Annie Besant and Charles Bradlaugh were charged with publishing an obscene book.[19] The text in question was Charles Knowlton's *Fruits of Philosophy*, an American birth control manual which had been in circulation since the 1830s. Bradlaugh asked why W. H. Smith was not prosecuted for selling expensive texts such as Chavasse's *Hints to Mothers* that contained much the same information. The English upper and middle classes had in fact already begun to restrict family size. The prosecution's main concern was that such a book as Knowlton's, at the low price of six pence, could end up in the hands of young girls. But as no couple should have more children than they could care for, argued Besant, it was necessary to make birth control texts cheap enough to be available to (in Bradlaugh's words) even the "squalid and poverty stricken."[20]

In June, Besant and Bradlaugh were found guilty, but the debate over birth control was far from over. In the three months during which the trial dragged on, 125,000 copies of *Fruits of Philosophy* were sold, and shortly thereafter the Malthusian League was established by Charles Drysdale with the goal of defending the morality of family restriction.[21] Annie Besant became the first English woman to produce a text on contraception. She ultimately dropped social criticism for the more abstract appeals of theosophy, but by the time she withdrew *The Law of Population* from circulation in 1890, 175,000 copies had been purchased.[22]

The respectable traditionally assumed that the moral issues posed by sexual practices were best dealt with by the clergy. In the nineteenth century the view was increasingly taken that doctors were as well, if not better, qualified to judge such questions. It was in this light that the bishop of London in July 1877, when distributing the prizes to the star pupils of St. Thomas's Medical School, referred to the doctor as a "domestic counsellor—almost the domestic confessor."[23] Cream was not among the recipients of a prize. In April 1877 he failed the anatomy and physiology examinations for entry to the Royal College of Surgeons, but in April 1878 he was admitted to the Royal Colleges of Physicians and Surgeons at Edinburgh and qualified for a license in midwifery.

Cream did not devote all his time to his studies. He was a womanizer. Archdeacon Lindsay, who had presided at his marriage in Quebec in September 1876, discovered Cream courting a woman in London in November.[24] Again in 1877, while living at Gough Square, Fleet Street, Cream began to "pay his addresses" to his landlady's daughter. In March, Charlotte Botteril of Montreal, who was visiting London and apparently knew Cream, wrote the young woman to warn her that her suitor was a married man. Cream obtained the letter and only withdrew his threat of a libel action after Botteril rendered an apology through a solicitor.[25]

Cream was not to be married long. In August 1877 Flora Brooks Cream, still residing in Waterloo, contracted bronchitis and died of consumption.[26] Or did she? Inspector Jarvis reported in July 1892 that Dr. Phelan had been suspicious.

> He states that the lady had undoubtedly had an abortion procured either by drugs or instruments but which, he is unable to say—Subsequent to the marriage when Mrs. Cream became ill, he was scarcely able to understand her symptoms and he asked the deceased if she had been taking anything and she said she had taken some medicine her husband sent her. He told her not to take anything except what he himself prescribed and she promised not to do so and the symptoms he had not understood gradually passed away. Dr. Phelan says he never saw any of the medicine Cream had sent his wife but he strongly suspected him of foul play.[27]

Whatever role Cream played in his wife's death did not deter him from claiming a thousand dollars from his father-in-law by rights of his marriage contract; he eventually settled for two hundred.

Cream returned to Canada in May 1878, setting up a medical practice in London, Ontario. This bustling little town, emerging as the financial and brewing center of the southwest portion of the province, needed professionals. Cream advertised himself in the local paper as "Dr. Cream: Physician and Surgeon. Office 204 Dundas Street. Residence 250 Queens Avenue." Because of his specialization in obstetrics, most of those he treated were presumably women.

Cream's office on Dundas Street was above Bennett's Fancy Store. On 3 May 1879 a little girl was horrified to discover slumped over in the outhouse behind Bennett's the body of Kate Hutchinson Gardener. Kate Gardener, who had succumbed to an overdose of chloroform, was one of Cream's patients.[28] The young woman had been working as a chambermaid at the Tecumseh House Hotel, where she shared a bed with Sarah Long. For the week previous to her death, however, Gardener had lodged at a boardinghouse. When she failed to appear one evening, suspicions were raised, a search started, and her body discovered.

At the inquest Sarah Long stated that Kate had been put "in the family way" by a Mr. Johnson of the nearby village of Listowel and that she went to Cream seeking an abortion. Cream's account was that on 5 April Gardener offered him the enormous sum of $100 for medicine to "bring her right" and mentioned "smut rye." But the doctor only admitted to having treated her for "senescence" and said he refused to provide her with abortifacients. He concluded that her death was a suicide.[29]

There was not enough evidence to indict Cream for Kate Gardener's death, but his reputation was badly tarnished. According to Long, Cream not only gave Gardener medicine but also suggested that money could be made if Gardener accused W. H. Birrell, a wealthy guest at the hotel, of being the father of her child.[30] Suspicions of Cream were further raised by the abrasions found on Gardener's face and by Dr. Niven's statement at the inquest that it was impossible for a would-be suicide to hold a chloroform-soaked sponge over her own nose long enough to cause death. The coroner's jury's final ruling was that Gardener's death was murder, caused by a person or persons unknown. Cream—viewed as an abortionist, a potential blackmailer, and a possible murderer—hurriedly left Canada for Chicago.[31]

Chicago was the classic North American "shock" city of the nineteenth century, dominated by its stockyards and assembly-line slaughterhouses in which death had become mechanized. As the continent's chief distribution center linking the industrial East and the agricultural West, the raw, young city attracted streams of immigrants, both respectable and rough, from round the world.[32] In the midst of recovering from the great fire of 1871, its population was soaring from some six hundred thousand citizens toward the million it would achieve in 1890. Its reputation for municipal graft, incompetent policing, and working-class radicalism had already won it the title of the "wickedest city in the world."[33] Cream would play his part in sustaining this reputation.

Cream obtained a license from the Illinois State Board of Health in August 1879 and set up a medical practice in rooms rented from Mrs. Adell Gridley at 434 West Madison Avenue, one of the business streets flanking Chicago's notorious West Side prostitution district. A census revealed that the city had at least thirty-five hundred women

working the streets, their standard price being fifty cents a customer.[34] Although he had moved from Canada, Cream appears not
to have changed his ways. By the summer of 1880 he was known to
the police as an abortionist sometimes assisted by a young Afro-
American midwife, Hattie Mack.[35]

Close to the edge of town, at 1056 West Madison Avenue, Mack
occupied the second floor of a two-story frame building. In the
early hours of the morning of Friday, 20 August, George Green, the
first-floor tenant, became suspicious when Mack hurriedly departed.
Where, Green wondered, was the delicate white woman who had
been staying at Mack's for the previous ten days? When that afternoon
a "horrible stench" spread through the building, Green alerted the
police. Lieutenant Steele of the West Lake Street substation broke
down the door and found on the bed the decomposing remains of a
young female. The police identified her as Mary Anne Faulkner of
Ottawa, Canada.[36] Provided by Green with a description of the physician who had repeatedly visited her, the police found at a drugstore
on Madison Avenue both Cream and an incriminating letter Mack
had written him saying she was leaving, as the woman was dead.

The decomposition of the body made the postmortem, carried out
on Saturday by Dr. Bluthardt, difficult, but Bluthardt concluded that
an abortion had probably been performed on Faulkner. Mack, who
had been arrested, was only too willing to testify against Cream. Her
story was that, being indebted to the doctor, she was forced to accept
Faulkner as a boarder on 11 August. Faulkner told Mack that, pregnant and recently deserted by her husband, she had to abort in order
to work to support herself. A Dr. Greer, in return for her gold watch,
gave her Cream's name as one who was "in the business." Mack
claimed not to have been present when Cream used instruments on
Faulkner, but the fetid odor of sepsis quickly made it apparent to
her that the operation—if that is what it was—had failed. Cream, according to Mack, in order to cover his tracks and destroy Faulkner's
body beyond recognition, went so far as to suggest burning down
the house.

At the inquest Mack, assisted by a "very gentlemanly colored young
man" continued her attack on Cream. Cream had boasted, she stated,
that "he had treated five hundred like cases either at the St. Johns or
some other hospital in Canada." And Mary Anne Faulkner had told
her that Cream was known to prostitutes seeking to terminate pregnancies and had operated on "as many as fifteen cases in one sporting
house with success."[37]

Cream countered that it was Mack who had sought him out sometime after midnight on Friday, 12 August, to assist the young woman whom Mack had already incompetently aborted. Faulkner had taken oil of cotton root and ergot of rye; when these abortifacients failed, Mack employed instruments. Cream protested that all he had done was to try his best to restore the woman's health and, that failing, she died the following Friday.[38] He called on Dr. Donald Fraser to testify to having been brought along to see the woman and having been notified by Cream by telephone of her death. Despite such protestations Cream was indicted for murder and jailed along with "Dr." Charles Earll, a well-known Chicago abortionist who in the last six years had been arrested at least eight times.[39]

Cream's indignation at having a "quack" as a cellmate must have been replaced by more worrying preoccupations once he saw the press coverage given their cases. The *Chicago Tribune*'s editor concluded a lengthy article by attacking the apparent leniency with which such abortionists were treated. "Let the law be invoked to its utmost limit. If Earll and Cream be the guilty persons, as seems to be the case from all the evidence at hand, let them hang. This is the surest remedy against the prevalence of abortion as a practice."[40] Cream's murder trial, set for 16 November 1880, was to be presided over by Judge Joseph S. Gary.[41]

Although the evidence against Cream seemed impressive, his aggressive attorney, the cigar-chomping Alfred S. Trude, had little difficulty in winning acquittal as it basically came down to the question of whether the jury would take a "colored" woman's word against that of a white male doctor.[42] Cream, with his intelligent blue eyes, brown hair, and beard closely trimmed in the fashionable "Burnside" fashion, made a good impression. He was, according to the court reporter of the *Chicago Tribune*, the best dressed and best looking defendant to appear before the bar since Charles Angell. The appearance and demeanor of the state's chief witness were mockingly contrasted. "Hattie Mack, the frowsy little negress charged with practicing abortion on Mary Anne Faulkner with Dr. Cream, tripped downstairs in an exceedingly dirty gown, to say that 'she didn't know nuffin' 'bout nuffin' 'n warnt goin to say nuffin' 'bout nuffin'.'"[43] Trude reiterated Cream's original alibi and closed the case before "about two hundred spectators, all men with one or two exceptions," claiming that Faulkner's death was obviously caused by Mack "since it was a bungling piece of work and could not have been done by an experienced physician." He had already called a half dozen character witnesses to speak on his client's behalf and asserted that it was an every day occurrence for doctors to be blamed for abortions that nurses like Mack performed or that women carried out on their own person. The all-male jury, accepting the argument that doctors who found themselves at the mercy of such vindictive females had to be protected, deliberated only fifteen minutes before returning a not-guilty verdict.[44]

Cream was not scared off by this close call. Two weeks later, on 2 December, he was present at the opening of the trial of his cellmate "Dr." Earll for an abortion-related murder and was obviously "deeply interested in the proceedings."[45]

Sometime later that same month Ellen Stack died after taking medicine that Cream had prescribed for her. Cream sought to hold responsible for her death, and so extort money from him, one Frank Pyatt, the druggist who had made up her prescriptions. Cream wrote Pyatt on 13 March: "For God's sake keep quiet and trust no one, my bitter experience taught me to be suspicious of everyone I meet." On 24 March Cream followed this up with a warning that the chemist's business would be destroyed if the purported prosecution being prepared against him by lawyers went through.[46] Cream began his blackmail attempt in January 1881, Pyatt complained to the authorities in March, and in April and May an inconclusive police investigation was carried out.[47]

Cream's next brush with the law came later that summer when he was charged with sending through the mail scurrilous postcards. Having convinced himself that Joseph Martin, a furrier at 129 West 13th Street, had not paid his medical bill, Cream plagued him with libelous letters stating that Martin's wife and children suffered from a disease contracted from Martin and threatening to expose this publicly. When this pressure tactic failed, Cream mailed three postcards that referred to Mrs. Martin as a "low, vulgar, vixen" and asserted that Mr. Martin had left a bastard child in England. Press reports made it clear that this practice of blackening people's reputations by making outrageous assertions on postcards that anyone could read had become common. Cream was arrested 18 June and held on twelve hundred dollars bail.[48] The money was put up by Mary McClellan, an elderly English woman of West 13th Street, to whose daughter Cream had recently become engaged.[49] It was forfeited within the week; Cream jumped bail and left for Canada.

Cream's departure from Chicago was precipitated by a more serious charge than blackmail. In February 1881 Daniel Stott, the sixty-one-year-old stationmaster of the Chicago and North Western Railroad in Grand Prairie, a township near Belvidere, Illinois, sent his pretty young wife to Chicago to obtain for him pills that Cream advertised as a cure for epilepsy. Julia Stott was happy to do such errands for several months. Stott seemed to be making some slight improvement, but after taking the medicine prescribed by Cream on 11 June, he suddenly died. Since the old man was known to have "fits," local doctors attributed his passing to yet another epileptic seizure and he was promptly buried. But Cream telegraphed the coroner of Boone County that he knew the patient and suspected that Stott's death was due to the druggist's at Buck and Rayner's having put too much strychnine into the prescription. At the same time, Cream undertook, on Julia Stott's behalf, to seek punitive damages from the drug firm.

The skeptical coroner, at Cream's suggestion, gave a dose of Stott's medicine to a dog; in fifteen minutes the poor animal was dead. Stott was disinterred, and his stomach removed and taken to Chicago for a postmortem examination by Professor Walter Haines of Rush Medical College. Enough strychnine was found in Stott's intestines to kill anyone three times over. But to his surprise and indignation, the vindicated Cream found that he, not the druggist, was charged with murder.[50] This was the reason that he fled Chicago for Canada.

On 27 July the readers of the *Chicago Tribune* were provided with a detailed account of Pat Garrett's tracking down and shooting in New Mexico of Billy the Kid. The capture of Cream the same day by the Boone County sheriff at Belle Rivière, Ontario, was a far more prosaic affair. Cream put up no struggle and, after being questioned in Windsor, was returned to Illinois to stand trial for murder. Interviewed at Chicago's Michigan Central Depot on the morning of 3 August while awaiting transportation to Belvidere, the handcuffed and unshaven Cream presented his waiving of formal extradition procedures as proof of his innocence.[51]

The *Chicago Tribune*'s front page of 20 September 1881 was bordered in black and carried the enormous headline, "HE IS DEAD": the Republican paper was mourning the death of President James Garfield, victim of the assassin Guiteau. The opening day of Cream's trial, hailed the most notorious to have ever taken place in Belvidere County, was covered on page 5. This time Cream did not have the assistance of a lawyer as skilled as Trude to counter the arguments of the state's attorneys, R. W. Coon and Senator Charles Fuller.[52] And Cream alone was tried for murder; the delicate-looking Julia Stott, who had also been indicted, turned state's evidence.[53] She admitted that Cream had seduced her and charged that the ambitious plan to murder Stott and blackmail the drug store was his. The story of Cream's earlier attempt to blackmail Pyatt—the chemist who had made up Miss Stack's prescriptions—much in the same way that he recently had attempted to extort money from Buck and Rayner's, now came out. On 11 June, according to Julia Stott, Cream tampered with a new batch of pills that the druggists had made up for Stott. She returned home by train and gave the medicine to her husband, who, taking it the next evening, died almost instantly.

Although Julia Stott was obviously out to save her own skin, she had probably come to the realization that she too would ultimately number among Cream's victims. Of course, her testimony was suspect. Cream's fate was finally sealed as a result of the evidence offered by another woman, Mary McClellan. McClellan, who had put up Cream's bail money in the Martin case only to have it forfeited, now retaliated with the damning testimony that she had heard Cream speak of Stott's death before it had actually been reported. Her revenge was especially sweet; although it was not public knowledge, the police were aware that Cream had seduced, aborted, and abandoned McClellan's daughter.[54]

Cream was disowned by his father, who refused to provide any financial assistance. His brother Daniel and a sister stood by him, but could only send a small amount of money to defray legal expenses. Cream's defense was that the wrong person was being tried; Julia Stott, a "bad woman" who had uttered threats against her husband, was the poisoner. But the counterevidence—including that of ten-year-old Amy Stott, who testified that Cream had said he loved her mother—was overwhelming. Cream's claim that he had neither had "criminal relations" with Mrs. Stott nor tampered with his patient's pills failed to impress the jury. On 23 September, Cream was found guilty of murder and sentenced to be imprisoned "for the term of his natural life," one day of each year to be spent in solitary confinement. The 182-pound, florid-complexioned murderer, inmate number 4374, began his sentence on 1 November 1881.[55] Secured behind the imposing walls—six-feet thick and twenty-five feet high—of the Illinois State Penitentiary at Joliet, it could be assumed that Thomas Neill Cream's career as abortionist, blackmailer, and murderer was over.

* * *

Henri Le Caron, the English secret agent who worked at Joliet, recalled that in an overcrowded prison where three commissioners were in charge of fifteen hundred inmates corruption was inevitably rife. "At the time of which I speak, money could accomplish everything, from the obtaining of luxuries in prison to the purchase of pardon and freedom itself. Everything connected with the prison administration was rotten to the core."[56] This no doubt goes some way in explaining why ten years later, in 1891, Daniel Cream was successful in having Governor Joseph W. Fifer declare Thomas Neill Cream a "fit and proper subject for executive clemency." Cream's life sentence was reduced to seventeen years, which, with time off for good behavior, allowed him to be released almost immediately, on 31 July 1891. Cream's successful bid for parole coincidentally followed his father's death, which left the prisoner an inheritance of sixteen thousand dollars.[57] Ironically, Senator Charles E. Fuller, who had prosecuted Cream in 1881, played a crucial role in having him released. Fuller, as a leading Republican, was closely associated with Governor Fifer.[58] Daniel Cream, who never ceased believing that his brother had only been convicted because of Julia Stott's perjured evidence, found that, to secure his freedom, the help of such "leading politicians" was essential.[59]

Upon his release Cream's first thought was to track down Julia Stott, whose testimony had sent him to prison. As early as 1890 he had sought the assistance of the Pinkerton Detective Agency in locating her, and he wrote them again in 1891 from both Joliet and Quebec City.[60] All these efforts failed. Cream returned to Canada and collected his estate. His brother and sister were shocked by the extent to which prison had changed him. The once dapper medical man was foulmouthed, frightening, and heavily addicted to drugs. Accepting their advice that a trip abroad might restore his health, he boarded the sailing ship the *Teutonic* in September, bound for England.[61] Cream arrived in London on 5 October and put up at Anderton's Hotel on Fleet Street; on 6 October, calling himself Dr. Neill, he took a front room on the second floor of 103 Lambeth Palace Road, directly across from St. Thomas's Hospital. He moved in the next day, explaining that he had come to England to rest.

Cream spent most of his time at home reading and writing.[62] He passed his evenings at the music halls, which offered more than music. "Professor Richard Landeman and a Seven foot Kangaroo," trumpeted a typical advertisement, "will box at the Imperial Theatre adjoining the Royal Aquarium—trained to never hit a man when down and retires to its corner after each round."[63] But what most attracted Cream's attention were the women who loitered at the entrances to such shows. In a portrait of Cream written later "By One Who Knew Him," the doctor was presented as a lonely, restless man, always pacing, always afraid of being alone. He talked constantly of women, money, and poison, carried pornographic photographs, and took enormous amounts of drugs.

Women were his preoccupation and his talk of them far from agreeable. He carried pornographic photographs, which he was ready to display. He was in the habit of taking pills, which, he said, were compounded of strychnine, morphia, and cocaine, and of which the effect, he declared, was aphrodisiac. In short he was a degenerate of filthy desires and practices.[64]

Neill needed diversions because he suffered from both weak eyes and headaches. On 9 October he visited an optician on Fleet Street to purchase spectacles. He was diagnosed as having hypermyopia, the left eye being much weaker than the right and turning in toward the nose.[65] On 12 October he informed John Kirby, assistant at a chemist's shop at 22 Parliament Street, that he was attending courses at St. Thomas's and required nux vomica (a combination of brucine and strychnine), which was on the list of scheduled poisons.[66] In signing for them, he gave his name as "Thomas Neill, M.D., 103 Lambeth Palace Road." He subsequently purchased gelatin capsules. Bitter medicine was customarily enclosed in such capsules to render it tasteless.[67] Cream continued to purchase nux vomica from time to time in quantities of one to four ounces. He also bought an ounce of opium at least once every fortnight. Sales of nux vomica were not registered, but those of opium and laudanum were. Seeking relief for his headaches, he frequently purchased opium at other chemists' shops as well.[68]

On 13 October, Ellen Donworth collapsed in the street, and her subsequent death was declared by the coroner's jury to have been caused by poisoning with strychnine and morphia by a person unknown. A week later Matilda Clover's death was attributed to alcoholism. In neither case was any evidence advanced to implicate Cream. But after reading in the *Daily Telegraph* of the Russell divorce proceedings, Cream told Emily Sleaper, his landlady's daughter, that Lord Russell had killed Clover and asked Sleaper to deliver a denunciatory note to Lambeth Road. The perplexed young woman refused, believing Cream to be unbalanced.[69]

In November, Cream met and began to court Laura Sabbatini, a respectable young lady of Berkhamstead, Hertfordshire, who had come up to London to learn dressmaking. Cream wrote Sabbatini's mother asking for permission to pay his respects; Mrs. Sabbatini, satisfied by his response to her request for information about his family, consented. By the end of the month Cream had made a proposal of marriage; Laura accepted.[70] Cream appeared to envisage establishing a traditional middle-class home; at his request Laura gave up dressmaking. In early January he announced to Laura and her mother that he had to make a trip to North America to see about his father's estate. Before leaving, he drew up a will, which Laura's sister witnessed, leaving all his possessions to his betrothed, Laura Sabbatini.[71]

On 7 January, Cream set sail from Liverpool on board the *Sarnia* for Quebec City, where he said he could be reached in care of his brother Daniel. By the 1890s such trips back and forth across the Atlantic were not all that exceptional. The popular press carried advertisements for reduced fares to Canada from eighteen guineas all the way down to three pounds. The *Sarnia,* steaming across the wintry Atlantic, bore a curious mix of passengers. Cream—a convicted murderer—had as his dining companions Lieutenant-Colonel Vohl, chief of police of Quebec City, and the Reverend Robert Caswell, chaplain of the Toronto jail. Not surprisingly crime emerged as a topic of dinner conversation. John Cautle, a representative of a firm of Toronto oil merchants, heard Cream say that he knew something about a woman poisoned in London. Cream, having turned to whiskey to wean himself away from morphine, was intoxicated for most of the voyage. His drunkenness and constantly disparaging talk of women eventually led most passengers to avoid his company.[72]

In Quebec City Daniel Cream's wife found her brother-in-law's manner so unnerving that it was decided that everyone would be better off if he stayed at a hotel. But Cream never seemed to lack male friends. At Blanchard's Hotel in early March he formed a relationship with John Wilson McCulloch, a salesman for Jardine and Company, the Toronto grocery wholesalers. When McCulloch felt unwell, Cream, who occupied the room next to his, gave him an "anti-bilious pill and a blue mass pill." Cream, who complained himself of not being able to sleep at night, took large numbers of morphia pills.[73] He was fascinated by pharmaceuticals. He claimed he would make a fortune by the sale of pills and showed McCulloch capsules he used to get women "out of the family way."

Cream likely visited the brothels of Quebec City; he certainly showed McCulloch his pornographic photographs and spoke of the cheapness of London prostitutes, claiming he had had three women between 10:00 P.M. and 3:00 A.M. for a shilling each. But he also allowed McCulloch to see a photograph of Laura Sabbatini, whom he said he was going to marry, and jewelry that he asserted had been returned to him by a woman to whom he had been engaged who had married someone else.[74] At Quebec City, Cream also socialized with M. A. Kingman, a representative of a Saratoga Springs, New York, drug manufacturer, from whom he ordered five hundred 1/16th grain strychnine pills. In late March he went with Kingman to Saratoga Springs to pick up the pills, and on 23 March he sailed from New York aboard the *Britannic* for Liverpool.[75] He was back in London on 2 April.[76]

When Cream went to Montreal on 19 March to purchase his return ticket on the *Britannic,* he also ordered the printing of bizarre circulars in which he claimed to know who was responsible for the death of Ellen Donworth.[77] Cream arranged for them to be sent separately to England on board the *Labrador.* In his crazed way he probably thought he was thus protecting himself.[78] Of course, he was mad to have had such circulars made up in the first place. As it happened their contents were quickly discovered. Mr. Battersby, the curious shipping clerk, opened the package containing the circulars, later explaining, "It might have been dynamite for all I knew."[79] Reports of anarchist outrages around the world were making the authorities suspicious of any parcels sent on by third parties. But though the circulars were read, the police were not notified of their ominous message, the clerk's assumption being that they were part of an elaborate hoax.[80]

Back in London, Cream took up lodgings again at 103 Lambeth Palace Road and now described himself as an agent of the Harvey Drug Company. He spent weekends at Berkhamstead with his fiancée, employing a speaking tube to converse with the deaf Mrs. Sabbatini and attending local church services with Laura.[81] His routine in the city was much the same as it had been the previous autumn, but his fellow lodgers noted that he seemed to have given up opium. He took his meals out except for Sunday dinners. On Monday, 11 April, however, he dined at Lambeth Palace Road and went out at 10:00 P.M., explaining to his landlady that he had a late appointment. Marsh and Shrivell were killed that night.

Reading of their deaths in the following Easter Sunday edition of *Lloyd's Weekly Newspaper,* Cream made to Miss Sleaper, his landlady's daughter, the startling assertion that Walter Harper, a student at St. Thomas's and also a resident of 103, was responsible for these cold-blooded murders. Cream had earlier poked around Harper's room. The dark, thin twenty-six-year-old medical intern who came from a professional family in Barnstaple, Devonshire, had lived at 103 for the past three years. When Sleaper protested that he was the last man in the world to be involved in such crimes, Cream replied that he had his information from an American detective friend and that she was not to say anything.[82] He related much the same story to Laura Sabbatini on 2 May when asking her to write a number of letters for him in the name of a detective called "Murray."[83]

It is not surprising that Cream, a lonely, restless, inquisitive man, was drawn to the world of private detectives.[84] In April, as we have seen, he struck up a friendship at the home of his photographer, William Armstead, with Haynes, who in turn introduced him to Sergeant McIntyre of Scotland Yard. Cream was at first open in his dealings with his detective friends. His desire to impress them at the Armsteads' or at the nearby Crown and Cushion Pub with his knowledge of the London world of crime and prostitution seemed natural enough given the fact that the English papers in April and May were filled with reports of the murders of Frederick Deeming, who some thought was Jack the Ripper.[85] Cream told Margaret Armstead that he was shocked to hear of the deaths of Marsh and Shrivell.

> Neill said, "Whoever poisoned these girls in Stamford Street, they ought to be hanged."
> I said, "Yes, they ought to be."
> I said, "Did you know the girls, doctor?"
> He said, "I knew them well, they used to solicit up at the Bridge of an evening."[86]

By mid-May, however, Cream had become more circumspect.[87] Knowing that the police were watching him, he nervously began to dress differently and alter the course of his walks around Lambeth.[88] But if the police had viewed Cream as a killer, they presumably would not have simply watched as he continued to accost prostitutes. The truth was that as late as 23 May they regarded him as no more than a blackmailer who had tried to turn to his own purposes gossip picked up from streetwalkers. The police concluded that Cream "doubtless heard Clover's case spoken of by them" and simply sought to make something of it.[89]

To provide evidence that he was an agent for a drug company and not a confidence man, Cream went along with his friend McIntyre on 19 May to the Pheasant Public House on Lambeth Palace Road to meet Inspector Harvey and Chief Inspector Mulvaney of the Lambeth Division.[90] But after Harvey and Mulvaney left, Cream complained to his friend McIntyre of being spied on and failed to appear for the 24 May meeting McIntyre and Mulvaney had tried to arrange between Cream and women who knew the dead prostitutes.[91] Yet Cream and McIntyre had drinks together again on 26 May and parted "good friends." Later that day Cream formally complained to the chief commissioner of being followed. Finally, the police decided it was time to make their move; that same evening Inspector Tunbridge of the Criminal Investigation Department officially interrogated Cream about his movements and his possession of strychnine.[92]

On 1 June Tunbridge proceeded to interview Walter Harper, about whom Cream had made such wild allegations and at Barnstaple Tunbridge obtained from Joseph Harper the letter in which his son had been accused of the Marsh and Shrivell murders. Tunbridge immediately recognized that the letter was in Cream's handwriting and written on the same sort of unusual American writing paper that Cream habitually used.[93] More exciting was the fact that the letter contained, in addition to a newspaper cutting concerning the Stamford Street deaths, three circulars relating to Ellen Donworth's murder.[94]

By 3 June J. Braman, superintendent of L Division, was convinced that Cream was tied to the murders. To prevent his slipping away, the police arrested him on the blackmail charge that very day.[95] But it was chiefly the problem of linking Cream to Alice Marsh's and Emma Shrivell's deaths that preoccupied Scotland Yard. On 4 June 1892 Robert Anderson, head of C.I.D., wrote exasperatedly to the Secretary of State of the Home Office, "The moral proof of his guilt is ample, but my utmost efforts have so far failed to procure any direct evidence connecting him with these crimes."[96]

In the hope of finding some evidence that might incriminate Cream in the murders in which he appeared to be so obviously implicated Scotland Yard dispatched Inspector Frederick Jarvis on 18 June to retrace Cream's career in North America. Well before Jarvis returned to England that August on board the *Mongolian* he had provided Scotland Yard with abundant proof that in North America Cream had been an abortionist, a blackmailer, and a murderer. But the question still remained—where was the evidence to convict him of the London poisonings?

5

THE TRIAL

The law courts of England are open to all men, like the doors of the Ritz Hotel.

Attributed to Lord Darling

Matilda Clover's body was exhumed 5 May 1892 at Tooting Cemetery. On 23 May, the same day that a police report was filed stating that Cream could not be the murderer, Dr. Stevenson completed his post-mortem investigations, concluding that Clover had died of strychnine poisoning.[1]

Haynes was with Cream on 2 June. They still were apparently friends; on 3 June it was Haynes whom Cream sought to contact when Inspector Tunbridge of the C.I.D. at the Bow Street Magistrates Court charged him with attempting to extort money from Dr. Harper of Barnstaple. The blackmail accusation was only made by the authorities to give the police additional time to locate evidence linking Cream to the Lambeth poisonings.[2] Such links began to be forged on 11 June, when Eliza Masters and Elizabeth May, the prostitutes who had followed Matilda Clover and her client, were interviewed; on 17 June they identified Cream in the yard of the Bow Street Police Station as the man who in October had passed Hercules Road and entered Clover's House on Lambeth Road.[3]

The Clover inquest began on 22 June at the Vestry Hall, Tooting, before Mr. A. Braxton Hicks.[4] Its sensational nature attracted a crowd

of hundreds of spectators; with adjournments it did not conclude until 7 July. The evidence produced against Cream appeared to the public to be overwhelming. Albert Kirby testified to having sold Cream
strychnine, Eliza Masters and Elizabeth May identified him as the man
seen with Clover, Dr. Broadbent described the letter sent him on
30 November saying Matilda Clover had been murdered, and Emily
Sleaper reported that Cream had told her in October that a woman
in the Lambeth Road had been poisoned.[5] Cream was moreover
linked to the other killings when Battersby telegraphed from Montreal giving an account of Cream's possession of the "Metropole circular" describing Ellen Donsworth's death and Inspector Tunbridge
introduced an envelope found in Cream's room on which were written the initials of the murdered women and the dates of their deaths.[6]
Cream refused to testify, but Haynes included in his testimony references made by Cream to other prostitutes' deaths. By 4 July Cream's
daily trips in handcuffs between Holloway Prison and Tooting were
enlivened by youths running alongside his warder's hansom cab boo-
ing and jeering.[7]

The most sensational event in the inquest was undoubtedly the appearance of "Lou Harvey." Early on in the inquest Haynes mentioned
the fact that Cream had linked the names of Matilda Clover and Lou
Harvey. The police still had no idea who the Harvey woman was until
she, having read that her name had been mentioned at the inquest,
wrote to Sir John Bridge, the Bow Street magistrate, and Braxton
Hicks, the Tooting coroner, giving the following account.

> Met a man outside of St. James Hall Regent St. 12.30 one
> night in October, about the 20th. Had been to the Alham-
> bra and seen him there earlier the same night. Went with
> him from St. James to a hotel in Berwick St., Oxford St.
> Stayed there with him all night left about 8 oc. in the morn-
> ing. Made an appointment with him to meet the same night
> at 7.30 on the Embankment.[8]

Lou Harvey's real name was Louisa Harris; she took the surname of
Charles Harvey, an omnibus man, with whom she lived just below
Primrose Hill in North London at 44 Townsend Street, St. John's
Wood. As her testimony concerning Cream made clear, she was very
observant.

> He wore Gold rimmed Glasses and had very Peculiar eyes.
> As far as I can remember he had [a] dress suit on, and [a]
> long mackintosh on his arm. He spoke with a foreign
> Twang. He asked me if I had ever been in America. I said

no. He had an Old fashioned Gold Watch, with an Hair or silk fob Chain and seal. Said he had been in the army. I noticed he was a very hairy man. He said he had never been married.[9]

Louisa Harris was also a cautious woman. She told her client that she was a servant, which was not true, and that she lived at 55, rather than 44, Townsend Road. The doctor's announcement that he would bring her some pills which he wanted her to take she thought odd and, feeling a need for protection, asked Harvey to follow her to the rendezvous on the Embankment.

> Met him the same night opposite Charing X [Cross] Underground R. [railway] Station. Walked with him to the Northumberland Public-house, had glass of wine, and then walked back to the Embankment. Were [sic] he gave me two capsules. But not liking the look of the thing, I pretended to put them in my mouth. But kept them in my hand. And when he happened to look away, I threw them over the Embankment. He then said that he had to be at St. Thomas's Hospital, left me, and gave me 5s. to go to the Oxford Music Hall. Promising to meet me outside at 11 oc. But he never came. I told him that I was living at Townsend Rd., St. Johns Wood but I gave him the wrong number.

Charles Harvey, standing a little way off, saw the doctor give Harris something. They were two long pills wrapped in tissue which he took from his waistcoat pocket, put in her right hand, and told her to swallow, not bite, there and then. He also gave her one or two figs, which she was to eat after taking the pills. Louisa Harris was suddenly afraid. In the darkness she put her hand to her mouth, pretended to take the capsules, but transferred them from one hand to the other. When the man asked to see her hands she let the pills fall behind her. Satisfied, the doctor said he had to go to St. Thomas's Hospital but would meet her at eleven, and he quickly went off toward Westminster Bridge. Harris waited for him at the Oxford Music Hall until eleven thirty; he never came.

A few weeks later Louisa Harris saw the man again, but he did not recognize her.

> I never saw him again until about three weeks after. When I moved from St. Johns Wood to Stamford St. When I happened to be in Piccadilly Circus and I saw him. I spoke to him. He asked me to have a drink, in the Regent, Air St. He promised to meet me at 11 on the same night. He had

> not seemed as if he knew me while we were drinking. So I
> said to him don't you remember me. He said no. I said not
> that night when you promised to meet me outside the Ox-
> ford. He then said whats your name. I said Louisa Harvey.
> He seemed surprised, said no more, and walked quickly
> away. And never turned up that night. I saw him once
> again, about a month afterward with a young lady down
> the Strand, and I never saw him again.

Harris was not sure what the problem was. She was not a woman who
liked playing games. "'I was the woman you went with to such and
such a hotel.' I told him plainly, and he did not believe it."

Harris, after reading the press reports, saw that she had been one
of Cream's intended victims. Now she was out to get him.

> I have a witness who saw him give me capsules on the Em-
> bankment who could Identify him. I had not troubled to
> read the case particular [*sic*] till Friday night, when I hap-
> pened to read it in the *Star*. I was struck by the resem-
> blance. So I got the *Telegraph* next morning, saw my name
> mentioned, so I was almost sure. He being under the im-
> pression that I took the capsules, and either dropped dead
> in the street, or music hall.[10]

The jury's finding on 13 July was that Matilda Clover had died of
strychnine poisoning administered by Cream with the intent to murder. On 18 July Tunbridge officially charged him with Clover's death.
Ultimately he was charged with the murders of Clover, Donworth,
Marsh, and Shrivell, the attempted murder of Louisa Harris, and the
sending of extortion letters to Drs. Broadbent and Harper.[11] On
4 July Cream had written his fiancée asking that she not visit him in
Holloway Prison since the police were on the lookout for any incriminating evidence. On 26 July he was more optimistic; he sent Laura
the unlikely news that a member of Parliament had two hundred witnesses who would testify on his behalf.[12]

In the summer and early fall of 1892 the police and the Home
Office continued to collect evidence. The country turned its attention
in late July to Gladstone's new government and in August to the ap-
proaching cholera epidemic that was sweeping west through Germany and France. In September and October accounts of the illness
and death of Lord Alfred Tennyson, the poet laureate, dominated
the pages of the English press.[13]

Thomas Neill Cream, having markedly changed his appearance by
growing a reddish brown beard, appeared before a grand jury on
13 September, and "true bills," or indictments, were issued.[14] The

trial in what the press referred to as the "Lambeth Poisoning Mystery" took place between 17 and 21 October 1892 in one of the central oak-paneled court rooms of the Old Bailey. Mr. Justice Henry Hawkins, the presiding judge, was a small, slight man who reserved his affections for dogs and racehorses. He was so feared by prisoners as a brutal magistrate, having pronounced the death sentence on so many murderers, including those involved in the famous Penge case of 1877, that he was tagged "Hanging Hawkins."[15] The leading members of the bar regarded him as biased and unfair.[16] Unable to tolerate drafts, he subjected counsel to long days in stuffy courtrooms, having ordered every window to be firmly sealed.

In the 1890s famous barristers were as well known as music hall artistes.[17] This was certainly true of the barristers who appeared in the Cream trial. The crown counsel was one of England's most skilled lawmen, the attorney-general in Gladstone's new government, Sir Charles Russell, Q.C., M.P., soon to be Lord Russell of Killowen.[18] The accused's own counsel was Gerald Geoghegan, a brilliant but erratic and alcoholic Irish barrister. Geoghegan had advanced the defense of necessity in the famous *Mignonette* cannibalism case of 1884, had defended the poisoner Israel Lipski in 1887, and was fresh from assisting Marshall Hall as counsel for the infamous Deeming accused of the Rainhill murders. His colleagues were to remember Geoghegan as a great orator with a marvelous Irish brogue who, once unleashed, was impossible to stop.[19] A notorious trial with such a cast of players naturally attracted large numbers of spectators. Members of the "smart set" jammed the court, and hundreds waited outside. Ladies, the press reported with some annoyance, seemed to predominate.[20]

The chief legal interest of Cream's trial lay in the fact that there was not enough damning evidence to link him inextricably to any one of the deaths of which he was accused. Only because the court allowed the cumulative evidence of all the cases to be presented, which revealed a "systematic and deliberate course of action," could the crown hope to prove Cream's guilt.[21] The defense objected that Cream's being tried for seven crimes at once violated the general rule. Mr. Justice Hawkins allowed the prosecution to proceed, being of the opinion that evidence could be admitted to prove the intention or patterning of the crimes.

The crown's central argument was that the fact that Cream possessed strychnine, that four women died of strychnine poisoning, that the same pattern was discernible in each murder, and that the accused himself had lumped the deaths together in attributing them to young

Dr. Harper had the cumulative effect of proving Cream guilty. Advancing such a "chain of testimony" had its risks; the destruction of any one link could shatter the entire case.

The crown's presentation of its argument was fairly straightforward.[22] It set out to prove that Matilda Clover had been poisoned and that the poison had been murderously administered to her by Cream. J. G. Kirby, a chemist's assistant, told of selling Cream strychnine in the form of nux vomica. McCulloch testified that Cream had showed him the poison in Quebec, claiming that he used it as an abortifacient.[23] Dr. Thomas Stevenson, the crown's medical expert, testified that Cream's pill box contained seven bottles of strychnine pills and that postmortem examinations indicated that Matilda Clover, Alice Marsh, and Emma Shrivell had all died of strychnine poisoning.

Eliza Masters and Elizabeth May testified that they had seen Cream follow Clover; Emily Sleaper, his landlady's daughter, stated that sometime in the autumn of 1891 Cream had told her that a young woman in the Lambeth Road had been poisoned and that Lord Russell had committed the crime. Similarly, in April 1892, Cream had told her that Dr. Walter Harper, a fellow lodger, was responsible for the poisoning deaths of Alice Marsh and Emma Shrivell. Sleaper recalled that she had told Cream that he must be mad, but he had countered by saying he was well informed by a detective friend from America.[24]

The "M. Malone" letter sent to Dr. W. H. Broadbent accusing him of Clover's murder and the letter sent to Frederick Smith were declared by Walter de Grey Birch, handwriting expert of the Manuscripts Department of the British Museum, to be by Cream.[25] The letter to Broadbent stating that Matilda Clover had died of strychnine poisoning, written at a time when no one else suspected that she had been killed, was likely the single most telling piece of evidence against the accused.[26]

Haynes testified that Cream had attributed the deaths of Clover, Marsh, Shrivell, and Lou Harvey all to Walter Harper. This had occurred at a time when Matilda Clover's murder was still not suspected and the police knew nothing about Lou Harvey. Haynes reported that when he wanted to know more about Harvey, Cream took him to 55 Townsend Road, where she supposedly lived. Sergeant McIntyre confirmed much of what Haynes stated and produced copies of Cream's handwriting and American brand of writing paper that matched that sent to Dr. Harper. "The greatest interest was taken, however," reported the *Penny Illustrated Paper*, "in the appearance of the smartly dressed, Italian-looking young lady, Miss Sabatini [*sic*], to whom Neill had been betrothed."[27] Laura Sabbatini testified that in May Cream had had her write the mysterious letters signed "Wm. H. Murray" that were sent to the Alice Marsh and Emma Shrivell coroner's jury and to George Clarke, private detective, accusing Walter Harper of murder.[28] But the most dramatic evidence was offered by Louisa Harris (alias Lou Harvey), who recounted how Cream had attempted to get her to take pills and his fright when he later saw that she was still alive.

Geoghegan called no witnesses for the defense. Cream himself could not testify inasmuch as in the nineteenth century the accused in a capital case was not allowed to take the stand.[29] His counsel, of course, would not have wanted him to enter the witness box; had he done so, the crown in cross-examination could have extracted a damaging account of the crimes of which he had been convicted in North America. The defense counsel's strategy consisted simply of seeking to undermine the case built by the prosecution, based as it was entirely on circumstantial evidence. Was the jury, asked Geoghegan, convinced beyond a shadow of a doubt that Cream had poisoned Matilda Clover?

The defense's first line of attack was to suggest that Matilda Clover's death was not due to strychnine poisoning. Dr. Graham conceded that the bromide of potassium he had prescribed for Clover, if mixed with excessive amounts of brandy, could bring on seizures.[30] The defense's next strategy was to point out that the crown had failed to produce a single witness who could place Cream at the scene of any of the crimes. Lucy Rose, the only one to see the man to whom Matilda Clover had said good-night, had, as the crown counsel admitted, not identified Cream.[31] Another witness who could have made a valuable addition to this line of argument was Constance Linfield. She told the police she had seen her friend Ellen Donworth enter Morpeth Court with a tall gentleman. When they emerged, Donworth had touched Linfield with her umbrella and had spoken to her. Linfield noted that the man, who was not wearing spectacles, had a strange look in his eye. Although she later saw Cream at both the inquest and Bow Street, she stated that he definitely was not the man she had seen with Ellen Donworth. Constance Linfield was referred to by the crown counsel in his opening speech but was not called by him as a witness, and was therefore unavailable to the defense.[32]

Geoghegan's third gambit was to undermine the credibility of the crown's witnesses. He suggested that the lineup in which Eliza Masters and Elizabeth May identified Cream was rigged. Curiously enough, the police allowed the artist of the *Penny Illustrated Paper* to be included, but Cream was apparently the only bald-headed man with a squint in the lineup.[33] Geoghegan conceded that Masters and May remembered Cream from Gatti's Music Hall, but, he asked, could one be sure he was the same man they had glimpsed from an upper-story window following Matilda Clover?

As for Haynes, Geoghegan argued that Cream had simply made up stories for his gullible friend. But Geoghegan also suggested another reason why Haynes was not a believable witness: had Haynes not accepted Cream's stolen photograph of Harper and for some time gone along with Cream's blackmailing scheme? Geoghegan similarly sought to tarnish McCulloch's testimony by pointing out that McCulloch had not been particularly shocked by Cream's references to abortion, prostitution, and pornography.[34] Finally, Louisa Harris's evidence was dismissed by Geoghegan as at best no more than hearsay and at worst simply a sign of Cream's peculiar sense of humor. Since Cream knew in November 1891 that she was alive, why was he telling Haynes in April 1892 that she was dead?

Geoghegan knew he could not present his client as a complete innocent. He was willing to admit that Cream had toyed with the idea of becoming a blackmailer and that he had sent extortionate letters to Drs. Harper and Broadbent. The defense's argument was that Cream had heard of Matilda Clover's death and, as a medical man who recognized that the symptoms indicated poisoning, had hatched the idea of demanding money from dupes. But he had never gone through with it. Indeed, the fact that Cream was addicted to opium, morphia, and strychnine would explain why he had broached such a ridiculous blackmail scheme, one he never had any serious intention of pursuing. Even in this lesser affair of extortion, argued Geoghegan, Cream's guilt was mitigated by his drug taking.

Geoghegan was also willing to admit that Cream was addicted to the company of "loose women"; Cream had in his possession a note from Alice Marsh with her address on it and may have known both Marsh and Emma Shrivell, but what did that prove?

Given his lack of resources Geoghegan did a creditable job of defending Cream, but his arguments were seriously undermined by Mr. Justice Hawkins's summing up of the evidence. Geoghegan had told the jury they had to be convinced of Cream's guilt "beyond a shadow of a doubt." Hawkins directed them to find him guilty if the evidence reasonably satisfied them. He stressed the fact that in many of the cases under consideration eyewitness evidence was not available and that it "was not to be expected in every case that there should be mathematical proof of the commission of the crime."[35]

The jury needed only ten minutes to arrive at its verdict—guilty. Cream, who until the last moment appeared to be confident of acquittal, was dazed by the outcome and had nothing to say. He was sentenced to be hanged after the customary three Sundays had passed. Once Mr. Justice Hawkins had finished passing sentence, the warder touched the condemned on the shoulder and quickly led him down the steps from the dock that communicated directly with Newgate Prison.

Cream apparently carried out his crimes with cool calculation. But was he sane? An editorial in the *Lancet*, having noted that Cream was obviously guilty, went on to say:

> To the psychologist, however, his case is one of absorbing interest. That he willed to do the murderous deed, or, in other words, acted under conscious motive there appears to be no shadow of doubt, leaving aside the absurd legal proof of criminal responsibility—"the knowledge of right and wrong, or of the nature and quality of the act." Nor can we argue in NEILL's favour impulsive homicidal insanity as usually understood. At the same time it is difficult to believe that the convict perpetrated these unutterable crimes with a mind constituted to realize their enormity and with a power of will equal to inhibit their commission.[36]

The *Pall Mall Gazette* was willing to accept the idea that Cream was mad but insisted that he, like Deeming and the Whitechapel Fiend, who also were clearly insane, had to die. Insanity defenses had been made prior to the nineteenth century, but it was only as a result of McNaughton's killing of Peel's secretary in the belief that the secretary was the prime minister that the "McNaughton Rules" of 1843 codified the insanity defense.[37] Theretofore to be excused one had to be totally incapable of distinguishing between good and evil. The simply deluded would be considered mad in civil, but not in criminal, law. The new rules relaxed the criterion somewhat, although much confusion still existed. In theory, one was not to be held responsible if it could be proved that because of a "defect of reason" one did not know a specific act was wrong.[38]

Few murderers successfully employed the insanity plea. A parliamentary committee reported in 1893 that, of the 256 prisoners sentenced to death for murder in the past nine years, 145 had been hanged; of the remainder, 102 had been committed to penal servitude (45 for life), 1 pardoned, and only 8 declared insane and committed to Broadmoor.[39] Deeming, tried in the spring of 1892 for murdering two sets of wives and children in both England and Australia, appeared to be a perfect candidate for Broadmoor. The son of lunatics, he had spent his early years in an asylum and had a history of epileptic fits. The doctors who examined him in Australia found signs of blows on his head and deep syphilitic scars on his body.[40] But the tide of revulsion caused by the discovery of his murder victims swept aside all exculpating evidence; Deeming hanged.[41]

Lou Harvey's testimony clinched Cream's guilt; it could just as well have been used to demonstrate the unbalanced state of his mind. In October Cream apparently believed that he had poisoned her. But his mind was so disturbed that three weeks later he did not recognize her. When she finally succeeded in reminding him of who she was, he was accordingly shocked. But five months later he was telling Haynes that Harvey was dead. Clearly, Cream no longer had the ability to sort out fact from fiction. But the defense passed this off as a sign of his curious sense of humor rather than of his madness. The press reported that the Treasury had four expert witnesses waiting to testify to Cream's sanity should such a defense be raised.[42] Curiously enough, it was not.

Only after he was found guilty did Cream's solicitors turn to an insanity plea.[43] His execution was postponed a week while his lawyers assembled a dossier to prove his unbalanced state of mind. They based their appeal primarily on the argument that during his ten years in prison he had been allowed the free use of opiates, which undermined his sanity. Thomas Davidson, of John Ross and Company, the executor of William Cream's estate, stated that Cream had written him letters from Joliet "in a most extraordinary and incoherent style which led him [Davidson] to believe that his mind had become unhinged and this opinion was strengthened in his seeing him after liberation by his wild and eccentric demeanor."[44] This was given as the explanation of why Cream's life sentence at Joliet was not carried out. He was judged to be insane, "on which grounds his release was ordered on the 31st of July, 1891."[45] Senator Fuller, who had prosecuted Cream in Illinois, accepted this diagnosis and supported the argument for early release. A. C. Trude, Cream's American defense lawyer, gave a slightly different account, however, attributing his release primarily to purchased political influence. Trude noted that already in 1881 Cream was exhibiting a crazed desire for anatomical knowledge and a homicidal view of women, whom he saw as a "threat" to society.

Cream's family claimed that after his release from Joliet his behavior in Quebec in August 1891 had been noticeably peculiar. Not content with having called his sister a "streetwalker," Cream included the libel in letters he sent to her friends. Jessie Read Cream, his brother Daniel's wife, wrote that during his stay of 2 August to 15 September 1891 she was struck by his vacant eyes and frightened by his creeping up on her from behind.[46] Daniel hoped that a trip by sailing ship to England would help. Davidson concluded that it did not. Cream, he wrote, "appears to have become much weaker mentally than they supposed and utterly unable to resist it, he fell a ready victim to 'the stream of vice always flowing in the metropolis.'"[47] Davidson, in trying to get Cream to return to Canada, sought the help of an old family friend, Rev. Dr. George Duncan Matthews of Bondesbury. Matthews wrote to Daniel Cream that the "family should have had the Dr. placed under restraint as he did not think he was in a fit state to be at large."[48]

Affidavits were submitted by Matthews and James Aitchison, Cream's Fleet Street optician, testifying to Cream's irrational behavior. Matthews, who had seen Cream when he first arrived in London in October 1891 at Anderton's Hotel, doubted his mental competence and believed there was some question of "hereditary insanity" in the family. Aitchison, who diagnosed Cream as suffering from "hypermyopia," felt that his inordinate use of drugs had made it impossible for him to know right from wrong.[49]

William Sellar of Montreal, who in January 1892 had the cabin across the gangway from Cream's on the *Sarnia*, reported that he and the other passengers believed Cream was not in his right mind. Cream, according to Sellar, spoke of nothing but women, how he met them in the street or accosted them at show places such as the Royal Aquarium. During the entire voyage he drank heavily in an attempt to overcome his addiction to opium. Waking up Sellar in the middle of the night to continue his vulgar monologues, Cream would become angry if his neighbor refused to drink with him. Sellar, believing Cream was "not quite right in the head," was frightened by a man who seemed to have "no refinement and an utter absence of morality." When Cream offered him pills, the seasick Sellar prudently declined.[50]

Cream's family likewise testified that when Cream returned to Canada in the winter of 1891–92 they were convinced that he was insane. Daniel Cream's wife did not want him in the house "as she did not like his manner and thought he wasn't right in his mind."[51]

The members of Cream's family who sought to save him from hanging claimed he was mad. Those who wanted him executed stressed his rationality, his ability to make choices, his individualism. The press warned Home Secretary Asquith not to give vent to any "sentimental nonsense."[52] Asquith seems to have followed this advice since no great effort was made to determine the prisoner's state of mind. The report made by Dr. Gilbert, the medical officer of Holloway Prison, who declared that in his opinion Cream was sane, appeared to be sufficient.[53] The Secretary of State, after rapidly weighing the evidence, denied Cream's appeal on 11 November.[54]

On 12 November the *Illustrated Police News* carried the following advertisement for the benefit of its distributors.

Execution of Dr. Neill
Next Week (November 19th)
Illustrated Police News
(Unless the respite is extended)
Will Contain a Full Page Illustration of the
EXECUTION OF
DR NEILL CREAM
Give early orders. An enormous sale is expected
All unsold copies exchanged[55]

Cream was executed 15 November 1892. In the United States "execution by electricity" was being experimented with, but England remained loyal to the noose.[56] Billington, the hangman, followed the Home Office's new directives concerning the type of rope and length of drop. Public hangings had been brought to an end in 1868; hangings now took place within the prison walls witnessed only by the sheriff, surgeon, justice of the peace, and close relatives. Similarly, with the intent of putting an end to the unseemly spectacle of mobs celebrating the deaths of villains, the Home Office insisted that the subsequent inquest and burial also be carried out at Newgate.[57] Nevertheless, a crowd of four to five thousand "drink sodden men and repulsive females," the largest crowd to gather at an execution since they had ceased to be public, waited in a fine drizzle outside Newgate Prison on the morning of Tuesday, 15 November, for the news of Cream's death. "Probably no criminal was ever executed in London," declared a Canadian newspaper, "who had a less pitying mob awaiting his execution."[58] The appearance of the black flag was greeted by hoarse cries and cheers: "Now 'ee's a danglin'." Billington left soon after, followed by small boys who "regarded him with considerable awe."[59] Those who felt they had not seen enough went along to Madame Tussaud's, where as early as 23 October a special display depicting Cream's murders and those of the Rainhill Tragedy had been put up alongside the effigies of Horatio Nelson and the recently departed Lord Alfred Tennyson.[60] In November the waxworks paid £200 for Cream's clothes; the money was distributed among his solicitors.[61]

Illustrations

1. A page of advertisements for abortifacients from *Pick-Me-Up*, 24 February 1894.

2. A cartoon from *Punch* (8 September 1849) noting the ease with which poisons could be purchased.

FATAL FACILITY; OR, POISONS FOR THE ASKING.

Child: "Please, Mister, will you be so good as to fill this bottle again with Lodnum, and let Mother have another pound and a half of arsenic for the rats(!)"

Duly qualified chemist: "Certainly, Ma'am. Is there any other article?"

DR. THOMAS NEILL CREAM AND HIS BETROTHED AT THE INQUEST ON MATILDA CLOVER; AND "NEILL" AT BOW STREET
CHARGED WITH WRITING BLACKMAILING LETTERS.

"DR. NEILL" AND THE SOUTH
LONDON STRYCHNINE CASES.

Far graver even than the Deeming charges appear to be the appalling allegations against the man accused at Bow Street Police Court under the name of "Thomas Neill," who is portrayed afresh as he reappeared at the Court on Monday last, and as he appeared before Mr. Braxton Hicks at the inquest held on the exhumed body of Matilda Clover.

With an American accent spoke Neill when he was brought up at the Tooting Vestry Hall, where Coroner Hicks opened the inquiry into the death of Matilda Clover, who was known to Neill, according to the evidence of her uncle, Robert Taylor, who identified a photograph of Neill as that of a man he had seen drinking with deceased. Lucy Rose, servant at the Lambeth dwelling in which the poor girl died in agony, deposed that Clover said on her deathbed—"That wretch has given me some pills which have made me ill."

But Lucy Rose did not identify Neill as the man last seen with Clover. Neither did the landlady, a Mrs. Phillips or Mr. Vowles. But two women in whose company Neill had been at Gatti's Music Hall, as they said, declared they had seen Neill follow a girl into the house in Lambeth Road where Clover lived. Mr. Gill, who stated that Neill had bought quantities of nux vomica and gelatine capsules at Priest's chemist-shop, 22, Parliament Street. Neill's landlady, Emily Sleaper, was also called, and referred to a remark by Neill as to a girl having been poisoned in the Lambeth Road.

The greatest interest was taken, however, in the appearance of the smartly dressed, Italian-looking young lady, Miss Sabatini, to whom Neill had been betrothed. Her appearance in court naturally made a marked impression upon Neill. Miss Laura Sabatini, of Chapel Street, Berkhampsted, said she was introduced to him last November as Dr. Thomas Neill Cream, and that she accepted his proposal of marriage. At his dictation she wrote the letters to the Coroner, in which suspicion was attempted to be thrown upon a young medical man. She asked Neill for information about the substance of the letters, and he refused to give her any information. A young man who met Neill at a photographer's in Westminster Bridge Road in April said that in the course of their walks together the prisoner told him that a young woman named Clover had died from strychnine poisoning at a house in Lambeth Road in the previous October. The inquest was adjourned from June 24 to July 7.

On Monday last Thomas Neill, or Cream, was again brought up, on remand, before Sir John Bridge at Bow Street, charged with sending a letter to Dr. Harper, of Barnstaple, threatening to accuse his son of being concerned in the death of two girls who died from the effects of poisoning in Stamford Street in October last. The proceedings were formal, and Mr. Stephenson, on behalf of the Treasury, having asked for a remand for a week, the magistrate acceded.

4.   "London poisoning horror," *Penny Illustrated Paper*, 16 July 1892. The three photographs of Cream were the work of William Armstead. By permission of the British Library.

MATILDA CLOVER,
WHO DIED FROM STRYCHNINE IN SOUTH LONDON.

5. "Matilda Clover, who died from strychnine in South London," *Penny Illustrated Paper,* 22 October 1892. The sketch was apparently based on a photograph of Clover taken by William Armstead. By permission of the British Library.

6. "Neill at the Old Bailey; sketches of important persons connected with the case," *Illustrated Police News,* 22 October 1892. By permission of the British Library.

7. "The Lambeth poisoning case: Neill's career," *Illustrated Police News*, 29 October 1892. By permission of the British Library.

8.   "The just end of a monster of iniquity; the condemned man, Neill, mentally reviews his awful past," *Illustrated Police News*, 5 November 1892. By permission of the British Library.

9. "The execution of Dr. Thomas Neill Cream: Closing scenes in the career of a great criminal," *Illustrated Police News*, 19 November 1892. By permission of the British Library.

PART TWO: THE CONTEXT

Of all offences, it might well be supposed that the crime of
murder is one of the most arbitrary and irregular . . . The
fact is that murder is committed with as much regularity,
and bears as uniform a relation to certain known circum-
stances, as do the movements of the tides, and the rotation
of the seasons.

Henry Thomas Buckle, *The History of Civilization in
England* (1857–61)

All executions, even ones like Cream's that take place behind the walls
of a prison, are "public executions."[1] Both the public and the authorities take the opportunity to draw a moral from the event. In Cream's
case, both those who thought he was guilty and those who thought he
was insane agreed at least on the incomprehensibility of what he had
done. Some called for his blood; others inundated Newgate with religious tracts and pamphlets seeking his conversion.

After Cream had been found guilty, *Lloyd's Weekly London Newspaper*
printed a telegram sent by Mr. Charles Morrell, a wealthy resident of
Kent Mills, Ontario. Morrell described a conversation he had had in
1881 with Cream concerning the assassination of President James
Garfield by Charles Jules Guiteau. In response to Morrell's musing
about how difficult it was for him to imagine how anyone could carry
out such a cold-blooded act, Cream reportedly said, "Well, it might

not appear so hard to some people when they are used to it."[2] Such statements were reported with the intent of showing how remote men like Cream and Guiteau were from sharing the feelings of the normal. But as Guiteau's biographer has pointed out, the very "madness" from which such men suffer is a product of the society in which they live.

> It has frequently been noted that the delusional systems of the mentally ill have a chameleon-like quality, an ability to find themes, tunes, specific menaces in the atmosphere and events of their times . . . [Guiteau] had the ability to portray tragically and unselfconsciously a drama characteristically American as he acted out his sickness.[3]

Much the same could be said about Cream. In turning from his trial to the social context in which he operated, one can see that his thoughts and deeds, as "crazed" as they were, in many ways reflected the central preoccupations of the age.

In part 1 of this study we moved from the general context of nineteenth-century Lambeth to the killings, to the police and their suspects, and finally to the killer. In part 2 we reverse this process, moving from the most specific and localized issues, the murder of the prostitutes, to the ways in which women were treated in society, to the larger question of how deviancy was explained and policed. Chapters 6–8 explain why prostitution, abortion, and blackmail posed particular threats to Victorian society. In chapters 9–11 the complex ways in which doctors, police, and criminologists both created and responded to new forms of criminality are examined. These new professionals all too often regarded women as—indeed, sought to make them into—passive objects of investigation. But the ways in which women actively sought to make the world respond to their needs is the focus of the final chapter, chapter 12. Cream is in a sense the guide who leads us through this culture. Ideas and feelings common to late-nineteenth-century society—the adulation of the doctor, the fascination with the investigative aspects of policing, the fear of blackmail, the simultaneous preoccupation with and hatred of women as sexual beings—were to find in his thoughts and behavior their most exaggerated expression.

6

PROSTITUTION

We enact many laws that manufacture criminals, and then
a few that punish them.

Benjamin R. Tucker, *Instead of a Book* (1893)

All the Whitechapel women who fell victim to Jack the Ripper were
prostitutes—the drunken forty-two-year-old Mary Ann Nicholls,
known as "Polly," found disemboweled on 31 August 1888; forty-
seven-year-old Annie Chapman, who not being able to afford lodgings,
was butchered in the streets on the night of 8 September; forty-year-old
Elizabeth Stride and forty-three-year-old Catherine Eddowes, just released from the Bishopsgate police station, who were both murdered
on 30 September; and twenty-four-year-old Mary Kelly, the Ripper's
last and youngest victim, killed 9 November. The police noted that
the murders were linked by clear signs of the "frenzy" in which the
attacker had wielded his knife. Although all the women but Kelly
were killed in the street, none of the crimes were witnessed.

In the midst of the murders letters began to be received, purportedly written by the killer. These helped crystallize the fear that a
madman was carrying out, not random attacks, but some sort of pre-
meditated campaign against women. A note signed "Jack the Ripper"
was sent to the Central News Agency on 28 September; its publication
on 30 September caused an outcry. A second letter, received after the
Eddowes and Stride murders, furthered the public panic.[1]

The panic could have been even greater. The police dossiers contained references to the murders of many other women in London's East End that were not attributed to "Jack the Ripper": Martha Tabram, alias Turner, killed on 7 August 1888; Catherine Millet, an "unfortunate," whose body was found 20 December 1888 in Clarke's Yard, Poplar; Alice MacKenzie, murdered 19 July 1889; an unidentified headless female found under the arches off Pinchin Street on 10 September 1889; and Frances Coles, a Whitechapel woman, whose throat was cut 13 February 1891.[2]

Why were prostitutes singled out as victims by serial murderers like the Ripper and later Cream? Part of the answer must be that these killers shared in the general preoccupation with the "prostitution problem" that gripped nineteenth-century society. Attitudes toward prostitution had traditionally been divided, some seeing it as a necessary evil, others as a form of "slavery" that had to be eradicated. In the 1860s the British government, seized with an enthusiasm for the efficacy of medical surveillance, followed the lead of its continental neighbors in attempting to regulate prostitution through the Contagious Diseases Acts.[3]

France's chief advocate of regulation was Dr. Parent-Duchâtelet, a public health expert who in the 1830s had moved easily from an exploration of Paris's sewers to a study of the city's prostitutes. Feeling obliged to defend the propriety of his new investigations, he began his account of prostitution by asking,

> If, without scandalizing anyone, I was able to enter the sewers, handle putrid matter, spend part of my time in the refuse pits, and live as it were in the midst of the most abject and disgusting products of human congregations, why should I blush to tackle a sewer of another kind (more unspeakably foul, I admit, than all the others) in the well-grounded hope of effecting some good by examining all the facets it may offer?[4]

Such dehumanizing rhetoric was employed by men who saw themselves as progressive reformers. Regulation, which was fully elaborated under the July Monarchy, entailed the establishment of brothels where registered prostitutes could be policed and medically examined. French health officials candidly defended the system on the grounds that it would provide both a moral sequestering of disorder and a containment of disease; the intent was not to eliminate prostitution but to control it.

In England the Society for the Suppression of Vice's expression of alarm at the parading of immorality in West End London was met by William Acton's argument that a new policing mechanism of prostitution modeled on French practices was needed.[5] The sensational trial in 1858 of Giovanni Lani for the murder of a prostitute in Arundel Court reinforced middle-class fears of the disorders created by "gay women."[6] Although some proponents hoped eventually to extend such regulations across the entire country, the initially modest ambition of the Contagious Diseases Acts was the detention of diseased prostitutes in order to protect from venereal complaints the armed forces of a dozen port and garrison towns. Such diseases were held responsible for constantly rendering unfit for duty the equivalent of several battalions.[7] Women whom the police judged to be prostitutes were forced to undergo medical examination and in effect could be imprisoned, not for any crime but for merely being sick.[8] The defenders of the Acts argued that since women freely entered the profession they had to obey the rules that governed it.[9]

Despite such protestations the legislation infringed on individual rights and unabashedly sustained the sexual double standard: women were examined; men were not. Given these limitations it is difficult to imagine how such inspections were supposed to eradicate disease. In any event, since doctors at the time could not always diagnose venereal diseases and were unable to cure them the legislation had no prospect of fulfilling its therapeutic purpose.[10] But the Acts could be considered a political success: for doctors inasmuch as the Acts asserted that the well-being of the state depended on the expertise of the medical profession and for the police inasmuch as their new power to label and detain prostitutes increased their ability to intervene in working-class neighborhoods.[11] Prostitutes, in being labelled, found themselves socially cut off, further marginalized, and their relationship with the larger working-class society made more difficult.

But the Contagious Diseases Acts, in attributing the spread of venereal disease solely to women, created a backlash; even respectable, church-going matrons who viewed prostitutes with distaste were affronted by laws that allowed men to shirk their own responsibilities. The campaign for the repeal of the Acts, led by the Ladies National Association, created in 1869 by Josephine Butler, played a key role in the emergence of the late-nineteenth-century women's movement. Drawing on working-class, nonconformist, and liberal sentiment, the opponents of regulation achieved victory in 1886.[12] Even convictions for "annoying male persons for purposes of prostitution" dropped from 3,233 in 1886 to 1,475 in 1888.[13]

For feminists the campaign against the Contagious Diseases Acts provided a political apprenticeship and left a legacy of anger at male sexual license. The discoveries, made between the 1870s and the 1890s, that gonorrhea was a cause of sterility in women and that neurosyphilis led to insanity, raised in middle-class women new fears of both prostitution and male sexual demands. In this context the suffragist cry of "votes for women and chastity for men" was raised.

Feminists and their allies, having put an end to the state regulation of prostitution, were immediately divided on the question of whether the profession should be tolerated in any form.[14] In the last decades of the century the main wing of the women's movement swung around in support of a "social purity" campaign aimed at completely eradicating what was increasingly called "white slavery." The view now taken was that women never rationally entered the trade; they were entrapped. Ignored were prostitutes' own assertions that they had not been seduced by gentlemen but had "gone wrong" with members of their own class.[15] That prostitution might be the most beneficial economic choice for women was also not considered. *Mrs. Warren's Profession* (1892), in which George Bernard Shaw dared to broach such an argument, was banned for eight years. This failure to recognize such practical motivations underlay the puzzled irritation with which the respectable regarded what they took to be poor women's perverse insistence on taking their chances with a life on the street.[16]

To justify a more preventive, repressive approach to sex, social purity tracts portrayed prostitutes as young innocents who had to be protected—even against their own desires. Doctors had largely supported the earlier regulationist cause, and their powers had been accordingly increased. But they also took a leading role in the subsequent social purity campaigns of the 1880s and 1890s, arguing that chastity was the best defense against venereal disease. The women's movement for its part fell back on an argument which held that females were morally superior to males and that moral regulation was therefore required to raise men to the level of women. But such an argument led not simply to the policing of male behavior; it had the perhaps more important effect of preventing the emergence of any positive view of female sexuality.

The sexual activities of young women or "girls" was a growing source of anxiety to the late Victorian middle class, manifesting itself in preoccupations with prostitution and pornography.[17] Even the opponents of such practices indulged in an ambiguous prurience. W. T. Stead, the best known of the social purity campaigners, focused on the issue of child prostitution. In a series of sensational articles entitled "Maiden Tribute to Modern Babylon" which ran in the *Pall Mall*

Gazette in July 1885, he described how he "bought" a thirteen-year-old girl for five pounds.[18] Some castigated the muckraking journalism of "Bed-Stead" as voyeuristic; indeed, he was prosecuted for abduction.[19] Nevertheless, his actions contributed to the passing of the Criminal Law Amendment Act of 1885, which raised the age of consent for girls to sixteen.[20] The irony was that many of those opposed to the Contagious Diseases Acts supported a law by which the police's control of young women was extended.[21]

The leading activists in the campaign against the Contagious Diseases Acts moved on to join the National Vigilance Association, which attacked the immoral excesses of music halls and theaters on one hand and established rescue homes for "fallen" women on the other.[22] A sense of the movement's agenda was given at its sixth annual meeting, presided over by Millicent Garrett Fawcett, Josephine Butler, and W. A. Coote. The association, having received Gladstone's best wishes and heard Fawcett set as its next goals the winning of the female franchise and the creation of a force of woman police inspectors, congratulated itself on its successful prosecution of the publishers of Rabelais and its establishment of homes for fallen women.[23] Prostitutes, who earlier in the century had been harassed by the defenders of the Contagious Diseases Acts, in its closing decades found themselves badgered by such vigilant groups out to "rescue" them.[24] It was the strength of this new puritanism that explains why a serious play like Ibsen's *Ghosts* that broached the topic of venereal disease was condemned in the press for being "as foul and filthy a concoction as has ever been allowed to disgrace the boards of an English theatre."[25]

The Rev. G. P. Merrick was one of the few clergymen to question the zeal of the moral purity activists. Illiteracy and irreligion might, he pointed out, have kept some prostitutes from responding to the calls of their "rescuers," but most simply did not understand them.

> I am convinced that there are many poor men and women who do not in the least understand what is implied in the term "immorality." Out of courtesy to you, they may assent to what you say, but they do not comprehend your meaning when you talk of virtue or purity; you are simply talking over their heads.[26]

Few members of the police or judiciary entertained the view that prostitution could be eliminated. They took it as a "normal" institution that had to be tolerated. The keeping of a bawdy house was always considered a nuisance in English common law, but while brothels were prosecuted, streetwalking was not. But whatever laws were in force, the results were usually the same: women were punished and men let off. Prostitution offenses formed the overwhelming proportion of criminal charges against women in the nineteenth century.[27]

In this context it is possible to understand why prostitutes became the classic victims of the serial murderer. They were, as the Cream case made clear, often isolated and vulnerable. Many reformers were more interested in rescuing women from the trade than in assuring their safety on the street. The police considered them a nuisance, creators of disorderly conduct, rather than worthy of protection. In the late 1860s experts estimated that about six thousand of England and Wales' twenty-five thousand "known" prostitutes worked the streets of London; close to a thousand were found in Lambeth.[28] Cream told McCulloch in Quebec City that women were to be found on Waterloo Road, Westminster Bridge Road, London Road, and Victoria Road.[29]

Prostitutes lived in poverty. The police knew Alice Marsh had not been a robbery victim; she still had all her money—23s 8d and two cheap rings.[30] Matilda Clover was drawn by the presumed generosity of the man who bought her a pair of boots. "I saw her the day she bought them," Lucy Rose recalled, "in the morning, and again in the evening; she bought them in the evening when she was out. She was drunk when she came home. She said the gentleman had given her the money to buy them."[31] Marsh, according to her landlady, was swept away by her benefactor's lavish promise that he "was going to allow her £2.10 a week, and keep her in off the streets all the winter."[32] These women's backgrounds were much like those of the fourteen thousand prostitutes whose dossiers were kept by G. P. Merrick, chaplain of Millbank Prison. Most came from poor laboring families and eked out a living as domestics, laundresses, or barmaids. They tried to "keep within doors" and only took to the streets when there was no other option.[33]

The middle class attributed the women's "fall" to their "broken" homes. Eight thousand of the 13,915 "immoral women" who passed through Millbank Prison had lost one or both parents.[34] Emma Shrivell had lost her mother; Alice Marsh, her father. They led a life of irregular relationships. Shrivell had lodged for a short time in Brighton with Frank Pimm before coming up to London.[35] In Brighton Marsh had a male friend: twenty-one-year-old Charles Robinson had "walked out with her" for two months.[36] In the capital she was pursued by a "sea captain." "He wanted to keep her," a friend recalled, "as it was a shame for a fine girl like her to be on the street."[37] Eliza Masters was married but separated from her husband. The point that escaped middle-class observers was that the women took up prostitution to sustain family relationships, not to break them.[38]

Ellen Donworth, whose child had recently died, lived the last eighteen months of her life with Ernest Linnell, a private in the Second Battalion of the East Surrey Regiment. "I knew," he told the police, "Donworth went out and met men and got money in that way."[39] He earned eight to nine shillings a week; the rent was six shillings. Ellen Donworth made up the difference. "She used to walk the streets at night, and bring the money home. She was a very sober girl."[40] At the time of her death Linnell's regiment was about to be transferred to Tipperary.

Matilda Clover was even less fortunate in her choice of mates; she had a child by "Fred," who eventually abandoned her. After he left, she had to earn her keep by spending even longer hours on the streets.

The expectation that their male partners would take care of them was not indulged in by such women. Louisa Harris, when asked if she lived with Harvey, replied, "Yes, sometimes; not all the time."[41] Charles Harvey insisted that he did not live on the money Lou earned; he described himself as having been a painter in Brighton and an occasional omnibus conductor in London. By the time of Cream's trial he was no longer living with Harris. "I am in no particular trade now. I live on help from my relations. I am now living at 148 Stamford Street. I am living with someone there, on the same terms as I lived with Lou Harvey . . . I know she supports herself on the streets."[42] The coroner in the Ellen Donworth inquest was outraged by such casual relationships. Ernest Linnell was given a gratuitous dressing down for candidly admitting that he did not know the contents of the letters Donworth received.

> CORONER: "It appears to me that you didn't care. Who's keeping you now?"
> WITNESS: "My mother."
> CORONER: "She ought to kick you out and let you shift for yourself."[43]

To the young Thomas Holmes, fresh out of Staffordshire when appointed Lambeth police court missionary in 1885, the discovery of such prostitutes' networks of relationships was an appalling revelation. "I hear stories of lust, drunkenness, and theft. I see the smartly-dressed harpies who farm them waiting to pay their fines. I see the most despicable of all mankind, the fellows who live upon them, hovering like beasts of prey."[44]

The Cream trial revealed that constant moves, in addition to their transient relationships, were a part of the prostitutes' lives. Alice Marsh and Emma Shrivell had only come up to London from Brighton a few weeks previous to their deaths but had made the trip once before. Eliza Masters lived at Hercules Road in October 1891, at 121 Lambeth Road in May 1892. Her friend Elizabeth May moved from Hercules Road in 1891 to 45 Ponsonby Buildings, Charles Street, Blackwell, in May 1892. Louisa Harris lodged in St. John's Wood in 1891; had returned to Upper North Street, Brighton, by May 1892; and was back living on Stamford Street, London, in October. Single, unskilled woman workers such as domestic servants seemed to live equally peripatetic existences. Lucy Rose had only been at 27 Lambeth Road for a month in October 1891 when Matilda Clover died; Lucy Rose left after a few weeks for 88 Lambeth Road; in May 1892 she was at 90 Merrow Street, Walworth Road. Three days before Cream's trial the police, having lost track of her moves, launched a frantic search for her.[45]

The traditional view was that prostitution was the last recourse of the most desperate. Of course, not every woman who came from an impoverished, unhappy home became a prostitute. The Irish of York, although the most destitute in their community, were the least likely to enter the trade.[46] What often seemed to separate prostitutes from their sisters was a driving desire for something better. They were not impressed by expressions of disapproval. When Matilda Clover's uncle became too curious about her life, "she told him he might form his own opinion as how she earned her living."[47]

Most nineteenth-century moralists believed that prostitutes paid for their immorality by having a short career that ended in death. The evidence suggests, however, that for many women streetwalking was an option taken up for a relatively short time and that after this temporary stage they went to live more or less normal working-class lives. Police surveillance and harassment, however, made this sort of slipping back and forth between "moral" and "immoral" pursuits increasingly difficult.

Undoubtedly the most peripatetic prostitutes working on Stamford Street in the 1890s were the Jewish women from Poland, whom pimps exploited in London and then shipped off to South America or South Africa. The "Stamford Street Gang" was run by Joe Silver, who was born in Poland in 1869, emigrated to the United States in 1888, and arrived in London in 1895. Silver and his accomplices, who had their headquarters at the American Hotel, Stamford Street, preyed upon young women recently arrived from eastern Europe. Eventually, the London Jewish philanthropic societies succeeded in driving Silver out, but when he and fourteen fellow traffickers sailed for South Africa in 1898 they took with them twenty to twenty-five "girls."[48] The authorities were perplexed that so many prostitutes would allow themselves to be taken off to Africa and would refuse to be "rescued." But rescued to do what? They received no job offers. Such perplexities were continually experienced by those who refused to recognize the economic impetus that drove women into prostitution.

In the Cream case two attempts at rescue were documented. The first was brought to light when the Brighton police, in assisting their colleagues in Lambeth, uncovered a curious letter dated 9 April 1892 sent to Emma Shrivell's home.

> What has become of you? I got no letter from you so don't know whether you are in Brighton or in London with Alice which latter arrangement I should much regret as I know but too well the only work you would find with her and from which I finally thought I had saved you.

The letter was signed "Joe" and the return address given as care of Preston, 1 Cambridge Place, Kensington. In an earlier letter of February it was made clear that from this posh address in West London Joseph Simpson, a middle-class philanthropist, had been sending Emma Shrivell money for the purpose of weaning her away from a life on the streets. Simpson did not want his dealings with prostitutes to be made public knowledge; on occasion he called himself "Pedro Glenzo" and the "Marquis de Santurae."[49]

Simpson's friends Arthur and Herbert Preston, who were partners on the stock exchange, apparently allowed him to use their address as a mail drop. When in Brighton they stayed at Mutton's Hotel, where Emma Shrivell's sister, Nelly Washer, worked. Presumably that was where Simpson met Shrivell. Nelly told the police that Simpson was on the stock exchange and lived an elegant upper-class life in London complete with carriage, maids, and cooks in a house with a large garden. All this had been reported to her by Emma, who had taken tea with him.

This account was substantiated by the recollection of Lizzie Sullivan, who had known Alice Marsh and Emma Shrivell when they were in London two years previous, that "a gentleman friend of theirs paid their fare [back to Brighton] and persuaded them to go back to service." When Sullivan met Emma in March 1892 at the Old Crown and Cushion Pub in Lambeth, she said Emma had pawned her clothes to obtain the money to get back to London. She was looking for her benefactor, who, she now claimed, was a member of Parliament![50]

After the deaths of Emma Shrivell and Alice Marsh the press reported that there were rumors that some eminent public personalities had used their services. The police investigated and found that this was not in fact true. But *Lloyd's Weekly London Newspaper,* having heard of Joe Simpson's involvement, announced that a member of Parliament who had tried to save the young woman from going on the streets had been interviewed by Scotland Yard.[51]

The police determined that Simpson, whom they questioned 21 April and who actually lived at 18 Carlton House Terrace, had about two years before gotten Emma Shrivell off the streets. But since Shrivell did not mention him in her dying statement and his handwriting did not match that of "Clifton," the C.I.D. concluded he had no hand in her murder. After Shrivell's death he lay low. Frank Pimm, with whom Emma had lived in Brighton, futilely sought to have him pay for her burial.[52] Emma Shrivell and Alice Marsh received only a humble funeral in Brighton on 20 April.

As hard as it is to believe that Simpson's involvement with Emma Shrivell was as innocent as he made out, it has to be remembered that the Liberal prime minister William Ewart Gladstone was himself involved in just such "rescue" activities. With the benefit of Freudian hindsight it is easy to appreciate the sexual ambiguities with which such relationships were likely riddled.[53] But whatever their motivations, the fact remains that some members of the Victorian upper classes felt driven to respond personally to the prostitution "problem." In the very midst of Cream's trial the Victorian reading public took it as natural that Catherine Gladstone, the prime minister's wife, should officiate at the opening of a home in Liverpool for "female inebriates."[54]

The same week that Cream was executed a second "rescue" attempt failed when Annie Donworth, the seventeen-year-old sister of Cream's first London victim, Ellen, fought off her family's efforts to save her from a life of prostitution. Mary Ann Donworth, her mother, tracked Annie from Vauxhall to Ann's Place, Westminster, where she was harbored by Henry Liveter, a twenty-five-year-old fitter. Her parents, as they later explained to the police, were afraid that Annie, who had been away from home for a week, "was going wrong." Her mother protested that it was not right for a girl to "stop from home and go astray" and attacked Liveter. He retaliated with an iron pipe, breaking her nose and knocking her unconscious. Annie rallied to her man's defense, telling Constable Sandercock that some unknown person had assaulted her mother. Both Annie and Henry were remanded at the Westminster Police Court.[55]

We do not know what eventually became of Annie Donworth. What is clear is that despite both the "rescue" attempts of family and social purity activists and the violent dangers posed by men like Cream, young women would continue to be driven by poverty and lured by the hopes of something better to walk the streets of London.[56] "It's Jack the Ripper or the bridge with me," declared one prostitute. "What's the odds?"[57]

Social and economic factors exacerbated by police harassment that made it increasingly difficult for prostitutes to enjoy the tolerance and protection of the surrounding working-class community were largely responsible for making such women vulnerable to attack. Actual incitements to attack them could be found in doctors' statements that prostitutes were the chief cause of the spread of venereal disease that endangered innocent middle-class wives and children, and social purists' assertions that these women out of sheer evil-minded willfulness refused to abandon their lives of crime. It is in this context that Cream's murders have to be situated. A. S. Trude, the lawyer who defended him in Chicago in 1881, said Cream had two manias. The first was to know all there was to know about medicine. "His other mania was a desire to get rid of women who were in a condition in which they were a menace to society."[58] After Cream's conviction Haynes was reported as saying that the doctor had boasted of killing prostitutes. "'Pshaw! I have killed lots of that cattle.' I said, 'Do you really say you have killed women?' 'Yes, all of that class are to be killed.'"[59] How could such views be expressed? At the time some suggested that Cream was "inspired" by the example of Jack the Ripper. Given that Cream shifted from killing women who sought abortions to killing prostitutes, it is likely that there were elements of the "copycat" murderer at work here. But Cream did not have to look far afield for assertions that prostitutes were less than human.

An article in the *St. James's Gazette* of 22 October 1892 asked whether the rash of attacks on women by Jack the Ripper, Cream, and others might not have been due to some "subtle influence in the air." The author of the article did not appear to notice that he had answered his own question by going on to say, "Of course, the woman Clover was only a miserable street outcast, whose life was of no particular value to anybody."[60] This same denigration took place throughout Cream's trial. The crown counsel referred to prostitutes by the circumlocution "the class of persons known as 'unfortunates.'"[61] He took it for granted that they were alcoholics, describing Matilda Clover as "given to excess of drinking, like so many of her class."[62] Cream's barrister said of her, "She was a woman of the town; depending for her bread upon prostitution in the streets—one of that vast army, the legion of the lost, that was to be seen in our midst."[63] Geoghegan described Alice Marsh and Emma Shrivell as "loose women" "leading an immoral life." Even the respectable, he argued, could not avoid them: "Men of experience could speak to the manner in which women solicited them in the street."[64] The great interest of Cream's trial, according to the *British Medical Journal,* was that it revealed "the manner of life led by the degraded women who haunt the street, the gin palace, and the music hall."[65]

Implicit in such arguments was the belief that these women were already "lost." A police court missionary described them as no longer real human beings. "I see some young in years who have already come to the wayside of life, for their bones are full of their sin. I see young women, sometimes fair and sometimes foul to look upon, but whether fair or foul, half beast and half human."[66] Indeed, the easiest way to explain, if not to sanction, the actions of their murderers was to attribute to such men a desire to end the evil that prostitutes were spreading. William Acton, England's leading exponent of the regulation of prostitution, after referring to the streetwalker's spreading of venereal disease as a "crime against society," concluded that she was a "distributor of poison to others and herself."[67] Such an attitude helps one to understand why the popular belief that Jack the Ripper suffered from syphilis was taken by some as in some sense justifying his crimes.

> So I used to imagine the half-crazed sufferer, his bones being gnawed away by this terrible ailment, determining to revenge himself on the class of women from whom he had caught it. It must have been in an almost moral urge to purify the East End of these plague-bearing Harpies that he set himself this task, and the revolting sexual refinements must have been the culmination of his destructive orgy of collective vengeance.[68]

Why did the prostitutes take the pills Cream offered them? Lou Harvey said that he told her the medicine would improve her complexion. More believable was Lucy Rose's statement that "Fred," who made up four pills for Matilda Clover, claimed that they would prevent her from "catching the disease," that is, venereal disease.[69] Cream, who regarded prostitutes as a "menace," had struck on the diabolical idea of appealing to their concern to protect themselves from the most obvious danger to which their profession exposed them.

The court condemned Cream; it also condemned his victims. At the Old Bailey and in the press Cream's victims were described as the "wretched," "dissolute" women who posed a "menace to society." Their fates were held up as a warning to others. The hidden, or not so hidden, message was that women who were independent, incautious, or without male supervision could expect to be subjected to such terrors.[70] Of course, the point was made that only "deviant" women were at risk; those who knew their place were in no danger.[71] Robert Anderson, the assistant commissioner of the Metropolitan Police, expressed his amazement that respectable women were frightened by Jack the Ripper; after all, he only preyed on lower-class prostitutes.

> No amount of silly hysterics could alter the fact that these crimes were a cause of danger only to a particular section of a small and definite class of women, in a limited district of the East End; and that the inhabitants of the metropolis were just as secure during the weeks the fiend was on the prowl, as they were before the mania seized him.[72]

The "silly hysterics" of Anderson's remarks realized in at least a subjective way that violent attacks upon a "definite class of women" were in fact attacks upon all women. The comments made by the police, judge, and lawyers whenever men like Cream were on trial defined and differentiated the roles of respectable versus immoral women. Implicit in such arguments was the notion that all women were being judged by men, that all possibly warranted discipline and punishment.

7

ABORTION

The most horrid social enormity of this age, this city, and
this world.

A. K. Gardner, *Conjugal Sins* (1860)

In the late 1890s women dressed as hospital nurses fanned out across
the more modest suburbs of London and Manchester distributing
advertising postcards puffing the ability of Madame Frain's pills to
remove "obstructions"—a code word for unwanted fetuses. The medicine, which cost 7 1/2d a bottle to produce but which sold at prices
ranging from 7s 6d to 22s, was completely useless and could not serve,
as the advertising implied, as an abortifacient. But the proprietors of
"Madame Frain's Herbal or Medical Institute" of Hackney Road, London, by declaring that they would only sell to customers who swore
that they were not pregnant, *thought* they had struck on a shrewd way
of both legally protecting themselves and boosting their product.[1] Indeed, between 1897 and 1899 thirteen hundred women who refused
to make such a declaration were sent back their money by registered
mail.[2] Undeterred, the police raided the institute and charged its
owners with inciting "women who should read and become cognizant
of pamphlets and circulars published in the name of Madame Frain
to attempt to administer to themselves noxious things with intent to
procure a miscarriage."[3] Why, asked the crown counsel, would women
in needy households pay up to the equivalent of a laborer's weekly

salary if not with the serious intent of inducing a miscarriage? Defense counsel for the institute responded that, although the customers may have thought the concoction could cause a miscarriage, the defendants knew it could not and therefore there was no case. Dr. Luff, Fellow of the Royal College of Physicians, agreed that the medicine was useless. But Mr. Justice Darling, the presiding judge, countered that any sort of pill, if taken in sufficient quantities, could be noxious, and the case was sent to the jury. The defendants—William Brown, Emmanuel Abrahams, and James Fox—were found guilty and sentenced from nine to twelve months' hard labor in Pentonville Prison.[4]

Most striking about the Madame Frain trial was not so much Mr. Justice Darling's creative lawmaking as the case's revelation that thousands of women across England in the 1890s were willing to go to enormous lengths to restrict their fertility.[5] In response to the growing expense of maintaining gentility the middle and upper classes had been limiting family size from the mid-century.[6] If middle-class men turned to contraception largely out of a concern at the expenses posed by the large family, middle-class women, though no doubt sharing such concerns, were drawn to the same tactics out of a desire for some life beyond that of producing and rearing offspring. In the last decades of the century even laboring families restricted their fertility. The imposition of compulsory education on one hand and the growing prohibition of child labor on the other meant that large numbers of children, once a valuable asset in the working-class home, were increasingly viewed as a burden.[7]

The socially conservative Malthusian League began in the 1870s to trumpet the advantages of the small family.[8] Although socialists were generally reluctant to broach the issue, even the *Clarion,* a popular labor paper, was in February 1892 running advertisements for a tract provocatively entitled *Ought Women to Be Punished for Having Too Many Children?*[9] But when one moved from theory to practice, problems arose. Although a Dubliner on a visit to London was shocked to see the number of "antigestatory appliances shown in chemists' windows," condoms, diaphragms, and douches were expensive and until well into the twentieth century employed by only a small portion of the population.[10] Withdrawal, or coitus interruptus, would remain in the working-class household the main method of contraception. What if it failed? The most desperate resorted to infanticide and abandonment; in 1895 the bodies of eleven infants were found in Lambeth's streets and gutters.[11] Far more common was the attempt to induce miscarriage.

Women seeking abortion had to face the hostility of clergy, police, and doctors.[12] Those few physicians who considered helping women to control their fertility were warned off by their peers.[13]

> To give directions for the prevention of conception, or instructions in the guilty use of syringes, and other expedients to aid crime or to defeat nature, although not offences within reach of the law, are nevertheless most derogatory and degrading to the assenting practitioner, and a gross abuse of his professional knowledge.[14]

Because the limitation of family size was very much a tabooed subject in both Britain and North America, some women were inevitably exploited by quacks like Madame Frain; others were operated on by incompetent abortionists; and the most unfortunate fell into the hands of someone like Thomas Neill Cream. It is quite possible that he killed more women seeking abortions than the ones he was actually accused of killing. While he was awaiting execution, the *Toronto Globe* reported that Mr. Waters, his solicitor, had a confession in which Cream admitted that "he made a practice of poisoning dissolute girls in Canada."[15]

The first point to be made in understanding Cream's career as an abortionist/murderer is that in the last decades of the nineteenth century women's need for assistance in terminating pregnancies had taken on a special urgency.[16] Social pressures to restrict family size had increased, but adequate contraception was simply not available. Women made unexpectedly pregnant, holding true to a traditional view that they had the right to "make themselves regular," often attempted to induce miscarriage. Estimates were made that between a sixth and a fifth of all pregnancies were terminated.[17]

The second point revealed by the Cream case is that in the late 1800s, because of new laws, the options of a woman seeking to induce a miscarriage were limited. Although doctors could safely carry out abortions, they attempted to do so only for therapeutic reasons and sought vigorously to drive out of business the irregular practitioners, midwives, and herbalists associated with the practice.[18]

Doctors deemed abortion "wrong" but sometimes necessary.[19] A conservative such as Dr. Robert Reid Rentoul believed that abortion was thinkable only when a mother's life was in extreme danger. In practice, as an 1896 secret report of the Royal College of Physicians indicated, the profession's policy was to leave to the discretion of the individual practitioner the question of when to act.[20] A therapeutic abortion was considered legitimate if it was carried out by a regular doctor after consultation with colleagues. And professional etiquette dictated that colleagues not look too closely into each other's affairs.

> Even if a medical practitioner is known to have procured abortion, the presumption is that it was done in the legal exercise of his calling; and the strongest evidence should be forthcoming before he is made answerable for his actions, or, peradventure, the death of his patient.[21]

Any abortion not carried out by a doctor was labeled a "criminal abortion." The campaign against such practices in both North America and Britain was part of the process by which the medical profession came to monopolize the delivery of health services.[22] By an "ideological sleight of hand" doctors declared that abortion was "murder." It was a legitimate operation only if physicians decided—in the privacy of their consulting rooms—that it had to be carried out.[23]

Nineteenth-century doctors helped push through a legal revolution. Until the early 1800s abortion before "quickening"—that is, before the woman could feel the fetus's movements at about thirteen weeks after conception—was not penalized. Abortion after quickening was only punished by a fine or short imprisonment. Even these levies were rarely imposed. In 1803 abortion both before and after quickening was made a crime; only in 1837 was the concept of quickening itself removed.[24] These early statutes were aimed at the abortionist; not until passage of the Offences against the Person Act of 1861 was the woman herself subject to prosecution. In the United States, where it was estimated that 10 to 30 percent of pregnancies were terminated, a similar rash of laws criminalizing abortion—warmly advocated by the medical profession—appeared on the statute books between the 1860s and 1880s.[25] Doctors, lawyers, and clergymen in carrying out their successful crusade to criminalize abortion created the conditions under which desperate women became Cream's potential victims.[26] A woman's worst nightmare—falling into the hands of a killer who posed as an abortionist in order to have his victim become an unwitting accomplice in her own murder—had become a reality.

Some middle-class women cajoled their doctors into providing abortions. Only the occasional tragedy brought such transactions before public scrutiny. Ethel Hall, the separated wife of Edward Marshall Hall, who was emerging as one of England's foremost barristers, died in 1890 as a result of being operated on and administered a noxious drug to terminate a pregnancy. Her doctor—suspected of forgery and drug trafficking as well—was committed to the Old Bailey to be tried for willful murder; the charge against her well-connected lover of being an accessory was dropped.[27] Other women, whose demands for medical assistance could not—given the law—be met in an open way, were forced into the back streets. Few working-class women had the temerity to try to convince a regular doctor of their need for an abortion; they continued to rely on the services of midwives, the "old queens" of the neighborhood, and if those were lacking, on quack products and commercial abortionists.[28]

A cursory glance at the columns of the popular press and even the religious press of the 1890s reveals dozens of advertisements for abortifacients—Towles Pennyroyal Pills, Blanchard's Pills, Fenn's Pennyroyal, Steel, Hiera Picra and Bitter Apple Pills, Ottey's Strong Female Pills, Apiol and Steel Pills for Ladies, Tuck's Female Mixture, and Widow Welch's Pills, to name only a few.[29] A typical advertisement in the *South London Mail* stated that those who wrote L. M. Dasmail of Walthamstowe would obtain "Dr. Monteith's Electric Female Pills for all Irregularities, Suppressions, and Obstructions of the Female System however Obstinate and Long-Standing." Some of these medicines contained a few elements of the traditional abortifacients such as aloes, savin, pennyroyal, and apiol, but many were no more than candy pills.

If drugs failed, as presumably most would, and self-induction with knitting needles or douches was unsuccessful, abortionists might be approached. The Chicago press, in reporting Cream's arrest in 1880 for abortion, noted the numbers of practitioners offering similar services.

> Some years since a sensational newspaper in this city published an article purporting to expose the professional abortionists. The list included a dozen or twenty quacks, more or less known as such, and we believe no libel suits ever came of the publication . . . It is certain that every large city contains a large number of persons calling themselves doctors or midwives, who undertake the crime of abortion for almost any fee that may be offered them.[30]

In England practitioners ranged from regular doctors such as Charles Whitefoord, convicted in July 1891 of procuring abortion, to irregulars who advertised their ability to treat "women's ailments."[31] Not surprisingly, midwives such as Elizabeth Berry, Dorothy Davis, Lizzie Ann Mitchell, Annie Stewart, and Dinah Clapp were frequently prosecuted for carrying out "illegal operations."[32] In 1893 Edith Bannister, an employee of the London newspaper the *Sun*, died as a result of a bungled abortion; two years later her newspaper exposed Dr. James Ady for using his "Lambeth Self-Supporting Dispensary" as an abortion clinic.[33] In this twilight world of legal and illegal operations, competent and incompetent practitioners, lurked Cream.[34]

At Blanchard's Hotel in Quebec City in March 1892 Cream struck up a friendship with John Wilson McCulloch. The two traveling agents' talk soon turned to women. Cream led McCulloch to understand that he was an abortionist. "He next took a bottle out of the cash box and said Do you known what this is? I replied No. He then said It is poison. I said For God's sake what do you do with that? He replied I give it to women to get them out of the family way." The bottle contained whitish crystals, the size of pinheads, presumably strychnine. When asked how he administered it, Cream showed his friend a box of capsules, saying "I give it to them in these." Cream also produced a pair of false whiskers. "I said What do you use these for? He replied To disguise my identity so that they would not recognize me again." [35]

Cream aborted his wife, Flora Brooks; whether he was responsible for her death a year later is impossible to say. He was guilty of the deaths of Kate Hutchinson Gardener in London, Ontario, and Mary Anne Faulkner and Ellen Stack in Chicago, Illinois. While Cream was awaiting execution in London, it was reported that in Chicago, where "he owned a house wherein young unmarried women were assisted over their troubles, he took the lives of many." [36] Killing women who sought abortions was diabolically clever; the victim pathetically made as many efforts as her murderer to hide their relationship.

The subject of abortion held a morbid fascination for Cream. In the letters in which he accused Frederick Smith and Walter Harper of giving women poisons that they thought were abortifacients it is difficult not to see a twisted account of his own actions. "I am writing now," he purportedly warned Ellen Donworth, "to say that if you take any of the medicine he [Smith] gave you for the purposes of bringing on your courses you will die." He likely accused Lord Russell of Matilda Clover's death not just because Russell's name was in the news due to his messy divorce but because the Russell family was associated with the defense of birth control. This connection had been made when in 1868 Lord Amberley (Bertrand Russell's father) lost a bitterly contested South Devon election after it was made public that he supported neo-Malthusian doctrines. [37] Amberley was vilified in the press and pulpits for having favored what the press referred to as "unnatural crimes."

Such were Victorian proprieties that at Cream's trial, although the topic of murder was openly discussed, the issue of abortion was carefully skirted. The crown counsel noted that in Quebec City Cream had spoken of having drugs "for the purposes of preventing childbirth" whereas Cream had made it clear they were for provoking miscarriages.[38] Likewise in referring to the letter sent to Frederick Smith containing the note purportedly written to Ellen Donworth, the crown counsel avoided any reference to the warning not to take drugs to miscarry.[39] The possible use of strychnine to bring on abortion was also presumably what Geoghegan was discreetly referring to when he put a question in writing to the medical expert, Dr. Thomas Stevenson. The court considered the question too indelicate to be aired in public, but one can infer the substance of the query from Stevenson's oral response that "it is a matter of common medical knowledge in this country. It is supposed to have come from America. It was mentioned in a notorious pamphlet."[40]

Abortionists sometimes accidentally killed; in 1875 Alfred Thomas Heap, having caused the death of a woman he was seeking to abort with a spindle, was executed in Manchester.[41] Some killers involved themselves in abortion. At the 1898 Huntingdon Assizes, Mr. Justice Hawkins sentenced to death a man who gave strychnine to his pregnant lover, having led her to believe it was an abortifacient.[42] Jack the Ripper was thought by some to be an abortionist; one of his victims—Mary Kelly—was three months pregnant.[43] On 10 September 1889 a woman's mutilated, headless body, wrapped in a garment marked with the name "L. E. Fisher," was found by the police under the arches off Pinchin Street, Whitechapel. Because of the locale her file was included in the Ripper dossier, but the *New York Herald* reported in its London edition of 11 September that Dr. Thomas Bond, chief surgeon of the Metropolitan Police, concluded that the death resulted not from decapitation but from an attempt to procure abortion.[44] Cream's career, linking as it did abortion and murder, was in short far from being unique. An analysis of his killing of women seeking to terminate a pregnancy directs our attention to the fact that the new abortion laws, in creating a new class of criminal, facilitated the ambitions of such a homicidal individual. Cream's victims in attempting to control their fertility had forfeited the protection of the state; indeed, the state, in declaring them outlaws, had driven them into the murderer's clutches.

The third point raised by an analysis of Cream's abortion-related murders is the intemperate language in which respectable society described those who sought to terminate their pregnancies. We know that Cream regarded women who sought abortions as a menace to society who should be exterminated. What comes as a shock is the discovery of the inflammatory rhetoric so many public commentators used to express similar feelings of hostility toward such women. Women seeking abortion were typified at best as having "fallen from virtue." The wife who intended to control her fertility was castigated by Sylvanus Stall as entering the marriage relationship "for the purpose of practically leading a life of legalized prostitution."[45] George H. Napheys declared with horror, "Hundreds of vile men and women in our large cities subsist by this slaughter of the innocents, and flaunt their ill-gotten gains—the price of blood—in our public thoroughfares." To his disgust he discovered that many of these clients were "virtuous matrons" of the middle classes.[46] Hugh L. Hodge in *Foeticide, or Criminal Abortion* (1869) berated such women for seeking abortions for the most "futile and trifling" reasons.[47]

At worst such women were described as murderers. Lord Brougham criticized single women seeking abortions for adding the "deliberate sin of murder to the former one of the passions."[48] Thomas Radford referred to the "diabolical arts" used to induce miscarriage.[49] P. H. Chavasse said abortion was simply murder.[50] In 1859 Harvard University professor Walter Channing attacked women for committing "foeticide, unborn child killing."[51] H. S. Pomeroy referred to the destruction of unborn life as the "American sin."[52] Emma Drake called it "antenatal infanticide" and in her popular North American tract, *What a Young Wife Ought to Know,* dealt with the issue in a chapter entitled, "The Destruction of Infant Life."[53] John Cowan similarly spoke, not of abortion but of "foeticide."[54] Augustus K. Gardner warned women, "You have no right to take precautions or failing in this to resort to murder."[55] The Canadian Medical Association bemoaned what it called the "slaughter of the unborn . . . whose destruction is equivalent to murder."[56] In such misogynistic rhetoric the fetus was always presented as male, as a "potential man."[57]

Such examples could be multiplied many times over. Of course, it is a large step to move from rhetoric to action. And one could argue that the fact that Cream was ultimately executed proves that the larger society in reality did not desire the deaths of women seeking abortion. But in looking for the sources that might have incited Cream, the public debate over abortion cannot be dismissed. If Cream sought sanctions for his crimes, he did not have far to look; the press was full of violent denunciations of women who had had recourse to abortion. The respectable referred to it as murder and to women who sought abortion as murderers. Was not death the appropriate penalty? Could not Cream, when murdering such women, imagine that he was acting in the interests of the greater society? The *Canada Lancet* coolly described the fate of women dying as a consequence of bungled abortions as "retributive deaths."[58] Cream, as a "madman," simply took to its murderously logical conclusion an argument that the rational meant to be no more than a rhetorical exercise.

Turning from the question of the possible source of Cream's motive to the means he adopted leads us to the fourth issue illuminated by an analysis of his crimes—the fact that being a doctor trained in obstetrics facilitated his murderous intentions. The late nineteenth century was the very time when obstetrics and gynecology were becoming respectable specialties, when the access of the male physician to the female patient finally received full legitimation.[59] James Murphy reminded his colleagues at the first conference of the British Gynaecological Society held in 1891 that a once disdained speciality was now in the forefront of surgery; ovariotomy had "opened up the whole field of abdominal surgery, so that many men who started as gynaecologists, are now our most brilliant surgeons, successfully attacking the uterus, the spleen, the liver and all the organs contained in the abdomen."[60] A feminist doctor like Elizabeth Blackwell believed that women's sexuality was indeed being "attacked."[61] Many leading gynecologists accepted with apparent equanimity the fact that the newest and most daring forms of surgery carried the highest risks for their female patients.[62]

A number of gynecologists were only too happy to parade a crude misogyny. At an 1886 meeting of the British Gynaecological Society, Charles Routh devoted a paper on the problems posed by "unfortunate and diseased women" who were under the delusion that they had been molested by their male relatives. As far as Routh was concerned such confidences had to be shown up for the lies that they were; incest was unthinkable.[63]

> Whenever I hear such stories, I suspect the women who tell them, for if, in the history they give of themselves, they can invent such terrible stories about those whom they ought most to love and revere, they seem to me to be very apt to invent and believe other and more terrible stories about their medical attendants, whom they know less of, and which might seriously affect their happiness and future career.[64]

Such perverts posed a danger to every man who came near them. Doctors called to testify in rape cases were accordingly warned by Routh to make every effort to see that no man was ever made a nymphomaniac's victim.

> It is not enough to see if she has been outraged or not; the sign of the rape should be certainly unequivocal. But is she addicted to masturbation? Has her mind been deteriorated

by prurient ideas? These peculiarities are seldom if ever noted. Juries and judges are completely ignorant of the tendencies of such women, and yet these tendencies are the keys to the whole situation.[65]

Routh concluded that great caution was necessary in dealing with any woman who claimed to have been molested. "Except upon the strongest corroborative evidence, the presumption is they are liars, plausible liars, cunning liars."[66]

Lawson Tait, the Birmingham surgeon who did more than any other single individual in making gynecology a specialty, was equally convinced that men were sexually exploited by women.[67] He seriously believed that boys were as often raped by women as girls were by men and protested that males were offered no legal protection. During the centuries when rape was a capital crime, Tait speculated, "thousands of innocent men must have been practically murdered." Enraged by the passage of the 1885 Criminal Law Amendment Act, which appeared to him to make it even easier for girls under sixteen to file rape charges, Tait persuaded the authorities to allow him to investigate all such complaints made in the Birmingham area. Disregarding the tremendous courage required of a young girl to file such charges, Tait concluded to his own satisfaction that out of a hundred cases a mere six prosecutions should be proceeded with. As regards the children and mothers in the other cases, Tait cruelly concluded that it was

> an open question as to whether it would not have been far better that many of these children, and the mothers and women concerned with them, aiding, abetting and originating their vile sins, better that one and all of them had been prostitutes openly plying for hire in the market place than have been the vile conspirators and blackmailers that many of them, the great bulk of them, prove to be.[68]

The middle-class "fussy women" of the Vigilance Committees and the typical twelve-year-old girl, a dirty little wretch of a "bragging, lying disposition, a not unusual disposition of her class," were in concert, according to Tait, making martyrs of defenseless men.[69]

One would not have to be psychoanalytically inclined to suspect that men such as Tait and Routh were drawn to the field of gynecological surgery by some psychological fear of female sexuality.[70] A more mundane explanation would be that since the term "woman's doctor" could conjure up the image of the abortionist, some gynecologists sought to prove their loyalty to other males and their respectability by parading an exaggerated suspicion of women.[71]

The breaking of gender boundaries, which interventionist gynecological surgery represented, created ripples of disquiet in late Victorian society. One is reminded that the antivivisection campaign was in part fueled by middle-class women's outrage that they, like animals, were being experimented on by male surgeons.[72] The straps and stirrups of the obstetrical consulting room conjured up too readily images of pornographic bondage, a pornography in which Cream indulged.[73] Feminists referred to the use of the speculum for the forcible examination of prostitutes under the Contagious Diseases Act as "instrumental rape"; it continued to be associated with assaults on female dignity long after the Acts were repealed. Antivivisection fiction, in playing on the theme of the villainous surgeon who begins by murdering animals and ends up poisoning his wife, unintentionally provided a portrait of a man not unlike Cream.[74]

Such preoccupations help explain why the image of the murdering mad doctor emerged even before Cream appeared on the scene.[75] Jack the Ripper was believed by many to be a doctor. Cream himself believed that murder and medicine were easily linked. In attempting to blame others for his crimes, he blackmailed a chemist, an intern, and an eminent physician.

A psychopath would no doubt have been drawn to the powerful role played by the physician. Why? Because as criminologists tell us, murder is the most "personalized" crime in our society inasmuch as friends and family are the usual victims and perpetrators. In acting as a doctor, the potential killer was facilitated because only he could rival friends or relatives in intimacy and contact: "He wasn't a stranger, he was a doctor." He could demand from women the sort of trust that would be denied any other man. Women, an obstetrician reminded his colleagues, "are obliged to believe all that we tell them. They are not in a position to dispute anything we say to them, and we, therefore, may be said to have them at our mercy."[76]

The fifth point raised by the Cream case relates to this power doctors had over their patients, in particular those seeking abortion. Cream gave prostitutes hoping to avoid venereal disease and women seeking to terminate a pregnancy drugs which killed them. He took advantage of the injunction that doctors were to be trusted. But respectable doctors certainly never lied to their patients regarding the medicines they prescribed. Or did they? Some nineteenth-century physicians, besieged by women seeking to induce a miscarriage, felt that this was one occasion in which honesty was not the best policy. A number flaunted their ability to trick patients who sought abortifacients. The French physician Dr. J. P. Munaret, early in the century, boasted that it was his practice to give such women candy pills. "The foetus has the time to grow and strengthen itself while my pills are being used which makes all the more difficult, and dangerous new attempts at abortion. To save a child from death, and a mother from crime, what could be a more wonderful result."[77] The English author of *The Young Practitioner* wrote in 1890 that doctors should keep such women "in ignorance of the innocuousness of the patient assumed abortifacient, lest other means be sought to effect the desired wish and interest."[78] Similar stratagems were employed in the United States.

> Druggists are often asked for substances to produce abortion, and in order not to offend by refusing to sell, yet not involve themselves in a criminal act, dispense harmless powders, such as milk-sugar or starch mixed with a small amount of quinine to give a marked taste, and thus lead the person to believe that an active drug is being used.[79]

In short, when it came to abortion, medical men felt they had a right to lie.[80] Doctors applauded themselves for such trickery and were not bothered by the ethics of their dissimulations.[81] After all, they were administering placebos, not poisons, and were smug in the conviction that they were doing right. But such stratagems were not innocent; as Munaret stated, they made other attempts at abortion "more difficult and dangerous." What is really germane was how symbolically important it was that the doctor alone determined what to give his patient while keeping her in ignorance of its effects.[82] Given this professional justification of deceit, Cream's acts—the administering of poisons in the place of abortifacients—appear not a completely isolated incident but the ultimate form of betrayal of the patient.

Cream's atrocious crimes were more understandable than the respectable society of the 1890s cared to admit. This was a world in which experts in medical ethics unapologetically declared that when it came to sexual questions, the violation of the trust of female patients was warranted, even to the point of lying to them about their medications; in which leading gynecologists openly paraded their misogyny; in which the press was full of violent rhetoric denouncing women who aborted as murderers. All of this suggests that although Cream was obviously disturbed, the "voices" that drove him on in his killing came as much from the society around him as from any devil lurking within.[83]

8

BLACKMAIL

I will free the world of a poisonous thing. Take that, you
hound, and that!—and that!—and that!—and that!
Arthur Conan Doyle, "Charles Augustus Milverton" (1899)

Sir Henry Hawkins, Cream's trial judge, made his name while a young
barrister in the 1860s representing the infant heir in the case of the
"Tichborne claimant," probably the most famous nineteenth-century
attempt at fraud. With the benefit of hindsight one can only marvel
that Arthur Orton, a Wapping butcher's son, came so close to passing
himself off as the missing claimant to the Tichborne fortune. At the
time the dramatic appeal of a shipwrecked prodigal son returning
home after years of exile drew many to his side. The haunting specter
of a legitimate heir possibly being deprived of his rightful due obviously hit a nerve in Victorian society; the case dragged on for years,
splitting many English families into two warring camps.[1]

There have always been frauds, people passing themselves off as
someone they are not. In late Victorian London a more modest
example of the confidence man was Augustus Wilhelm Mayer, who
posed as "Lord Hilton." His simple scheme consisted of promising the
women whose acquaintance he made a lavish trip to Europe. Before
embarking, he would write a large check to cover the cost of their
travel wardrobe and ask if he might borrow their rings in order to
size the other jewelry he intended to buy them. Mayer then disap-

peared with the rings; the women were left with a worthless check.[2]

Mayer practiced a classic form of fraud. There was a timeless quality to his trick of callously turning other people's pursuit of profit to his own purposes. But the last decades of the nineteenth century created unparalleled opportunities for more complicated deceptions.[3] The revolutions in communications and transportation meant that both legal and illegal business transactions now took place in enormous markets.[4] The cheap press publicized business transactions. Ready access to advertising, the public mails, post office boxes, cheap offices, letterheads, and mimeograph machines allowed the enterprising confidence man to pass himself off as a reputable businessman.[5]

Take, for example, the remarkable career of Horatio Buckland.[6] Buckland, born in 1856, entered the Grenadier Guards as a young man. Tiring of the military life, he deserted in 1888 and again in 1889 to plunge at the turn of the century into a bewildering number of shady deals. He first came to the police's attention in 1897 while posing as the president of the Klondyke Cooperative Prospecting Society, which charged up to £20 per person for transportation to the Canadian goldfields. A similar scheme went under the name of the Eldorado Traffic Syndicate. In neither case were any services ever provided. Buckland was arrested and sentenced to eighteen months for fraud; he somehow managed to avoid serving his time.

Undeterred by this brush with the law, Buckland, who was also a bigamist and employed several aliases, attempted a number of other swindles, including the selling of coal he did not have and pretending to operate a ship that did not exist. Perhaps his most ambitious scheme was hatched during the 1905 Russo-Japanese war when he offered to provide the Russians with information (which he, of course, did not possess) on colliers bound for Japan. Buckland was arrested in 1899, 1902, and 1905. On the last occasion he received a stiff sentence of five years in Dartmoor Prison. He was released in 1907, jailed again, and discharged in 1909. The last reference to him in the police files noted his having been sentenced in 1910 to three years in prison for a fraudulent ice rink scheme which bilked the workers and contractors of Gloucester out of £1400.

Even behind bars Buckland could not stop telling tales. In the hopes of winning an early release from Dartmoor he roamed the cells collecting information and peppered the wardens with confidential reports on prison gossip. He was especially proud of the knowledge he gained of a gang run by a man called Montague that blackmailed homosexuals. "Montague also supplies young boy[s] for sodomites and then blackmails them. Montague meets his friends of the jewel-

lery and forging business at the 'White Horse PH' [public house] Stepney and at his flat, he meets the boys at The Bond Street Tube
Station."[7] One of the tactics employed by the gang, reported Buckland, was for the boys to follow older men into public lavatories, expose themselves, and then call for help. An accomplice would then
arrive on the scene and threaten to have the dupe arrested if hush
money was not forthcoming.

The wardens, although titillated, came to treat all of Buckland's
baroque revelations with weary contempt, judging them to be a mixture of truths and falsehoods simply concocted to win parole. But
what is of importance is not whether the Fagin-like character of Montague and his blackmail ring actually existed but the fact that such a
blackmail scheme could be envisaged.

In the traditional version of the old "badger game" a prostitute lured
a client into a compromising situation whereupon a fake brother or
father suddenly appeared to demand money. Prostitutes were, for
obvious reasons, long thought to be well situated to engage in such
schemes.[8] Buckland's homosexual variation on this theme suggests
that possibilities of blackmail were widening at the end of the century.
Of course, the blackmail victim and the fraud artist were in some
senses much alike; both sought to keep hidden from the public some
aspect of their true identity. But they were also quite different; the
blackmail victim sought to protect his or her privacy while the fraud
artist sought to foist his or her version of the truth on a trusting
public.

Thomas Neill Cream was a fraud, selling pills in Chicago to cure
epilepsy and posing in London as "Dr. Neill" and "Major Hamilton."
He was also an incorrigible blackmailer. Blackmail appeared to be a
preoccupation of the world in which he moved, tainting even the lives
of his victims.

Emma Shrivell had lived in Brighton with Frank Pimm. "I used to
walk out with her," he told the police, "and for about fourteen months
up to five weeks ago I used to cohabit with her." Hearing of her death,
he went up to London with Emma's mother and searched the rooms
at Stamford Street, uncovering two letters from Joe Simpson, whom
he then sought to confront at the Prestons' home at 1 Cambridge
Place. Why? Pimm told the police he simply wanted Simpson to help
pay for Emma's funeral. The Prestons were convinced he was trying
to blackmail Simpson. A servant at first would not even let Pimm in-
side the house; then Mrs. Preston appeared in a dressing gown to ask
if there was anything wrong, if Emma was ill. Pimm replied she had
been murdered and that, though he had destroyed some of the letters

Simpson had sent her, he had kept two. Mr. Preston, who now appeared, exclaimed, "How cute you are." Together the Prestons faced Pimm down. Simpson, they said, could not be seen because he was going on holiday; he could not help with Emma's burial because he was short of money. At a loss as to how to respond, the defeated Pimm accepted Mrs. Preston's patronizing offer of a half crown to get him back to Blackfriars; he handed the letters over to the police.[9]

Blackmail letters figured centrally in the Cream case. Approached from a psychological perspective the letters he sent could be taken as signifying little more than his egotistical desire to publicize his crimes, to be caught and punished. But when placed in their social context these letters, which threatened the respectable with revelations of their links to the secret worlds of abortion, prostitution, medical malpractice, and murder, accurately indicated what would most menace a Victorian's reputation. Indeed, the very notion of the enormous dangers posed by blackmail was a product of the unprecedented importance nineteenth-century society attributed to "reputation."[10]

The term "blackmail" was first used in a quite different manner by sixteenth-century English jurists to describe the openly extortionate practices of Scottish brigands in the border counties of Cumberland, Northumberland, Westmoreland, and Duresme. The word was similarly employed by parliamentarians pushing for the passage of the 1722 and 1754 "Black Acts" aimed at putting an end to farm laborers' threats against landlords. The sending of threatening letters, which under common law was a high misdemeanor, was made a felony punishable by death.[11] In the nineteenth century, magistrates continued to talk of "blackmail" when describing disgruntled ex-employees demanding redress from their bosses. But threatening to use physical force if money was not forthcoming was really a form of robbery and qualitatively different from the modern notion of blackmail, in which the threat consists of revealing information. When in 1779 James Donally extorted money from Charles Feilding, son of the earl of Denbigh, with the threat of charging the latter with having committed buggery, a new form of crime emerged.[12] Accordingly, in the course of the nineteenth century the image of the blackmailer changed from one who physically threatened a person to one who threatened a person's reputation. Legally blackmail consisted of making knowledge of another person's past a source of profit.[13] The essential proof of the crime did not depend on whether what the blackmailer threatened to reveal was true (as was the case in slander or libel) but whether he or she knew that such demands for money were illegal.[14]

Why this new concern for reputation? In the preindustrial world aristocrats who enjoyed a secure, ascribed status could be largely indifferent to what was said about them. Even in the nineteenth century the duke of Wellington responded to extortionate threats with his famous "Publish and be damned" challenge. But less-favored Victorians viewed with increasing anxiety any threat of exposure of private matters. Judges agreed with them and continued to reduce the level of threats they believed the "firm and constant man" could withstand. Reputations in a nineteenth-century careerist, mobile, middle-class society were increasingly important and fragile, in particular those of men in sensitive positions such as doctors and politicians. Cream, of course, sought to blackmail chemists, doctors, and politicians.

Respectability in the Victorian world was itself demonstrated by the ability to draw a clear line between one's public and private lives. The middle class treasured the privacy of the walled gardens of their suburban villas whereas the "roughs" were under the constant scrutiny of neighbors, police constables, health visitors, and settlement workers. Accordingly, middle-class Victorians regarded the blackmailer who threatened to violate the sanctity of their privacy as the lowest of blackguards. Even the murder of a blackmailer by one of his victims was portrayed in Arthur Conan Doyle's "Charles Augustus Milverton" as something that Holmes and Watson were right to sanction; "justice had overtaken a villain." [15] How else could an end be put to such harassment?

Even the powerful were open to extortion. Few people in England could have been unaware of the letters forged by Richard Pigott that the *Times* unsuccessfully employed in 1887 to portray Charles Parnell, the Irish parliamentary leader, as a supporter of terrorism. Pigott had offered them to the highest bidder, and they thus served the purposes of both blackmail and slander. In the end Parnell's defense counsel Charles Russell (who later prosecuted Cream) provided the proof that the letters were in fact manufactured. The unlucky Pigott, pursued by the police to Madrid, committed suicide in November 1889.[16]

"Some foreign countries say," noted Mr. Justice Phillimore, "that England with all her pretended virtues is the home of the blackmailer." [17] The more "respectable" Victorian society prided itself in being, the more the individual had to take into account public opinion, and the more vulnerable he or she was made to blackmailers. And their numbers were increasing. The passage of the 1857 Divorce Act with the provision requiring evidence of adultery spawned the private detective profession and provided new opportunities for muckraking journalists, whom the respectable viewed as little better than extortionists. "Le chantage," observed Balzac, "est une invention de la presse anglaise." [18] Did not these new professionals seek to profit from the ferreting out of secrets? More important, the legal process itself—by criminalizing certain activities such as inducing abortion or engaging in homosexual practices—produced enormous new classes of potential blackmail victims.

Buggery was punished with the death penalty until 1830; the law making this practice a capital offense was only revoked in 1861. But if in the early nineteenth century certain sexual acts were prosecuted, homosexuality per se was not. In the late nineteenth century the situation was reversed; the Labouchère Amendment to the 1885 Criminal Law Amendment Act targeted a particular sort of person rather than any particular act. Indeed, the law did much to crystallize the concept of "homosexuality." In France the labeling of homosexuality was also under way as a result of Tardieu's medical investigations, but the French did not criminalize adult homosexuality, only "indecent assaults" on minors. [19] English legislation referred more vaguely to "gross indecency" and criminalized acts committed in private by consenting adults. Prosecutors did not even have to outrage the public by revelations of what exactly they meant by such a catchall phrase as "unnatural acts." The Labouchère Amendment was in effect a "blackmailers' charter." [20] It would be going too far to say that it created the possibility of homosexuals being blackmailed—after all, the blackmail of homosexuals had occurred in the eighteenth century—but the law did publicize their vulnerability and simplified their persecution. [21] It made the homosexual the ideal blackmail victim. [22]

In July 1886 the gay brothel run by Newlove and Veck on Cleveland Street employing telegraph messenger boys was raided. The clients exposed in what became know as the "Cleveland Street Scandal" included Lord Arthur Somerset, the earl of Euston, and possibly Prince Eddy—the duke of Clarence (1864–92), subsequently suspected by some of being Jack the Ripper but who conveniently died before inquiries could be pursued. Attempts were made by Hammond, a blackmailer, to exploit the situation, but an 1889–90 police coverup prevented this from occurring. [23]

Oscar Wilde, whose novel *The Picture of Dorian Gray* (1890) was suffused with themes of secrecy and homoeroticism, was probably blackmailed from 1892 on. [24] His trial in 1895 inextricably associated his name with homosexuality. Two men, who were charged at Marlborough Police Station in May 1895 with seeking to extort money from a hairdresser whom they accused of accosting a youth in a public lavatory, described themselves as detectives on the lookout for "some Oscar Wilde business." [25]

Homosexuals might have been the ideal blackmail victims, but we simply do not know how many were blackmailed. The nineteenth-century "record" for the number of individuals victimized in one blackmail scheme was established by the three Chrimes brothers, who in 1898 set out to exploit, not homosexuals but women seeking abortion through the purchase of abortifacients.

Abortion was certainly not new to the nineteenth century, but its "commercialization," the sale of products that purported to provide a safe termination of pregnancy, was. Women seeking such patent medicines in the advertising columns of the popular press found themselves in an unregulated world. In the growing anonymity of the mass market, buyers no longer knew producers and so depended increasingly on advertisements, testimonial letters, patents, and copyrights for assurance of the quality of the products they purchased. All such guarantees could, of course, be faked. In the popular press of the 1890s appeared masses of advertisements for fraudulent products like Professor Holt's "Hair Destroying Fluid" and the shoe "elevators" peddled by A. L. Pointing of the Oriental Toilet Company.[26] In fact Professor Holt—as well as Dr. Boyd, Dr. Frank Lesley, and Dr. Field—was a nom de guerre of Arthur Lewis Pointing. Pointing had run the Reliable Apartment Agency and the Universal Employment Agency in 1893 but by 1896 seemed to have found quack medicines more profitable. He advertised his products widely in mass circulation papers such as *Answers*. He was successful. At the Argyle Chambers on the West Strand he received up to three hundred letters a day from women requesting his Hair Destroying Fluid. The police were frustrated by the fact that, although the product was apparently useless, no complaints were made. Presumably, the clients' embarrassment deterred them from going public with their complaints. Equally useless was Pointing's "Obesity Pill" sold under the name of "Dr. Frank Lesley." A seventeen-year-old girl in Bromley, Kent, who took the pill died, but fortunately for Pointing the coroner's jury decided that pleurisy was the cause of her death. Pointing's career came to an end only when customers' complaints about his shoe "elevators" led to his being charged in May 1897 with obtaining money under false pretenses.[27]

The irony was that the Chrimes brothers, who sold a reputed abortifacient—the use of which was a criminal offense—ran less of a risk than Pointing of being reported by a customer. Edward, Richard, and Leonard Chrimes from 1896 on advertised "Lady Montrose Tablets," the "Mona Specific," and "Panolia" sugar pills, which supposedly would remove "obstructions." After two years they had on file the names of something like ten thousand women who had sent for these useless products. The brothers then took the cruel decision to extort a few pounds from each victim by threatening to reveal that they had attempted to induce a miscarriage. The Chrimeses rented an office on Northumberland Avenue, purchased twenty-five reams of paper and a cyclostyle, and ordered printers to prepare twelve thousand letterheads and addressed envelopes. A typewriter was rented, the threatening letter cyclostyled, and the machine returned to the dealer. The letter the Chrimeses concocted asserted that an official had proof of the woman's attempt to abort and that, unless she returned £2 2s and swore never again to prevent a birth, legal proceedings would commence. The letter was signed "Chas. J. Mitchell, Public Official."

Despite the precaution the Chrimeses took of sending their letter in three envelopes—an outer one, one for returning the funds, and a safety envelope in case the outer envelope was opened accidentally—they had foolishly assumed that the Victorian husband would respect the privacy of his wife's correspondence. But a Mr. Clifford went through all three envelopes and alerted the police. The failure of this grandiose scheme—the Chrimeses were soon tracked down and sentenced by Mr. Justice Hawkins to prison terms of seven to twelve years—could not cloak the enormity of the blackmail attempt. In the end something like 8,100 women had been sent threatening letters and close to 3,000 had responded. Contemporary observers were shocked that a crime on such a scale should have been attempted. What they curiously failed to note was that it was only because abortion had recently been declared a statutory offense that women seeking to regulate their fertility could be made the victims of such extortion attempts.[28]

Cream as a doctor was drawn to abortion and prostitution, which in addition to homosexuality were "victimless crimes" that had been made criminal offenses in the late nineteenth century. Drug addiction, in which Cream was also involved, would be added to their number in the early twentieth century. All these "crimes" were medically related; deviancy was simultaneously criminalized and medicalized.

Doctors, because of the nature of their calling, found themselves the custodians of increasing amounts of information that, if made public, could be damaging. The growing public concern with hereditary taints, degeneracy, and venereal disease focused attention on what a doctor could or should make public.[29] The protection of the right of "medical secrecy," viewed increasingly as a legal rather than a simple moral question, accordingly became a preoccupation of the profession.[30] The ability to protect one's privacy was the benchmark of Victorian respectability. This was a new world, Georg Simmel pointed out, in which "what is public becomes even more public; and what is private becomes ever more private."[31] For this reason the threat of exposing unpleasant truths and family secrets could be devastating.[32]

The police for their part found that the criminalization of deviancy also expanded their potential powers. But both the police and the public were ambivalent about the seriousness of such crimes as abortion, prostitution, and homosexuality, and therefore the laws against these practices were not enforced uniformly; indeed, such laws created other, far more serious crimes like the Chrimeses' blackmail attempts and creeping police corruption. At the very least the police found themselves, when dealing with "crimes" where it was unlikely that anyone would file a complaint, reduced to entrapment or spying to attain arrests. This created the very climate in which blackmail would flourish.[33] The fact that the roles of detective and blackmailer were very close explains in part why Cream was attracted to detectives like Haynes and McIntyre. Their world of spying, tracking, disguises, and duplicity was much like his own.

A Freudian analysis of his activities might lead to the conclusion that the blackmail letters Cream sent following his murders were a manifestation of an unresolved relationship with his father. "W.H." were not only the initials of William Henry Cream but also those of Dr. W. H. Broadbent, W. H. Smith, and the fictitious detective W. H. Murray.[34] Or perhaps Cream just suffered from a lack of imagination. Given the absence of any information on his childhood, such speculations cannot be pursued. But if we know little of the inner workings of his mind, we know a good deal about the age in which he lived. His fraudulent and extortionist activities begin to become comprehensible when placed in the context of a society increasingly preoccupied by questions of secrecy and surveillance. The nineteenth-century middle classes, in attempting to separate rigidly the private and public realms and in pursuing the fiction that criminalization could obliterate a range of sexual practices, had created a world in which fraud, blackmail, and sex crimes would flourish.[35]

DOCTORS

The fact of a man being a poisoner is nothing against his prose.

Oscar Wilde, "Pen, Pencil and Poison." (1889)

In turning to the question of the way in which the professions responded to the disturbingly new forms of late-nineteenth-century criminality committed by a man like Cream, it is appropriate to begin with his own, the medical profession. To have the title of doctor meant having power; it gave Cream the ability to prescribe death-dealing drugs. And yet late-nineteenth-century medicine was well aware of the fragility of its reputation. In cramming into his brief career almost every vice to which his colleagues were exposed, Cream was the archetypical doctor "gone bad." Much of the interest of his trial lay in what it revealed of both the new powers of the profession and the pitfalls into which its members, more than any other group, were likely to fall. One finds regular practitioners, who were only too aware of the incompetence of some of their colleagues, insisting that marked improvements would be made once the "irregulars" had been eliminated, others are seen falling to the temptation posed by easy access to drugs, and a notorious few were caught attempting to deal with their private devils by employing poisons.

Late-nineteenth-century doctors were far from monopolizing medical care. On the occasion of Cream's prosecution Sir Douglas Straight recalled that in the 1872 trial of Christina Edmunds a "jury of matrons" had been employed.[1] The accused murderer, seeking to avoid execution, had declared that she was pregnant. The society ladies attending the trial were to their shock and consternation forcibly impaneled by the sheriffs to sit as a "jury of matrons" with the duty of determining there and then if Edmunds were in fact "quick with child." According to Straight the confusion which reigned reached ludicrous heights:

> The doctor who was assisting them sent a message to say he wanted a stethoscope, and instructions were given to one of the court officials to see that it was at once obtained. After a considerable interval the messenger returned bearing a *telescope* which he said was what he understood he had been ordered to bring.[2]

The idea that a group of untutored women, merely "assisted" by a doctor, should determine a medical issue was taken by doctors as an insult to their profession. The moral they drew from cases such as this and Cream's was that where medical problems were concerned only regular doctors could be relied upon.[3]

Medical expertise was increasingly called for in an age of greater government intervention in the lives of the public via compulsory schooling, medical inspections, and the Contagious Diseases Acts. New concerns for hygiene and bacteriology raised the possibility of a conflict between social needs—in particular as more public money was invested in social insurance schemes—and individual rights.[4] It was thus deemed all the more important that doctors impress upon the public their competence and professional propriety.

What the Cream case revealed was that in practice regular physicians were far from monopolizing the health care of the poor. In the first instance slum dwellers doctored themselves, turning to chemists, herbalists, and suppliers of patent medicines for drugs and advice. In more serious cases the poor relied on a variety of irregular medical caregivers. Ellen Donworth was attended by John M. Johnson, an unqualified assistant to Dr. Lowe, medical officer of the South London Medical Institute.[5] Matilda Clover was negligently diagnosed in her last hours by Dr. McCarthy's assistant Francis Coppin, who "had no qualifications whatever" and could not provide a death certificate. Coppin had worked for fourteen years in South London and must have been experienced. Nevertheless, he had never treated a case of strychnine poisoning and put down Clover's convulsions to delirium tremens.[6] Dr. Graham, Clover's physician, claimed he did not come to see Clover himself because he was tied down by a labor case. He further asserted that he had seen her eight or nine times in the twelve days prior to her death, but because she was a club patient he had kept no records of these consultations.[7]

A concern to limit the practice of unqualified assistants came to light in March 1893 when a regular physician and confirmed drunkard, John Hurson, M.D., committed suicide after being fired by Dr. J. S. Casterman, the proprietor of a Stockwell Road dispensary. A. Braxton Hicks, the coroner, was disturbed by Hurson's death but clearly more preoccupied with the fact that much of the dispensary's work was carried out by H. E. Jones, an unqualified assistant. When Casterman protested that his business was legitimate, Braxton Hicks replied: "Then keep your eye on Mr. Jones and do not let him see so many patients as he did last night, when my officers called at your dispensary." Casterman, who clearly had a less exalted view of medical certification than the coroner, responded with the practical observation that "Mr. Jones was there before I took the place, and the patients know him; in many cases they would rather see him than myself." They apparently continued to do so; an investigator later discovered they went on seeing Jones for vaccination and school board certificates.[8]

Of greater concern to the profession than assistants were the "irregulars" whom the Medical Defense Union, led by Lawson Tait, were seeking to drive out of business.[9] In Lambeth a number of people were attended by a "Dr." Henry Sampey of the Metropolitan Dispensary located at 154 Wandsworth Road run by "Dr." Clayton and "Dr." Sweeney. Sampey signed medical certificates for the Hearts of Oak and similar local friendly societies. Following the death of a twelve-year-old girl in South Lambeth and the local coroner's investigations, Sampey disappeared.[10]

The police also knew of a Mr. Park who styled himself "Dr." Park. He worked out of a dispensary at 203 Blackfriars Road and served as club doctor for the theatrical members of the Society of the Comical Fellows. In Rotherhithe, a J. Haynes charged a mere shilling a visit, buying what drugs he needed at retail outlets. Haynes was trained as a chemist and so knew what he was about. The investigation focused on whether he had been calling himself a doctor rather than on what nonphysicians would have regarded as the presumably more significant question of his competency to prescribe medicine.[11]

Medical societies wanted such unqualified practitioners driven out of business but did not want to foot the bill for their prosecutions. Since few patients ever complained, the government did not view irregulars as a major problem. Nevertheless, in 1892, the Home Office informed the commissioner of police that the Medical Defense Union had been told that in the future it would be awarded costs in such trials. The Medical Acts Amendment Bill of 1900 regularized the paying of such fines to the General Medical Council and also gave it the power not only to erase but to suspend members.[12]

Largely skirted in such discussions were the possibilities of regular doctors' abusing their powers. The person undoubtedly most responsible for allowing Cream's rampage to go undetected was a regular physician, Dr. Robert Graham, who provided the inaccurate death certificate for Matilda Clover. The writing of this certificate was evidence, declared the crown counsel, of the "grossest culpability."[13] How often did this sort of thing occur? It is impossible to say, but one is reminded of Dr. Pritchard, the murderer, who in 1865 filled out the death certificates for his wife and mother-in-law. Investigations were only made after officials were alerted by anonymous letters; fellow doctors did not want to interfere. A Dr. Paterson, when asked why he, though suspecting these poisonings, did not protest his colleague's filling out possibly fraudulent death certificates, replied: "It is the etiquette of our profession."[14]

Doctors like Pritchard and Cream were associated with dispensing poisons; they were also known for their use of drugs. The question of what, if any, harm opiates posed was, in the 1890s, very much a subject of public debate. Until the coming of aspirin narcotics constituted the most common pain killers, even serving as the key ingredients in infant cordials. For most of the century Britain had forcibly countered Chinese government attempts to check the importation of Indian opium, but in 1893 the Opium Commission reviewed the situation, taking evidence from cultivators, manufacturers, and those seeking to restrict or prohibit the trade.[15] In the Western world the morphine syringe was already displacing the opium pipe. The medicinal use of morphine, the main alkaloid found in opium, was as a sedative and analgesic.

Doctors, not surprisingly, given their access to pharmaceuticals, were overrepresented among the first generation of morphine addicts. The first 3 addicts admitted to the Bethlam Royal Hospital were all doctors; 289 of France's 545 "morphine maniacs" were physicians, according to Lacassagne's figures.[16] If used in excess, the drug caused poisoning with symptoms of pinpoint pupils, shallow and slowed respiration, coma, and finally death. The succumbing to morphine in the 1890s of a number of English medical professionals prompted colleagues' pleas that doctors not allow the "habit of indulgence to take root."[17] In 1892 cocaine was added to the roster of recreational drugs reputed to have the insidious effect of producing a breakdown in the moral and the intellectual spheres. Sherlock Holmes's 7 percent solution was injected cocaine.[18] But drug use only began to be perceived by doctors as a serious problem when used by "others"—the working class and the Chinese who lacked the willpower to fight off addiction—or when, as in the case of the morphine syringe, it posed the threat of a medical procedure being usurped by nonprofessionals.[19]

Emily Sleaper testified that Cream was in the habit of taking opium in water and eating a lump of sugar afterward. John McCulloch was told by Cream that he took large quantities of morphia and opium for relief of insomnia and headaches. Sabbatini and Haynes concurred that at times he appeared almost comatose. There is the possibility that some of Cream's victims died of the combination of strychnine, morphine, and cocaine, for which he had developed a tolerance. He perhaps employed them as an aphrodisiac, but he also knew that they could kill.[20]

Cream exploited his position as a doctor while in North America to commit at least four murders; in London in 1891 and 1892 he had no difficulty either in obtaining poisons or in continuing to pass himself off as a physician to carry out an additional four. In having recourse to poison, Cream was following in the footsteps of a line of famous or infamous nineteenth-century medical murderers such as Pritchard and Palmer. After seeing Cream sentenced to death, the editor of the *Pall Mall Gazette* recollected that as a boy he had attended the trial in May 1856 of Dr. William Palmer which first made strychnine's poisonous powers notorious.[21]

In the nineteenth century, reports of poisoning deaths held a lurid fascination.[22] Oscar Wilde was drawn to the story of Thomas Griffiths Wainewright (1794–1852), an artist friend of Lamb, de Quincy, and Hazlitt who poisoned his uncle, mother-in-law, and step-sister-in-law. In "Pen, Pencil, and Poison" (1889) Wilde presented Wainewright, though actually knowing very little about him, as the archetypical dandy who led the double life of the aesthete and the killer.[23] Wilde more fully explored the dangerous theme of crime stimulating art in *The Picture of Dorian Gray*. He was no doubt drawn to such ideas as much by a desire to provoke his middle-class readers as out of any inherent need to embrace the forbidden. He had Wainewright confess to the murder of Helen Abercrombie with the Wildean line, "Yes, it was a dreadful thing to do, but she had very thick ankles."[24] Yet Wilde was not tempted, despite the contemporary notoriety of Cream and Jack the Ripper, to explore the literary theme of the doctor as killer, perhaps because so many others were doing so.[25]

Sir Edward Marshall Hall, the eminent barrister, confessed that when only fourteen in 1872 he, like Edward Straight, followed with fascination the trial of Christina Edmunds, the Brighton poisoner, who concealed strychnine in chocolates and, in a manner somewhat akin to Cream's, tried to cover her tracks by sending anonymous letters warning against the confectioner.[26] Dr. Thomas Stevenson, the expert witness in the Cream trial, testified to strychnine's effect in the Silas Barlow case of 1876.[27] Given in tiny doses, the alkaloid was prescribed by nineteenth-century doctors as a tonic for nervous diseases. Usually not more than 1/16 of a grain was given; 1/12 was the maximum medical dose. One grain was considered fatal.[28] Cream employed gelatin capsules into which he could insert up to eight grains. The time of death would depend on the form of strychnine, the length of time it took the capsule to dissolve away, and the contents of the stomach. In most cases the poison would likely begin to take effect in three-quarters of an hour.

Poisonings could touch anyone; they were difficult to detect; many undoubtedly went unreported.[29] But once a poisoner like Cream was exposed, there was an obvious inclination to attribute every unexpected death in the community to his or her handiwork.[30] Scotland Yard received a report in September 1892 that Cream, while in Quebec after his release from Joliet in the late summer of 1891, had been on "intimate terms" with Daniel Cream's mother-in-law, Mrs. Louisa Mary Hume Read of Pointe Louis, who died suddenly. After Cream was charged with the London murders, the Quebec authorities pondered the wisdom of ordering an exhumation.[31] But Henry Russell, the doctor of the Read and Cream families, told Inspector Jarvis that the death was not due to poisoning. Russell had been called to Daniel Cream's summer cottage at St. Joseph's, three miles below Quebec City, to attend Mrs. Read on 25 August; she died on 29 August, at age sixty-three, of what the doctor diagnosed as "Canadian cholera." Russell stressed that he knew of Cream's past and, seeing him at the cottage, was on his guard. The doctor took the fact that the body was not rigid as an indication that strychnine was not involved.[32]

An 1833 select committee noted that England, compared to the rest of Europe, lacked an efficient system of investigating deaths.[33] Only after 1836 were medical witnesses appearing regularly at coroners' inquests and were burials refused without a death certificate. The patient's doctor had the legal duty from 1874 on to provide such a certificate.[34] This requirement presumably made concealments of murders more difficult, but as the Matilda Clover case revealed mistakes were still made. The real problem, according to the medical profession, was that only a trained doctor could be a good coroner, but in the 1890s fewer than one-sixth were; the overwhelming majority were lawyers.[35]

Poisonings, however, were the murders most likely to pass unnoticed even by the medically trained.[36] At the 1859 trial of Dr. Smethurst, charged with murdering a mistress whom he had bigamously married, ten doctors said she was poisoned, while seven testified that she died of dysentery and the complications of pregnancy.[37] In the famous 1865 prosecution of Dr. Pritchard, who poisoned his wife and mother-in-law with antimony, medical men showed themselves reluctant to make any judgment as to cause of death.[38] As late as October 1891 an inquest jury was unable to determine how a death-dealing dose of strychnine had ended up in a young woman's Epsom salts.[39] The forensic uncertainties revealed in the Cream case, in which the deaths of Daniel Stott and Matilda Clover would have gone undetected if it had not been for Cream's letters alerting the authorities, were thus not all that unusual.

The French novelist Emile Zola provided in *La bête humaine,* published in January 1890, the classic portrayal of the husband as successful poisoner, but women, given their restricted access to other sorts of weapons and their lesser physical powers, were thought to be more likely than men to have recourse to poison.[40] Arsenic, readily available in a variety of nineteenth-century household products to control weeds and vermin, was the poison of choice.[41] Of the forty-nine women executed for murder in England between 1843 and 1890, twenty-nine had killed with poison; in twenty-three of the twenty-nine cases arsenic was employed.[42] The remarkable Mary Cotton, tried in 1873, was held responsible for the deaths of three husbands, fifteen children, and one lodger.[43] The sisters Catherine Flannagan and Margaret Higgins, with scant regard for appearances, took out three life insurance policies on Higgins's husband before poisoning him in 1883.[44] Florence Maybrick, perhaps the century's best-known female defendant, when accused in 1889 of using arsenic to kill her husband, admitted soaking flypaper but protested it was only done to retrieve the mineral coating which she employed as a cosmetic. Although Maybrick was ably defended by Sir Charles Russell, her access to the poison and the admission of an adulterous affair did her in.[45]

Even a child could employ poison. A little girl who "had taken a great interest in the Maybrick case" and who with another child "used to play at being Mrs. Maybrick, one pretending to be sick and the other pretending to be the poisoner," was charged in 1890 with attempting to poison her father's fiancée.[46] In the winter of 1891 eleven-year-old Lily Cartwright, a lonely, young domestic servant who desperately wanted to return home to her mother, put a large dose of aconite in her mistress's tea.[47]

Given the need to administer poison in food or drink, the likelihood was that it would most often be employed in domestic homicides. These sorts of preoccupations threw the police off Cream's trail. If it had not been for the flurry of accusatory letters that Cream himself had sent and the enormous assistance offered by prostitutes and the working women of Lambeth, he might never have been apprehended.

The Cream case, in exposing the doctor's power to do evil as well as good, might have provided medical men with food for thought. The pitfalls into which they, more than any other group, were likely to stumble, in particular the unwarranted use of poisons and drugs, had been well documented. But this was not a lesson on which doctors liked to linger. The medical press chose to use the Cream trial and similar cases as an argument that the powers of the medical profession should be extended rather than curtailed. Only with the carefully policing of "irregulars" and an elimination of degenerates, it argued, could such tragedies be avoided in the future.

10

DETECTIVES

He that spies is the one that kills.

Irish Proverb

Cream, for obvious reasons, presented himself at times as a doctor and at others as a confidant of detectives, a combining of identities which held a particular attraction in the late Victorian period.[1] Playing these roles gave him the power on one hand to prescribe death-dealing drugs and on the other to boast of his knowledge of the underworld. One is reminded that the authority of both the doctor and the policeman had only recently been won, and in the late nineteenth century the source of their special prerogatives still was not clear. Although both professions were making strenuous efforts to differentiate themselves from their "irregular" competitors, the truth was that anyone who claimed to be a doctor or a secret agent had a good chance of getting away with it. If late Victorian society was fascinated by the detective story, it was in part because cases like Cream's gave rise to the troubling suspicion that the lines separating caregiver and killer, constable and criminal, anarchist and *agent provocateur* were at times far from apparent.

In 1878 a remarkable young man by the name of Sherlock Holmes came down from university and took rooms just around the corner from the British Museum on Montague Street. Dissatisfied with these lodgings, he shortly thereafter moved further west, taking a flat on

Baker Street with a young doctor who had just received his medical degree from the University of London. Holmes was thrown to his apparent death in the Reichenbach Falls by the evil Moriarty on 4 May 1891 just a few weeks after the Stamford Street murders; he happily reappeared in 1894 but had missed the opportunity of tracking down Thomas Neill Cream.

Arthur Conan Doyle had introduced his detective to the reading public in 1887 in *A Study in Scarlet.* The mystery story could be traced back still earlier to the works of Wilkie Collins and Edgar Allen Poe, but the incredible popularity of Holmes and Watson firmly established the genre of the London detective story complete with foggy, gaslit streets, clattering horse-drawn hansom cabs, plodding constables, and brilliant sleuths.[2] Conan Doyle had many competitors. A generation of mystery and melodrama writers provided for a newly literate mass audience (produced in part by the 1870 Education Act) via the hundreds of outlets of new book distributors such as W. H. Smith.[3]

Ninety-five percent of nineteenth-century lawbreaking consisted of property crimes, but Victorian readers interested themselves primarily in crimes against the person.[4] Reading about violence was perhaps a compensation for not engaging in it; the growth of docility or civility seemed to be matched by the rise of the "thriller." Certainly the fascination with violent deaths increased as they declined in relative incidence. In past ages high levels of violence had been matched by high levels of illness. As sickness came increasingly under control, even declining rates of violence seemed all too high. Its literary depiction hypnotized the masses, but to describe the thriller as "in part a product of their intellectually empty and emotionally stunted lives, so tightly confined by economic and social circumstance," is no doubt going too far.[5] It still took courage and imagination to survive in the mean streets of London. The city had its own particular dangers; its deadly fog was responsible in the year of 1886 alone for over ten thousand bronchitis deaths.[6] Nevertheless, it is true that the attention of the reading public was won, not by the struggle of the health reformer against the microbe but by the contest between the detective and the archcriminal. The appeal of such conflicts was that they unambiguously demarcated the forces of good and evil.[7] What the Cream dossiers disturbingly reveal, however, is that in the real world such clear divisions could rarely be drawn.

The Metropolitan Police force of bobbies was created by Sir Robert Peel in 1829, originally operating out of an office in Whitehall Gardens. In 1891 headquarters for the new force at New Scotland Yard, an impressive, turreted edifice of white Portland stone and red brick on Derby Street between Whitehall and the Embankment, was opened. A commissioner oversaw London's twenty-two divisions made up of thirteen hundred sergeants and twelve thousand constables. There had initially been some opposition to the creation of a police force on the grounds that it represented an infringement on English liberty. The "myth" of the unarmed English police constable acting not like his continental counterpart as an instrument of repression but, rather, as an objective arbiter in neighborhood disputes, though ultimately embraced by the middle classes, was never firmly rooted among the poor.[8] The latter's cynicism was not misplaced. The original impetus for the creation of a modern police force was as much grounded in the government's concern to respond to political protests—of the Irish, Chartists, and agrarian agitators—as to prevent crime.[9]

Even some members of the middle class were made uneasy by the creation of a division of plainclothes detectives. Their anonymity and the "trickery" of their activities, it was feared, would end their accountability.[10] They might, by their very immersion in the world of criminality, become tainted by the vices they were supposed to be combating. Such fears were borne out in 1877 when three of the four chief inspectors in the detective branch were found guilty of corruption.[11] Howard Vincent, lawyer and Sandhurst graduate, was appointed by the Home Office to recommend reforms. Vincent put an end to blatant corruption, but in successfully reorganizing the Criminal Investigation Department along the lines of the preventive model of the French Police de Sûreté he opted for an increased use of undercover agents, whose dubious ethics were soon made embarrassingly public.[12]

On 25 November 1880 the readers of the *Times* were informed that Thomas Titley, a young chemist of Charlotte Street, had been charged at the Marlborough Street Police Court with "selling a noxious drug for an unlawful purpose."[13] Such arrests of sellers of abortifacients were not uncommon, but the story that emerged at Titley's trial was unusual to say the least. His lawyers protested that the charges were laid as a result of a "plant" and that Titley was the victim of a police conspiracy.[14]

The police claimed to have long suspected Titley of supplying abortifacients. The problem was that no one would file a complaint. To determine his guilt, E Division of the Metropolitan Police on 11 November had Martha Diffey, a "female searcher" and wife of a policeman, go to the Charlotte Street shop posing as the mother of a pregnant young woman who wished to have an abortion. Diffey's ploy was to say that her "daughter" would not come to Titley but would take anything he sent her. Titley, not surprisingly, was somewhat suspicious. To allay his fears, Inspector John O'Callaghan, under instructions from Superintendent Thomson, assumed the role of the young woman's seducer and wrote Titley a letter, dated 13 November 1880. This remarkable fabrication, which deserves to be quoted in full, proceeded as follows:

> Dear Sir—This woman's daughter who was in our service, is about 3 months advanced in pregnancy, and is naturally desirous of getting rid of her trouble. A friend has informed me of your skill in such matters, and I have advised the girl to call on you. She has, however, some hesitation in doing so; and the mother, who has been to me, informs me that in her absence you have some difficulty in prescribing effectually. As a man of the world you will understand my position in this matter. The mother is a virago, and constantly accuses me of having been the ruin of her family, and her daughter, though not so bad, is getting troublesome too. If the thing goes on to the end I shall have to pay. I should prefer doing so now, and so getting rid of this annoyance, which is becoming intolerable. I have, however, no desire to be seen in this matter. My part will be to pay; and I should be glad of your advice as to what is best to do in the circumstances. I can understand how desirable it is that you should see the girl herself, but I have hitherto failed to persuade her to go and see you. Kindly say whether you cannot possibly prescribe in her absence, and I shall be glad to pay any sum which may be reasonable for the service rendered, and I shall, moreover, be indebted to you for having relieved me of an annoyance which is becoming intolerable. I can send no money by this woman, as I have no certainty that it would reach you. In your note say how I am to remit.[15]

Some policeman obviously hankered after a literary career. This letter had all the elements of Victorian melodrama: the wealthy roué, the seduced young servant, and the mercenary mother. More to the point, however, is that the writer, not once, but four times in the course of the letter offered to pay whatever was necessary to end a pregnancy. Howard Vincent, the director of the C.I.D., had O'Callaghan provided with the sizable sum of twenty-five pounds with which to bait the trap.

Titley, still suspicious, replied that he would not discuss such a serious matter by correspondence but was willing to speak to the man. On 15 November Sergeant William Stroud, who presumably looked more like a gentleman than Inspector O'Callaghan, was brought to Charlotte Street by Mrs. Diffey and introduced as the seducer. Titley reiterated that it would be best if the young woman came herself and, according to the police, suggested that instruments could be used. Since this was not possible, the good-hearted Titley, in exchange for the modest sum of four shillings, gave the sergeant two bottles of "noxious drugs," cautioning that their successful use could not be assured. Titley was promptly arrested.

The defense, led by Edmund Clarke, argued that the case should be thrown out. Titley was indicted for supplying noxious drugs to the daughter of Martha Diffey, but no such person existed. And the seducer and mother were, of course, also fictions. Mr. Justice Stephen having allowed the indictment to stand, Clarke pleaded that the conduct of the police was "infamous," placing in question the "private safety and liberty of the subject." His client, he pointed out, had no way of defending himself against the "imputations made against him by the police spies, who had committed falsehood, forgery and bribery in order to induce the commission of the crime." This was a case in which the police had actually conceived the crime and invented it, held out inducements for another person to involve himself in it, and created an "imaginary" victim. The reports of their conversations with Titley could not be corroborated. Was the jury now to trust the evidence of constables who openly admitted employing falsehoods and were actual accomplices to the crime?

Mr. Justice Stephen, in summing up, admitted that the jury was undoubtedly disturbed by what they might take as the police's "ill-advised or . . . criminal course." But the real question, he insisted, was whether Titley had indeed supplied abortifacients. He asked the jury to remember "that if on the one hand they could not think well of a man who could write a letter in order to entrap a fellow being into crime; still on the other, they could hardly think too badly of a man if, as alleged, he was the habitual murderer of unborn children." Given such loaded language, it was clear where the judge's sympathies lay. The jury followed his direction in returning a verdict of guilty but, taking into account the police provocation, recommended mercy. Stephen sentenced Titley to eighteen months of hard labor.

The case did not end there. On 17 December the police who had entrapped Titley were indicted as accomplices and appeared before the same Mr. Justice Stephen. Although the legal cast was the same, the roles were reversed, with Edward Clarke now appearing as counsel for the prosecution and Harry Poland, "at the insistence of the Treasury," leading the defense. Ironically, Stephen quashed the in-

dictment because he declared the most important count—that the police had "incited Titley to supply a noxious thing, knowing that it was
intended to be used for an unlawful purpose"—faulty in not stating
for whom the drug was intended.[16] Yet the fact that Titley had been
indicted for providing drugs to a person who did not exist had not
prevented his being sent to prison.

An unanticipated wave of public indignation was elicited by this
revelation of police duplicity. An editorial in the *Times* reflected the
unease felt by the liberal middle classes on learning that their police
had acted as if any means were fair. The police might have had their
suspicions, but what, asked the editorialist, "if the temptation held out
by the police had induced Titley to take his first criminal step?" The
police were doing more than detecting crime; they were inciting it.
Who was to decide which limits were allowable?[17]

Finally, in January 1881 Sir William Harcourt, the Home Secretary,
was compelled by a parliamentary question to comment on the affair.
Stressing that there was some basis for the police's original suspicions
and at least one legal precedent for such tactics, Harcourt confessed
that he was "startled" when he first heard of the manner in which
Titley was ensnared.[18] "As a rule," Harcourt declared, "the police
ought not to set traps for people," and in the future the Home Office
would have to be informed if the police contemplated such actions.[19]
Such restraints on police conduct might make some crimes more difficult to pursue, but, conceded Harcourt, the "greater" evil, which
had to be avoided at all cost, was a possible loss of public confidence
in the police.[20]

Such precautions were cold comfort for Titley. Although his solicitors presented three memorials to the Home Secretary calling for the
reducing or reversing of Titley's sentence, including petitions signed
by 186 of his neighbors and 3,800 persons in London and the prov-
inces, their appeal was turned down.[21]

The Titley case was unusual, not so much because of its revelation
of unethical police undercover work but because it demonstrated that
such energies had been devoted to unearthing an offense of no great
obvious significance. Understandably enough, informers and spies
had been used by the government throughout the century to report
on the more serious threats posed by radical and working-class movements. In 1873 the Intelligence Department was created; in 1889 the
Official Secrets Act was passed. The same decades that saw the rise of
the detective story witnessed the emergence of modern spy fiction.[22]
The Fenian bombing campaign launched in 1881 and the Phoenix
Park assassinations of two English officials in Dublin in 1882 provided

the catalyst for creating a new secret service under a "spymaster-general," Sir Edward Jenkinson. The bombing campaign peaked in 1884 with the destruction of the Special Irish Branch itself in Scotland Yard and by 1885 was over.[23] The new "Special Branch" of the Metropolitan Police under the direction of Robert Anderson took over the surveillance of political radicals in the early 1890s, in particular anarchists thought sympathetic to continental policies of direct action.[24]

Cream was very much attracted to this murky world of plainclothes police agents and private detectives. On his last trip to Canada he passed many of the evenings on board the *Sarnia* with Lieutenant-Colonel Vohl, chief of the Quebec City Police.[25] Cream covered up his prison record by telling Vohl he had been "traveling" for the previous decade, but was more than willing to talk at length about his interest in women and the special study he had made of poisons. He even admitted that he had carried out several abortions. None of this seems to have offended Vohl, who invited Cream to his home.[26]

It is just possible that Cream's frequent trips back and forth across the Atlantic might have attracted the attention of agent Haynes, Sergeant McIntyre, and Inspector Tunbridge, who was described in the press as "engaged in dynamite enquiries" and whose job it was to watch just such movements.[27] To counter the threat of Fenian terrorism, Sir Edward Jenkinson had assembled a network of agents straddling England, Europe, and North America.

McIntyre and Haynes were both acquaintances of Henri Le Caron, who had recently emerged from his cloak of anonymity to be hailed as Britain's most daring secret agent. Le Caron, whose real name was Thomas Beach, emigrated to the United States in the 1860s, where he spent a year at Chicago Medical College in 1867 and worked briefly as resident medical health officer at Joliet State Prison (where Cream was incarcerated in 1881) before beginning his career as a British spy, infiltrating and reporting on Fenian activities in North America.[28] Le Caron communicated with Scotland Yard through Robert Anderson, adviser since 1868 to the Home Office, about the plans of the Irish revolutionaries.[29]

Le Caron only dropped his cover and revealed himself as a secret agent when asked by the *Times* to come forward in 1889 to provide evidence that Parnell, the Irish leader in the House of Commons, had secretly expressed support in 1881 for the Fenians' terrorist activities. Le Caron's testimony did not destroy Parnell's reputation—that was done by Captain O'Shea, the husband of Parnell's mistress—but Le Caron had made his own as the "prince of spies."[30] Though disparaged by Parnell's defenders Charles Russell (subsequently the crown counsel in Cream's trial) and H. H. Asquith (the future Liberal prime minister), he had the support of powerful men like Joseph Soames, solicitor of the *Times,* and police colleagues such as Sergeant Patrick McIntyre.[31]

McIntyre and his friend John Haynes—whom he "knew in a business capacity previous to the present case," as the press discreetly put it—had earlier worked with Le Caron in tracing the movements of suspects between America and Britain. Haynes was a curious character. He was trained as a ship's engineer and had worked for some time in the United States. He described himself as having made "inquiries for the British government" in both England and North America and spoke of knowing Le Caron "very well." How Haynes figured in Le Caron's penetration of the Fenian movement was never made clear, but Haynes intimated that he had worked for the British government in some capacity in America in 1890 and in London in 1892 regarding anarchist dynamite explosions. Haynes spotted the plainclothes officers tailing him and Cream along Westminster Bridge Road on 18 May and protested to the duty officer at the Kennington Road Police Station. To prove his importance, he stated that he thought that he was perhaps being tracked by "enemies of the government" and further declared that he knew Chief Inspector Littlechild.[32] Haynes, once informed of why the police were following Cream, offered his services in keeping him under observation. The subject of poisons was clearly broached since Haynes volunteered that he had seen Cream's leather case of pills. At the end of the report on Haynes's interview, the question was put forward whether Haynes could be relied on. An unidentified officer at Scotland Yard wrote in the margin, "no."[33]

At Cream's trial Geoghegan suggested that the unemployed Haynes was on the lookout for any information he could use to win the gratitude of the authorities, that Haynes believed he already had some sort of "claim" on the Home Office, and that he was seeking an appointment in either the London or Liverpool police forces. Haynes would not respond to such leading questions but did admit to having some link with Joseph Soames, solicitor to the *Times,* and to having been provided with a testimonial by the spymaster-general of the Home Office, Sir Edward Jenkinson.

Scotland Yard eventually found it necessary to give Haynes something, if only to keep him in London until Cream's trial. McIntyre and other police officers advanced him ten pounds, and a police memo explained that in addition he was going to be given an allowance of ten shillings a week. "Haynes has been unsuccessful in getting employment; he is entirely without means, and talks of putting an end to himself."[34] The Treasury, for reasons it did not want to put down on paper, refused to be a party to such a scheme. It informed Robert Anderson that

> the Treasury will *not* support or acknowledge the support of Hayes [*sic*] during the enquiries—or undertake in any way with the Police in their dealings with him . . . At present I do not think we shall want him as a *witness* but whether we call him or not we will not support him.[35]

Haynes had in some obscure way blotted his copybook; his old friends in high places wanted nothing more to do with him.

Sergeant McIntyre's career ended in a similarly rancorous fashion. McIntyre, originally from Northern Ireland, had joined Scotland Yard in 1878 and been recruited into political work in 1883.[36] For most of the 1880s he was employed in keeping Fenians under surveillance. In 1887, acting on a tip from Le Caron, he assisted in the arrest of two Irish bombers in Baxter Street.[37] During the subsequent decade his duties included the suppression of anarchist activities in England.

The popular press of the 1880s and 1890s, in part with police encouragement, kept the English reading public on edge with a constant stream of reports of terrorist outrages.[38] In December 1891 the terrorists' English campaign was launched when J. E. Barlas fired shots at the residence of the Speaker of the House of Commons. The tactic of "propaganda by the deed"—bomb throwings and assassinations— though denounced by leading anarchist theorists such as Kropotkin, was launched on the continent in March 1892.[39] The fear that any mysterious bundle could be an anarchist bomb was, of course, what led a clerk to read the circulars that Cream had sent from Montreal to Liverpool.

By a curious coincidence Sergeant McIntyre and Mr. Justice Hawkins, who both participated in Cream's prosecution, were also involved in March and April of 1892 in England's most famous anarchist trial. In January 1892 the police had arrested a group of continental and English anarchists at Walsall, near Birmingham, and charged them with possession of explosives. At the end of March the Walsall anarchists were put on trial at the Stafford Assizes, where Justice Hawkins sentenced them to prison terms ranging from five to seven years. Liberals and socialists were shocked at both the harsh penalties and the evidence made public in the course of the trial of the probable police use of *agents provocateurs*.[40] Certainly the uncovering of the Walsall plot had come at a very convenient time for the police; in providing "proof" of the importance of the Special Branch it fortuitously staved off threatened budget cuts.[41]

In an outraged response David Nicoll attacked Hawkins in the columns of the anarchist periodical *Commonweal* of 9 April as "Hangman Hawkins" and posed the rhetorical question of whether such magistrates should be allowed to live. On 19 April the offices of *Commonweal* were accordingly raided by the police and Sergeant McIntyre arrested its editor, Charles Mowbray. Mowbray, who had been for some time absent from the office attending to a wife who was dying of consumption and had had nothing to do with the article, won a good deal of public sympathy. Indeed, Mrs. Mowbray died only hours before his arrest.[42] William Morris offered to put up Mowbray's bail; his children were cared for while he was in jail by Annie Besant, once a pioneering advocate of contraception, now a lecturer on the occult and theosophy.[43] In court Mowbray was dealt with lightly; Nicoll was sentenced to eighteen months of hard labor for incitement to murder.[44]

McIntyre was himself demoted and then dismissed from the force under mysterious circumstances in October 1894. His dismissal might have been the result of what was considered his sympathetic handling of Mowbray. Certainly he considered the Tottenham Court Road anarchists impractical and harmless dreamers. It might have been because of his quarreling with Le Caron and the austere Plymouth Brother who now headed Scotland Yard, Robert Anderson. In any event McIntyre had his revenge in 1895 by providing *Reynold's Newspaper* with a serialized version of his memoirs, entitled "Scotland Yard—Its Mysteries and Methods." His most damaging revelation was that an *agent provocateur* by the name of Coulon had indeed been responsible for the entrapment of the Walsall group and that Fenian plots had been similarly orchestrated.[45]

Unperturbed by such revelations, the English press continued throughout 1892 to play up news of bombing scares from as far afield as Chicago, Liège, and Madrid. Socialist preparations for May Day demonstrations in favor of an eight-hour working day were viewed by the authorities with what proved to be unnecessary alarm. In mid-May hair-raising accounts came from France of Ravachol robbing the dead.[46] "The time is full of sensational crimes," noted the *Clarion*. "To Deeming succeeded Ravachol, to Ravachol succeeds the mystery of the Lambeth poison cases."[47] Cream's trial began on 17 October; he was found guilty on 21 October. The press and the police's attention swung around to the demonstrations of the unemployed in Trafalgar Square on 5 November. Cream was executed 15 November.

With the return of prosperity the political radicalism of the 1880s and early 1890s declined, leaving the Special Branch with little to do for the rest of the decade. In 1894 the French anarchist Martial Bourdin succeeded only in blowing himself up when trying to destroy the Greenwich Royal Observatory. The event's chief importance was to inspire Joseph Conrad to write his patronizing account of the London world of radicals *The Secret Agent*.[48] With the pickings so thin, Chief Inspector Melville of Special Branch convinced himself that the little-known Legitimation League was a cover for subversives. The League's journal, the *Adult*, edited by George Bedborough and the anarchist Henry Seymour, appeared in 1897 with the modest aim of securing the rights of illegitimate children and popularizing sex education. The program drew the support of such well-known progressives as Grant Allen, Edward Carpenter, and Mona Caird.[49] The League won brief notoriety during its successful campaign for the release of Edith Lanchester, a young Battersea woman who, having fallen in love with a socialist, had been committed by her father to an asylum. The Special Branch was sure that there was more to the League than the defense of children's rights. In 1898 Inspector John Sweeney purchased a copy of Havelock Ellis's pioneering study of homosexuality, *Sexual Inversion,* from Bedborough, whom he then arrested. The courts declared the work "obscene and filthy."[50] Protests were made by George Bernard Shaw and others, but the League collapsed and the police congratulated themselves on having destroyed what they were convinced was a front for anarchist activities.[51]

By the end of the 1890s the London police were pleased to believe that they had put an end to the campaigns of the Fenians, anarchists, and sex radicals. But in doing so, the police had created a world in which trickery and betrayal were lauded. They disguised themselves as criminals; they penetrated anarchist and Fenian groups with *agents provocateurs* for the purposes of entrapping them. Even simple chemists' shops like Titley's had provided a stage on which police constables played out elaborate roles in hopes of ensnaring a victim. Such police actions had the effect of blurring in the public mind the lines between crime and political protest, between sexual radicalism and anarchist terrorism.

The nineteenth-century English middle class was proud that systematic police enforcement had slowly replaced ad hoc and at times bloody forms of repression. In a similar sort of way medicine had been made more "preventive" with the public subject to medical inspection and vaccination even before illness struck. In the realm of policing, if the process was made more certain, it was at the price of being less public. The old liberal notion that police were only to respond to crises was displaced by new enthusiasms for observation, surveillance, and crime prevention.[52] Information was now not only collected and broken down statistically, but through the penny post, telegraph, and newspaper rapidly transmitted and diffused.

The greater the degree of the police's moral surveillance, the more possibilities were open to them for intimidation.[53] When the police played at being criminals, it was little wonder that a criminal like Cream would play at being detective. Their world of spying, tracking, disguises, and duplicity was much like Cream's own.[54] Cream did not conjure his "Bayne," "Malone," and "O'Brien" pseudonyms out of thin air; they were characters in search of an author.

11

DEGENERATES

We cannot consider society as entitled to exterminate all
people having defective structure of the brain . . . all idiots
do not become assassins.

Peter Kropotkin, *In Russian and French Prisons* (1887)

Cream's conviction and execution raised the police's hopes that Jack
the Ripper had finally been eliminated. Cream was obviously much
the same sort—a foreigner, often out of the country, who murdered
prostitutes for no apparent motive. If not the Ripper himself, Cream
was certainly the same "criminal type." The term was popularized by
those who laid the basis for the new science of criminology, which in
the 1890s was in the very process of emerging. In theory it promised
to protect society from people like Cream; in practice it espoused the
desire to eliminate in its own way the very class of poor women whom
Cream murdered.

One of the attractions of phrenology, the nineteenth-century science of reading character from the bumps on the head, was, as Gilbert and Sullivan noted, its promise to expose criminality.

Policeman nothing said
    (though he had much to say on it),
But from the bad man's head
    He took the cap that lay on it.

"Observe his various bumps,
    His head as I uncover it;
His morals lie in lumps
    All round about and over it.

"For Burglars, Thieves, and Co;
    Indeed I'm no apologist;
But I, some years ago,
    Assisted a phrenologist." [1]

Cream did not escape such attentions. L. N. Fowler of the Fowler
Phrenological Institute, Ludgate Circus, asked the authorities if a cast
of the murderer's head might be made before his death.[2] Francis
Thorburn, a rival phrenologist, assured the Home Office he would be
willing to read Cream's bumps even after his execution.[3]

These requests were turned down. Although phrenology had enjoyed an enormous mid-century vogue, the police and respectable
society were by the 1890s disdainful of such "quackery." The proponents of the science of criminology now dominated the discussion of
social deviants. But while those who formulated the concept of "criminal types" received a respectful hearing, it was a moot point if they
would be any more successful than the phrenologists in predicting
criminal behavior. Indeed, H. G. Wells warned that "a number of
cruel and mischievous ideas" were being advanced by those

> who would persuade the heedless reader that every social
> failure is necessarily a "degenerate," and who claim boldly
> that they can trace a distinctly evil and mischievous strain
> in that unfortunate miscellany which constitutes "the crimi-
> nal class." They invoke the name of "science" with just as
> much confidence and just as much claim as the early Vic-
> torian phrenologists. They speak and write with ineffable
> profundity about the "criminal" ear, the "criminal" thumb,
> the "criminal" glance. They gain access to gaols and pester
> unfortunate prisoners with callipers and cameras, and quite
> unforgivable prying into personal and private matters . . .
> Criminals are born, not made, they allege.[4]

What Wells put his finger on was the fact that criminologists were
not content with simply seeking to explain the emergence of a man
like Cream. They were asserting that a host of social problems could
be traced back to biological taints. They were, by presenting as inextricably entwined the problems of degeneration, criminality, and the
falling birthrate, "medicalizing" deviancy, which necessarily exalted
the importance of medical men.[5] They were condemning as lacking
in social worth the type of women whom Cream would murder.

Such pessimistic biological determinism was of relatively recent date. For most of the nineteenth century prosperous Britain was dominated by the progressive belief in inevitable social improvement. Darwin's theory of evolution was read in this optimistic light; the good and healthy would triumph over the bad and unhealthy. As artificial impediments to individual liberty fell away, society would become more peaceful and productive. And growing individualism would not result in anarchy; a society of free, rational creatures was bound together by innumerable contracts. Some, of course, were mentally unable to make such contracts; they were the insane. Others made, but broke, their contracts—the criminals. Such individuals in a previous unenlightened age were subjected to ferocious, irrational, and counterproductive punishments. In contrast, in nineteenth-century asylums a "moral treatment" was employed by custodians to fan into a flame any remaining spark of sanity. And in the new penitentiaries warders applied a "just measure of pain," not to extract retribution but to make prisoners see the error of their ways and so return to society productive citizens.[6]

The rash of penitentiary building that took place in the first half of the century, with London's Millbank Penitentiary (1821) as the model, was carried out in the expectation that in controlling the felons' environment society could in effect "cure" them. Although harsh, the mid-Victorian "separate system," in which prisoners were held in individual cells, premised that, if convicts were prevented from "contaminating" each other and subjected only to benign forces, their reform was possible.[7] Honest men, like criminals, according to such an environmentalist argument, were made, not born. By the 1870s, however, such expectations began to wane. Environmental improvements did not seem to work, recidivism rates remained high, and rehabilitation attempts flagged. The penitentiary, declared the pessimists, had failed.[8]

This decline of faith in environmentalism was not restricted to the world of corrections. With the rise of new industrial competitors like Germany and the United States, Britain lost its economic dominance and understandably reappraised the notion that, in the struggle for survival, the "good" necessarily triumphed. Something seemed wrong when shoddy products edged out quality goods, when the poor had large families while the prosperous had small ones. From the mid-century onward there accordingly coexisted in many middle-class minds, along with a basic belief in progress, the fear of social and moral "degeneration."

E. Ray Lankester, although restricting his discussion to the lower species, raised the specter in 1880 of actual biological degeneration, of a reversal of evolution, with species becoming less varied and less complex.[9] But fears of social degeneration had for some time been prominent on the continent, where the Lamarckian idea of acquired characteristics underlay the notion that degeneration could be caused by detrimental environmental forces. Drugs and alcohol were singled out for condemnation because of their ability to swamp the higher faculties and so allow the lower to take over. B. A. Morel argued in *Traité des dégénérescences* (1857) that a bad environment produced the degenerate individual, who carried a "morphological stigmata" which was passed on to subsequent generations.[10]

In 1870 the Italian physician Cesare Lombroso, after determining that the skull of an infamous brigand resembled that of an atavistic being, had the flash of insight that the constitutional criminal was an evolutionary throwback. In *L'Uomo delinquente* (1876), the century's most influential statement of biological determinism, Lombroso largely followed Morel but added the twist that degeneration represented a reversion to an earlier ancestral form. Lombroso in effect created criminal anthropology in defining various criminal types: the born or instinctual criminal; the criminal by chance, who was merely a reduced type of the born or instinctual criminal; the habitual criminal, who over time took on the attributes of the born criminal; and finally the insane, often epileptic, criminal. Only the criminal driven by a momentary outburst of passion and who was otherwise virtuous was considered by Lombroso free of hereditary taint.[11]

Criminal anthropologists suggested that preventive measures could be taken inasmuch as criminals manifested their atavistic or regressive nature by a variety of physical deformations. Crime was linked by Lombroso to

> the enormous jaws, high cheekbones, size of orbits, handle-shaped or sessile ears found in criminals, savages and apes, insensibility to pain, extremely acute sight, tattooing, excessive idleness, love of orgies and irresistible craving for evil for its own sake.[12]

Lombroso's main point was that if crime was in large part determined by heredity, it followed that forms of correction based on a belief in the ability to "reform" criminals were misplaced. Rather than punishing them for the particular crime they had committed, society should "treat" criminals for their problems and prevent them from reproducing their kind.

The continental school of criminal anthropology, materialistic and deterministic, was distinctly at odds with mid-Victorian liberalism. British criminology presented itself as avoiding the exaggerated theorizing of the French and Italians, as more skeptical and pragmatic. Its leaders were more psychiatric in orientation with a marked preoccupation with the insane and the feebleminded.[13] Nevertheless, in the later decades of the century currents of naturalism and determinism emerged in Britain similar to those prevalent on the continent. As faith in rehabilitation faltered, criminality was increasingly seen, not as a result of poor decision making or a lack of will, but as a "defect." Thomas Laycock asserted in 1862 that mental and moral qualities were hereditarily transmitted. Prisoners' heads were being measured by George Wilson in 1869.[14] In pursuit of a physiological basis of crime the great clinician William Osler dissected the brains of criminals.[15]

In the 1870s the degenerate or deviancy view was popularized in the works of such leading British psychiatrists as Henry Maudsley and Hack Tuke. The cause of crime was increasingly looked for in innate irrational forces. Uncontrolled rage, lust, and jealousy rather than cold calculation were assumed to lie at the roots of violence. All crime, according to Maudsley, was a result of insanity. The law attempted to have people control their impulses, but how, he asked, could it determine whether they were able to do so?[16] Criminals' ability to take responsibility for their actions was thus undermined. Women in particular were presented in medical discussions as influenced by "their special body functions."[17] The Home Office accordingly began routinely gathering medical testimony for trials; crime had become "medicalized."

Francis Galton, more than any other single individual, played the key role in linking up British anxieties concerning degeneration, criminality, and declining fertility.[18] A cousin of Darwin, Galton, who in 1883 coined the term "eugenics" to describe "the study of the agencies under social control that may improve or impair the racial qualities of future generations, either physically or mentally," asserted that the statistical approach, if used to encourage such selective breeding, could solve the problems besetting Britain.[19] Breeders had already succeeded in developing improved strains of plants and animals; could not techniques now be applied to human reproduction? As confidence in liberalism waned, such ideas began to receive the serious attention of academics. From the 1870s on, the British upper and middle classes, unlike the lower orders, were clearly limiting family size and, consequently, social commentators were becoming worried; by the turn of the century some had gone so far as to predict that the nation was facing "race suicide" and national degeneration. If a healthy demographic balance were to be maintained, they claimed, it would be necessary to entice the "fit" to breed and to take measures to restrict the reproduction of the "unfit."

Criminals were the least fit, those most lacking in civic worth. Turning to the question of correction, Galton asserted that the criminal—not the crime—had to be the focus of attention. There was no point, he declared in *Inquiries into Human Faculty,* in attempting to make the felon see the evil of his ways.

> The ideal criminal is, unhappily for him, deficient in qualities that are capable of restraining his unkindly or inconvenient instincts. He has neither sympathy for others nor the sense of duty, both of which lie at the back of conscience; nor has he sufficient self-control to accommodate himself to the society in which he has to live, and to promote his own selfish instincts in the long run. He cannot be preserved from criminal misadventure by either altruistic sentiments or by intelligently egotistic ones.[20]

The "natural criminal," according to Galton, was someone who had never grown up.[21] And because such an individual's "germ plasm" was an immutable hereditary substance, the unfit were doomed to pass on to their offspring traits that produced pauperism, criminality, and promiscuity.[22]

The Jack the Ripper scare in 1888 heightened interest in the question of criminal nature.[23] Havelock Ellis, a supporter of eugenics, responded to the scare by introducing the English reading public to the continental approach of "criminal anthropology" with *The Criminal* (1890). Ellis basically followed Lombroso in enumerating the different typologies of the habitual, occasional, and instinctual criminals and in sketching in the biological and social causes of crime. As in his later, better-known studies of sex, Ellis presented crime as a natural phenomenon. Organic malfunctions lay at its core. Vagrants and prostitutes, the noncriminal vicious, he presented as even more abnormal than the criminal. They too were degenerate, atavistic, and feebleminded.

Mendel's genetic theory was not yet available; therefore, hereditarians based the issue of "fitness" on external appearance. Physical stigmata were taken as signs of mental and physical failure.[24] The characteristics of the criminal, according to Ellis, included dark complexion, large hands, apelike agility, hairiness, vanity, and moral insensitivity.[25]

The "Criminology Series" that enlarged the British reading public's understanding of Lombroso, Enrico Ferri, and other continental, positive criminologists was edited by Rev. William Douglas Morrison, the Canadian chaplain of Wandsworth Prison, who in his own works, such as *Juvenile Offenders* (1896), focused, like Ellis, on the social and biological roots of crime.[26] Biological and social pressures, according to Morrison, led to degeneration by exacerbating existing moral defects. In proving to his own satisfaction that there was no necessary link between destitution and crime, he concluded that a "criminal class" existed. Prostitution, for example, was blamed by the sentimental on the poverty found in the slums of British cities. But since women also walked the streets in prosperous American and Australian towns, it was obvious to Morrison that they were motivated primarily by their innate slothfulness, vanity, and sensuality: "Very often crime is but the offspring of degeneracy and disease."[27] L. Gordon Rylands concurred; the criminal was not normal. Some minor crimes could be prevented by environmental improvements, but not theft, murder, and suicide.[28] Robert Anderson, head of Scotland Yard, reserved his criticism for the "short sentence craze." Since the character of the hardened criminal could not be changed, he had to be put away for life.[29]

Charles Booth's surveys of poverty in London seemed to support the notion that the city's squalid slums, as the Social Darwinists warned, were producing a degenerate race or "residuum." Alcoholism, tuberculosis, and venereal disease—all rife in the large towns—were assumed to be hereditary illnesses. Pessimists argued that social welfare programs, in blunting the struggle for survival—which in the world of nature effectively prevented the unfit from reproducing—would cause devolution rather than evolution. Arnold White, a vocal anti-Semite and leading member of the "yellow press," bewailed in the 1880s the rise of unhealthy cities, which spawned generations of the mentally, morally, and physically unfit. The danger, as he saw it, was that "the criminal and pauperized classes with low cerebral development renew their race more rapidly than those of higher nervous natures," and he accordingly called for the segregation of perpetual criminals and the sterilization of the "unfit."[30] John Berry Haycraft similarly argued, in *Darwinism and Race Progress*, that the criminal and vicious had to be rooted out. The goal he set was the nonperpetuation of the "worst strains."[31] Francis Galton, in giving the 1901 Huxley lecture, focused national attention on the proposal that such classes of "undesirables" be segregated and sterilized.[32] In the United States the rhetoric of the hereditarians, including Robert McClaughry, warden of Joliet Prison, where Cream was incarcerated, was even more inflammatory.[33] Henry M. Boies, a member of the Pennsylvania board of public charities, after declaring the institutional inmate a "worm-eaten, half-rotten fruit of the race," a "gangrened member," and a "horrid breed," called for the "extermination of the criminal class."[34]

The hereditarian argument was not without its critics.[35] The popular novelists Grant Allen and H. G. Wells, although not indifferent to the importance of science, subjected Galtonian eugenics to savage critiques.[36] Allen echoed biologist Alfred Russell Wallace's verdict that eugenics represented the "meddlesome interference of an arrogant scientific priestcraft."[37] Wells took pleasure in making the point that criminals, trying to escape their bad environment, might just be the hardiest human specimens and therefore the very ones whose reproduction should not be curbed. In any event, since next to nothing was yet known about hereditary ill health, Wells concluded that eugenicists were only parading their own inhumanity by presumptuously labeling social inferiors as "unfit." "No longer are we to say, 'There, but for the grace of God, go I'—when the convict tramps by us—but, 'There goes another sort of animal that is differentiating from my species and which I would like to see exterminated.'"[38] But in the last decades of the nineteenth century the tide was moving in the direction of the hereditarians.

Women—in particular, prostitutes—were not spared the appraising gaze of the criminal anthropologists. The female deviant was described as having lost her femininity.[39] She was darker and hairier than her law-abiding sister, had a smaller cranial capacity and a large "virile" jaw. Her "masculinism" was a sign of her criminality.[40] Her uncontrolled reproduction posed the greatest danger to the community.

At the same time that the fertility of the "unfit" was being lamented by the eugenicists, they were condemning any attempt by healthy women to shirk their childbearing role. "Birth control is poison to a race which has not legislatively organized a differential fertility of its castes; it is death to a race which has not regarded its own fertility in relation to that of its neighbors or possible enemies."[41] Indeed, fit women who refused to reproduce were declared degenerate. Mrs. E. Lynn Linton in her articles on "wild women" said that independent-minded women were revealing "certain qualities and practices hitherto confined to the uncultured and savages."[42] The linking of mental degeneration and a deterioration of the genital organs obviously manifested itself, so the biologist Walter Heape claimed, in the emergence of the women's movement.[43] Galton was himself a well-known antifeminist, a supporter of the Anti-Suffrage Society, and a defender of the Contagious Diseases Act that permitted the forcible medical inspection of prostitutes.[44]

This discussion among academics of hereditary criminality, degeneration, and atavistic tendencies in turn filtered down into popular consciousness through newspapers and novels.[45] Concerns for dual consciousness and degeneration were very much in the air in the 1880s and 1890s.[46] The portrayal of the double life of monster and medical man led by Cream had a particular resonance for a reading public that only six years earlier had shuddered at Robert Louis Stevenson's description of a similar villain in the *Strange Case of Dr. Jekyll and Mr. Hyde*. "He had now seen the full deformity of that creature that shared with him some of the phenomena of consciousness, and was co-heir with him to death."[47]

As famous a literary monster as Mr. Hyde was Count Dracula. The central theme in *Dracula* (1897)—the threat to the nation's blood posed by an atavistic, alien force—mirrored many of the eugenicists' preoccupations. Bram Stoker, the Irish author, certainly drew on Lombroso and Nordau for his description of the count's "high thin nose, massive eyebrows, pale pointed ears."[48]

Not surprisingly, the age's greatest detective revealed a familiarity with contemporary criminal anthropology. In 1893 Arthur Conan Doyle had Sherlock Holmes refer to Moriarty's "hereditary tendencies of the most diabolical kind."[49] Holmes later informed Watson, "I have a theory that the individual represents in his development the whole procession of his ancestors, and that such a sudden turn to the good or evil stands for some strange influence which came into the line of his pedigree."[50]

Given this cultural context, the representations made of Cream in the popular press were strongly influenced by an understanding of how such a killer should appear. When first on trial in Chicago in 1880, he was described in flattering terms: "In appearance, the Doctor is a highly intelligent Scotchman of medium build, with brown hair and blue eyes. He wears his beard in the Burnside fashion, closely trimmed."[51] "He is about 5 1/2 feet tall," reported an 1881 journalist, "very thick set, very good and intelligent-looking, and thirty-five years of age."[52] His ten years in prison necessarily had some effect on his appearance, but in 1891 and 1892 the only thing that the prostitutes noted out of the ordinary, aside from his expensive clothes, was Cream's crossed eyes. But once convicted, Cream was described in the press in terms that matched those of the criminal type—the restless creature craving stimulation, a vane, emotionally deficient but physically powerful man whose dark visage was dominated by a protruding jaw—and thus fit the typology elaborated by Lombroso and Ellis.[53] It was now recalled that there was some question of "hereditary insanity" in Cream's family. His unbridled use of opiates and the temptations of vice offered by the metropolis were trotted out as contributing causes of his degenerate state. Thus, when the *Illustrated Police News* hailed Cream's conviction with the headline "The End of a Monster of Iniquity," it meant just that; Cream was a "monster" produced by tainted stock and a corrupted environment.[54]

Of course, the insights of the criminologists had served no predictive purpose in tracking down Cream. They were only useful in explaining after the fact that what appeared to be a preeminently "fit" type—a white male doctor—could on closer examination be determined to be a degenerate. What is easy to forget is that the hereditarians regarded the prostitutes and vagrants on whom Cream preyed as equally dangerous. "The mental and physical peculiarities which are said to be characteristic of the criminal," Morrison reminded his readers, "are in reality common to him and the prostitute, the epileptic, the alcoholic, the habitual pauper."[55] Robert Reid Rentoul called for the sterilization of all degenerates including, according to his calculations, England's sixty thousand prostitutes and fifty thousand vagrants.[56]

On a general level this fear of a reversal of evolution appears to have been but one symptom of the anxieties felt by an elite faced with disturbingly new gender and class challenges.[57] Criminologists, by locating the source of criminal behavior within individuals, turned attention away from the social causes of crime and so justified the existing status quo.[58] Turning to specifics, it is obvious that theories of degeneration did nothing to *prevent* the crimes of a murderer like Cream. Indeed, a more convincing argument can be made that the criminologists' and eugenicists' attacks on the "unfit" could have actually been construed by such a man as an incitement to launch his attacks on the weak.[59]

12

WOMEN

"Criminals, idiots, women, minors, is the classification sound?"

Frances Power Cobbe, *Fraser's Magazine* (1869)

Even the enemies of capital punishment, declared the *South London Chronicle,* were only too eager to see Thomas Neill Cream in quick-lime. He was a "human tiger" whose cruelties were, according to this Conservative paper, even worse than those of the Irish. It found especially tragic that Cream, an educated man, "could prey upon these unfortunate women, whose degradation and defenceless condition appealed in vain for protection." [1]

One way of reading the Cream affair—the "official" reading—is that a madman who committed murders was tracked down by police-men, prosecuted by lawmen, found guilty by jurymen, and finally put to death by a hangman. All this is true, but given the fact that women figured so centrally in the story why, one might ask, is so little said about them? For the purposes of confirming Cream's guilt, it was, of course, in the prosecution's interest to portray the women as defense-less victims. It similarly better served the purposes of the police to suggest that Cream was tracked down due to their investigative abili-ties than to admit that if it had not been for his pestering letters and the prostitutes' rallying to protect themselves no prosecution could have been launched. Mr. Justice Hawkins at one point criticized Scotland Yard's mishandling of the Matilda Clover case; he later retracted his comments without stating why. Tunbridge, Harvey, McIntyre, Comley, Eversfield, and Ward were all ultimately praised by the court for their splendid conduct. The editor of the trial transcript declared that "this whole case is a striking example of the ceaseless care and vigilance which characterises Scotland Yard, but for which it is too seldom given credit."[2] But the prostitutes who came forward to testify received no praise. An injustice was done. A reappraisal of the evidence in the court dossiers reveals that the police were not masterful sleuths; the prostitutes were not helpless victims.

The police's most glaring oversight was their failure to investigate Matilda Clover's death. Her murder was not even recorded, let alone investigated, for half a year. And yet Cream had announced the murder to Broadbent and the Countess Russell. Even Mr. Justice Hawkins was shocked that Scotland Yard had had the influential Dr. Broadbent's house watched for several days in case his fictitious blackmailer should appear but had sent no one to look into Clover's passing. Why was it? he asked Inspector Tunbridge.

> Here is a real person who actually lived at 27 Lambeth Road, and it is said that this person was poisoned by strychnine. This information comes to Scotland Yard, within a quarter of an hour's walk of the place. How comes it that no one took the trouble to make an enquiry at Lambeth Road?—Well, it was not done, my lord.
> My surprise remains.[3]

The simple truth, of course, was that potential blackmail in the posh West End of London was of much greater concern to the police than a possible death in the slums south of the river. Even Cream was, in his manic fashion, annoyed that Matilda Clover's murder had gone undetected. Mr. Blumenfeld, London manager of the *New York Herald,* informed the police in September 1892 that in the previous autumn he had received a note saying that the police were covering up a Lambeth poisoning. Blumenfeld simply treated it as a hoax.[4]

The police likewise at first insisted on regarding Ellen Donworth's murder as a suicide. Her inquest jury was satisfied that her death was due to morphia and strychnine poisoning although it was unsure just how they were administered. The Lambeth Division officer in charge had no reservations. He reported to Scotland Yard on 23 October 1891: "There is little doubt that she took the poison herself knowing as she expected to die, and wished to expire at home." The argument was that Ellen Donworth—being only nineteen, her child having died a short time before, and her man unemployed—had little to live for. Despite Donworth's dying protests that a tall, dark, cross-eyed man with a black beard had given her white stuff to drink, Superintendent Braman of L Division reported that his men did not think there was the "slightest evidence of foul play."[5]

Finally, in the Alice Marsh and Emma Shrivell case, though the women protested that they had been given pills, the police were fixated on the idea that their deaths were caused by contaminated salmon.[6] "In all probability," concluded Superintendent Braman of L Division, this is "another case of poisoning by eating tinned salmon." The inquest led by Wyatt had determined by 13 April that the women had not died of ptomaine poisoning. Nevertheless, the police launched an unnecessary nationwide hunt for cases of Acme Flag Brand Salmon.[7] Dr. Stevenson reiterated on 28 April that strychnine had killed the women, but throughout the month of May Lambeth Division continued a pointless correspondence with the Liverpool police concerning the importation of canned fish.[8] The police's refusal to believe initially what prostitutes told them, statements that should have been given the respect of deathbed testimonies, provided the murderer with precious time. If it had not been for the flurry of accusatory letters that Cream himself sent and the enormous assistance offered by the prostitutes and the working women of Lambeth, he might never have been apprehended.

When Robert Anderson, head of C.I.D., wrote the Home Office of the frustration he felt finally knowing Cream was the murderer but not being able to prove it, he attributed the bulk of his problem to the prostitutes. "Due to the character and habits of the victims the same troubles are met with as in the Whitechapel murders."[9] These sorts of women, it was understood, could not be counted on to assist the police in their investigations. Anderson should not have been surprised. The Metropolitan Police had devoted decades to making the lives of such women as difficult as possible. In the 1860s prostitutes who were forced to bribe constables to avoid harassment were said to be "paying their footing."[10] In the 1870s the police nevertheless had closed down numerous casinos and dancing rooms, driving prostitutes into the more dangerous trade on the streets. In the 1880s the police pursued them into the public thoroughfares, employing vagrancy laws to arrest those simply suspected of soliciting. By 1890 the campaign had come to a disastrous end. Journalists played up reports that at least one respectable woman had been mistakenly jailed, and serious allegations were made in the press that constables were using the threat of arrest to extort money from streetwalkers.[11]

As far as the Cream affair was concerned, the problem was not that the police had difficulty getting prostitutes to assist them in their investigation; it was that these women had difficulty getting the police to assist them in theirs. One would not want to romanticize the efforts made by the women of the Lambeth slums by suggesting that they were self-consciously "policing" their neighborhood. But from the way the court record was assembled it is easy to miss seeing that a number of women shrewdly foiled Cream's murderous plans and that they and others played a vital role in his being tracked down and convicted.

The prostitutes appear to have kept track of each other. Networks of mutual aid were in evidence in the slums; streetwalkers were not as isolated or anonymous as they appeared to outsiders. Annie Clements, Constance Linfield, Eliza Heywood, and Eliza Northfield had all watched Ellen Donworth's comings and goings and had reported them to the police. Eliza Masters and Elizabeth May, the prostitutes who had followed Cream and Matilda Clover, kept tabs on each other's doings and their respective clients. In her deposition Masters mentioned that she was struck by the fact that she had heard of Clover's death only two or three weeks after seeing her with Cream.

Alice Marsh and Emma Shrivell, who died 12 April 1891, were also part of a female community. On 17 April two prostitutes visited the Lambeth Mortuary.[12] They had read of the murders of Marsh and Shrivell in the *People,* they told the keeper, and knew the deceased well. On the night of 11 April they had gone with them to a pub near Lower Marsh Street, where they had met "Fred" and together had drunk until closing time.[13] The police heard of this conversation at the mortuary on 28 April and hurriedly set out to find these potentially valuable witnesses.

Minnie Duncan (sometimes known as Jessie) was spending the month of May in Holloway Prison, which no doubt had some connection with her life on the streets. She had encountered Ward and Mulvaney on a previous occasion, and knowing of the police's interest in locating the prostitutes who had been at the mortuary, she said she could help. Braman noted that she owed a surety for good behavior of three pounds but had her released on the chance that she could be of assistance.[14]

Lizzie Sullivan, with whom Alice Marsh and Emma Shrivell had lived at 13 Blythe Terrace for a week in March before settling in at Stamford Street, spoke to Mulvaney and Ward on 26 May. Two years previous she had met the women on their first trip to London. When they returned in March 1892, they were penniless; Emma Shrivell had pawned her clothing for the fare to London. But on 9 April, three days before the boat race, Sullivan found that Emma was sporting a new pair of boots and appeared to be getting on well. It was agreed that they would have tea together on Easter Sunday. A few days later Sullivan read in the *People* of Emma's murder. On Sunday she and another prostitute, Emma James, set out on the sad and frustrating journey (about which the police heard) to pay their last respects to their friends. At St. Thomas's they were told the hospital no longer had Marsh's and Shrivell's bodies; at the mortuary the drunk keeper could provide no help. Finally an undertaker was found who told them that the bodies had already been sent on to Brighton, where they were buried 20 April. All Lizzie Sullivan was able to tell Ward and Mulvaney was that she recalled seeing Alice Marsh with a tall, dark, red-faced man.[15]

On 23 May, Ida St. Houstine, another prostitute, provided police with a description of the "Fred" who was the friend of Alice Marsh and Emma Shrivell. She remembered him as a man about five feet ten inches tall, twenty-six years of age, with gray-blue eyes, eye glasses, and a long moustache. "Whilst talking to him I noticed that his eyebrows met over his nose, and I said to him always beware of a man whose eyebrows meet. He laughed but said nothing." He was clearly not at all like the man seen with Matilda Clover and Ellen Donworth.[16] Ida St. Houstine believed that he was not from London, but from either Chatham or Gravesend. "But no importance can be attached to that," wrote Mulvaney in the margin of the report, "as these women are so unreliable." On the evening of 24 May, Ida St. Houstine and Lucy Rose were taken by McIntyre to Cream's lodgings to see if they could recognize him, but he failed to appear.[17]

On the evening of 13 May, when Comley and Ward first spotted Cream, they followed him to a prostitute's lodgings on Elliot Row. That prostitute later told them that Cream had said he lived "solely to indulge in women" and wanted to meet her again on Thursday, 19 May. The police did not tell her Cream was suspected of murder; they encouraged her to see him and find out all that she could.[18]

On 17 May Cream was taken by another prostitute, Violet Beverley, to her room in 3 North Street, Kennington. After having sex with her, he told her he was a representative of a New York firm of druggists and showed her his sample of pills. Probably this aroused her suspicions because she refused to sample the "American drink" which he prepared for her. On 18 May Cream visited Beverley again, "having connection twice with her," in the words of the police who had followed Cream and later interrogated Beverley.[19]

Violet Beverley was suspicious of Cream but at the same time un-willing to spy on him as the police asked. She responded to two needs: physical safety and economic need. The latter concern apparently be-ing of more importance to her, she immediately warned Cream that he was being followed. Cream in turn complained to Sergeant Mc-Intyre. The police were outraged by Beverley's actions. On the mar-gins of McIntyre's report Braman wrote, "I know from experience how unreliable these women are and I am sure this will be our great difficulty in getting evidence."[20] But the police expressed no qualms concerning their own policy of using these prostitutes as bait to trap a murderer.

In October 1891 Lucy Rose, the servant, provided a description of the man she had seen with Matilda Clover. More important, she was so impressed by Clover's death—which the doctors simply put down to drink—that six months later she alerted the police to its circum-stances. In June 1892 Eliza Masters and Elizabeth May identified Cream as the man they had seen with Clover.[21] But the most dramatic evidence at the Clover inquest and at Cream's trial was given by Louisa Harris, the only living person who could give a complete ac-count of the accused's modus operandi. Her partner Charles Harvey recalled that Harris had been suspicious of Cream from the begin-ning. "She told me she did not like the look of the man and was afraid of it and to see if it was all right."[22] Having survived her encounter with a murderer, Louisa Harris could have laid low; the police cer-tainly had no idea where she was. Why did she write the authorities and willingly testify in court? She wanted justice. This man had tried to kill her; in fact he thought that he had. He had given her poison and gone on happily with his life, "being under the impression that I took the capsules, and either dropped dead in the street, or music hall."[23] She was going to do all that she could to see that he did not get a second chance.

Not all prostitutes were cooperative. One, who the police thought might identify their suspect, was positively obstreperous.

> The woman Eliza Carter under sentence of six months h.l. [hard labor] was also in attendance having been brought up in custody from H. M. Prison Wormwood Scrubs, but she failed to recognize Neill as the man she saw in the com-pany of the deceased woman Donworth. Carter expressed an intention of not recognizing anyone, and when she is at liberty she is such a dissipated wretch that her evidence would be of little or no value whichever way she might go.[24]

Such expressions of contempt for female prisoners were not unusual. The medical officer at Millbank Penitentiary recalled that its warden viewed his female charges with fear and loathing. "If they were at all refractory, his sole idea was to hand them over to the medical officer as patients requiring medical care and treatment, and so to get them out of his jurisdiction for the time being. He seemed to have an idea that all the women were mad."[25]

Considering the disdain with which the authorities treated prostitutes, their lack of enthusiasm for assisting the police was understandable. These women were consistently described in the court and police dossiers as "girls." It was in part a question of gender; women were in fact legal minors—as were idiots and children—and would remain so all their lives. It was also a question of class. Prostitutes were not "ladies." In the police files they were referred to simply by name, for example, Matilda Clover, whereas Emily Sleaper was always identified as Miss Sleaper and Laura Sabbatini as Miss Sabbatini. The prostitutes, like everyone else, understood the importance of such designations; Louisa Harris described Laura Sabbatini as a tall, dark "young lady."[26]

Somewhere in between the "ladies" and the prostitutes one might locate Miss Emily Turner. Inspector Jarvis tracked her down in Montreal after being told by the chief engineer of the *Labrador* that a passenger had said she had been given pills by Cream. The story Turner told Jarvis was that she had lived in London between October 1891 and January 1892 working as a salesgirl at the Royal Aquarium in Tothill Street, Westminster. The Royal Aquarium contained within its canary yellow walls—in addition to a theater, a skating rink, a promenade, and a winter garden—thirteen fish tanks containing seven hundred thousand gallons of water.

> The Royal Aquarium, in short, was intended to be a sort of Crystal Palace in London within easy reach of Charing Cross, a covered-in promenade for the wet weather, with glass cases of fish thrown in. In truth, the attractions of the place began to be very "fishy" indeed. Ladies promenaded there up and down o'nights without the escort of any gentleman friend (till, maybe, they found one) and the appeal of the management to sensation-lovers was very wide indeed. Bare backed ladies dived from the roof or were shot out of a cannon, or sat in a cage covered with hair calling themselves "Missing Links."[27]

It was here that Miss Turner met a "Major Hamilton," who suffered from an eye complaint. He said he lived at the Metropole Hotel on

Northumberland Avenue. The major wooed Turner with suppers at Gatti's, outings to the Alhambra Music Hall, and the offer of two pounds a week and rooms on Lambeth Palace Road. But the idyll ended when, after sending Turner some gelatin capsules for her cough, the major disappeared. The pills made her sick, and she stopped taking them.

Turner mentioned the incident in January 1892 while steaming back to Canada on the *Labrador*. A doctor on board expressed interest in the story, and Turner gave him some of the capsules she had left. Scotland Yard eventually obtained the pills and had Stevenson analyze them. They contained only quinine.[28] Turner, when shown a picture of Cream, resolutely denied that he was "Major Hamilton" or anyone else she had ever seen. Jarvis knew she was lying but did not seem to understand why.[29] The point was that Turner inhabited a twilight world on the margins of female respectability. Though willing to take the chance of bargaining her sexual favors for financial support, she was not a common prostitute. Her desire not to appear as a witness at Cream's trial, where the world would be told of the sorts of calculations her life required, made perfectly good sense.

At the beginning of the nineteenth century when Mary Ashford was raped and murdered, the local minister had the following inscribed on her tomb:

> As a warning to female virtue, and a humble monument of female chastity, this stone marks the grave of Mary Ashford, who, in the 20th year of her age, having incautiously repaired to a scene of public amusement without proper protection was brutally violated and murdered on the 27th May, 1817.[30]

In a like manner Cream was not the only one held responsible for his murders. So too were his victims. In the press reports they were described as "wretched," "dissolute," and a "menace to society." Laura Sabbatini, who became engaged to him after a courtship lasting only four weeks, was declared by the press to be almost equally mad. The fate of such women was held up as a warning to others. The official account of the Cream case was that a madman had taken advantage of bad women. The moral drawn was that if women were virtuous and relied only on good men, such tragedies could be avoided. But the prostitutes clearly understood that they had to turn to each other for support. The press proved incapable of understanding such solidarity and reported with some puzzlement that the Cream case had attracted "many young women belonging to the same class as Neill's alleged victims. The trial appears to have a peculiar fascination for them."[31]

The stereotype of the inherently passive female did not go unchallenged. The same papers that carried accounts of the Alice Marsh and Emma Shrivell inquest and later Cream's trial also advertised public lectures on women's suffrage.[32] The English women's movement, in the process of emerging in the 1890s, advanced the argument that women had to be able to help themselves. Few went so far as to suggest that women were the equals of men. Late Victorian women saw themselves as different by nature; indeed, they exploited the idea of an innately more caring, sensitive female character to challenge male predominance.[33] Unconvinced, Gladstone came out against an extension of the franchise at the end of April 1892. But such was the public interest in the issue that a May meeting, organized by George Bernard Shaw at Great St. James Hall in favor of the vote, ended in a riot when Lady Florence Dixie, the star speaker, failed to appear.[34]

The movement was decidedly middle class. Millicent Garrett Fawcett traced her involvement back to the day in 1870 when her purse was stolen. She remembered feeling much like a thief herself upon hearing the culprit charged with the theft, not of her property but of her husband's. By law spinsters and unmarried women owned property; married women did not. To provide practical protection for needy women and self-respect for the middle class, Fawcett threw herself into the campaign for women's property rights, which finally came to fruition in the 1880s.[35]

Reforms in the areas of property and sexual morality were naturally enough of concern chiefly to the middle class. Working-class women's values were different. They were willing for practical purposes to put up with levels of drunkenness and violence that their social superiors found intolerable. There was no point in being "rescued" from a brutal husband if it meant a disruption of the family economy.[36]

In the first half of the century even middle-class women had little in the way of legal recourse in conflicts with their spouses. Men had the legal right to beat their wives "though not in a violent or cruel manner."[37] Wife murder was thought common enough in the 1870s for one Liverpool neighborhood to be described as its "kicking district."[38] A restricted, expensive, male-biased form of divorce was available after 1857, but aside from actual flight, poor women had no way to escape from disastrous marriages until an act of 1878, ex-

panded in 1895, allowed easy separation and maintenance. By the
end of the century nine thousand separations a year were being
granted.[39]

Although the Matrimonial Causes Act of 1884 extended to women
the right to end their marriage, the newspapers of the 1890s were full
of scandalous stories relating the difficulties that even the wealthy encountered in trying to escape unhappy unions. The 1891 divorce proceedings of Lord and Lady Russell, which attracted the attention of
Cream, dragged on for over a decade, culminating in the earl's trial
for bigamy before the House of Lords in 1901.[40] Eighteen ninety-one
also saw the resolution of the famous Clitheroe case in which a
Mr. Jackson abducted his wife, with whom he had not lived for three
years, and held her by force in Blackburn.[41] Mrs. Jackson's attempt to
win her freedom was initially turned back, but the Court of Appeal
made the historic judgment, though one met with a good deal of opposition, that a husband could not in future imprison his wife.[42] The
importance of the finding was reflected in the *Law Times*' hailing it as
the "charter of the married woman."[43] It was still the case, however,
that a man who raped his wife was not committing a crime. Mr. Justice
Hawkins commented that a jury was as likely to convict a husband for
rape as to find guilty of larceny a servant "who stealthily appropriated
to her own use a pin from her mistress's pin cushion."[44]

Ironically, the most dramatic change in late-nineteenth-century
women's lives—the sharp decline in the number of babies they bore—
found very few public defenders. The issue of controlling marital fertility remained a tabooed subject. It says something of the courage
and tenacity of so many ordinary women that they successfully sought
to control family size despite the opposition of the churches, the
medical profession, the law, and even, on occasion, their husbands.
Women's growing sense of individualism was both a cause and an
effect of the increased use of contraception. For the middle-class
woman at least, it was increasingly unlikely that she would, like her
mother, spend her entire married life bearing and rearing children.[45]

The reappraisal of gender roles was played out on the stage as well
as in court. Ibsen's *The Doll's House* opened in London in June 1889
and was followed by the marriage plays of Wilde and Shaw. The
new freedoms demanded by women were noted by novelists such as
H. G. Wells and George Gissing, the classic account being Grant Allen's *The Woman Who Did* (1895).[46] Although little-remembered novelists like Mona Caird and Ménie Muriel Dowie presented a generally
nonpolitical call for the social support of women, their exploration of

such themes as sexual disgust, the double standard, and trial marriage was remarkably daring for the time.[47]

The "new women" were not merely the products of novelists' imaginations. Women were demanding changes in the existing legal and social conventions pertaining to marriage and questioning the rigid separation of male and female spheres. By the 1890s many middle-class women were living independent lives, supporting themselves just as "redundant" females had to do.[48] The problem of how women who could not or would not marry might survive was attracting much public attention, and it was becoming widely recognized that sizable numbers would have no choice but to live by their own wits. No one suggested that these women should be envied or that their independence and lack of male supervision were grounds for terrorizing them. But a realistic acceptance of the changing nature of society was not infrequently expressed by persons who, in the next breath, could speak of women's "natural place." The pervasiveness of misogynistic themes in much of the art and literature of the last decades of the nineteenth century testified to the extent to which the new woman was regarded in some quarters as decidedly "unnatural."[49] The "revolt of women" thrilled and exhilarated some; it frightened and angered others.

Ironically, though the Cream case revealed the dangers a man could pose to women, no one took the occasion to challenge the assumption that women had to look to men for protection. Indeed, the specific "meaning" the courts and police gave to Cream's murders if anything strengthened such convictions.[50] The efforts made by prostitutes to defend themselves were not so much denigrated as not even noticed. Even middle-class feminists discounted the abilities of such women to survive without the safekeeping of their social superiors. The reality was that women on the streets, though they had to work within narrow margins of maneuver, utilized whatever means were available to protect themselves. They did not have to wait for the feminists to tell them to do so, though some might have incorporated into the sense of their rights the stress on independence popularized by the women's movement. The chief significance of the movement was that it had embarked on the long struggle not only to win legal equality, but to make visible and so gain some respect for the heroic efforts made daily by ordinary women to lead independent lives.

In November 1892 the commissioner of the Metropolitan Police rewarded those who he had determined had played the key roles in tracking down Cream. Police Constables McCarthy and Eversfield received, for their workmanlike assistance, 12s 6d; Police Constable Comley, who first spotted Cream, got £1 5s; Police Sergeant McIntyre was given the same amount for his surveillance of the suspect; Inspector Jarvis, who traced his activities in North America, got £2; Chief Inspector Mulvaney, who seemed to have played a minor part in surveillance, nevertheless was rewarded with £2 2s; Police Sergeant Ward, who tracked Cream relentlessly, received £3 3s; Inspector Harvey, who directed the Lambeth Division's investigation, walked away with £4; and Inspector Tunbridge, who was given full control of the case by the C.I.D., pocketed £5.[51] The prostitutes—who followed Cream, who identified him, who testified against him in court even when it meant broadcasting to the world their shameful occupation, who the police in the process of their investigations allowed to be preyed on by Cream—received nothing.[52]

It is hard to imagine a more eloquent expression of the official view of criminal justice than the commissioner's scale of rewards. The public was informed that the selfless service of police officers, in particular those of the higher grades attached to Scotland Yard, brought a villain like Cream to bay. The women's role was "hidden from history."

CONCLUSION

Middle-class society likes to represent the gulf between itself and the law breakers as unbridgeable, and is frightened to find that even mass-murderers are made of the same stuff and behave in all walks of life like the rest of us—your very neighbor might be a murderer.

Theodore Reik, *The Unknown Murderer* (1936)

In condemning Cream to death, the court did more than assert that the taking of life was not sanctioned. It presented his murders as the acts of an isolated, disturbed villain, and enormous efforts were made to personalize and individualize his guilt. On the one hand those who believed that Cream's murderous acts were part of God's mysterious plan, by which even the murderer in finding salvation might benefit, deluged Newgate Prison with religious tracts and pamphlets; on the other hand a drunken mob outside its gates, motivated chiefly by a thirst for revenge but partly by a confused expectation that a judicial killing could prevent other murders, bayed for his death.

The argument embraced by the enlightened when loathsome creatures like Cream were caught, tried, and executed was that such individuals were deranged, impelled by some inner force to commit evil. Jack the Ripper, speculated Dr. L. Forbes Winslow, "possibly imagined that he had received his commands from God."[1] To declare such individuals mad, insane, psychopathic, driven to commit their crimes by unknown, unknowable forces was certainly the easiest approach; it required no extensive analysis, merely a moral judgment. A contributor to the *Lancet* accordingly lumped together the era's most sensational crimes as evidence of some mysterious contagion of irrationality.

> The future historian of the latter part of this nineteenth century cannot fail to note the present epidemic of homicide; in the foreground of his picture he will place the dynamiting anarchist, and in the deepest shades of horror the crimes of Deeming, of the Whitechapel "ripper" and of this last, the poisoner of prostitutes; and he will comment on them probably as phases of a curious morbid and dangerous mental phenomenon.[2]

The man who penned those lines would necessarily be disappointed by the approach taken in this book. Little has been said about the state of Cream's mind; rather, the central contention has been that Cream is best understood if seen as a sick product of his society.

The contrary line of argument that holds that crimes of violence against women are "rips in the fabric of social order," of course, continues to have its defenders.[3] But the basic premise of this study is that a more compelling case can been made that violence is an intrinsic, not extrinsic, aspect of society. Even murder provides a distorted reflection of acceptable behavior. Cream was only one of eighteen murderers executed in England and Wales in 1892. They were all men. Two poachers killed two gamekeepers, a butcher killed a constable, and a lunatic attendant killed an acquaintance. Cream, of course, killed four prostitutes, and all the other murderers' victims were women—four wives, a mother, a "paramour," a "former cohabiter," a mistress, a landlady, a prostitute, two girls aged five and nine who were raped and killed, and a last victim identified in the parliamentary reports simply as a woman.[4] The fact that men were many times more likely to murder women than vice versa was—and remains—one extreme aspect of the general phenomenon of sexual domination.

But Cream was not a common murderer. His outrageous crimes were the result of an individual psychopathology wedded to a generalized misogyny or mistrust of women at a time when women were making a well-publicized bid for greater autonomy. The interest of his case accordingly lies not so much in what it can tell us about him as in what it reveals about nineteenth-century culture. After having provided a narrative account of his career, we began our analysis by examining the particular nature of his crimes—blackmail, fraud, and murder. His nefarious acts were shown to be fully intelligible only when seen in the framework of the particular sexual and cultural context of late Victorian society, a society made anxious by the rise in threats to reputation, the increased number of women in public life, the apparent blight of degeneration, and the erosion of gender boundaries symbolized by women's attempts to control their fertility.

A century ago a contributor to the socialist periodical the *Clarion* pointed out the self-serving way in which the respectable, in bewailing Cream's crimes and calling for his execution, sought to sweep such social issues aside and focus all attention on the psychology of the murderer.

> We are entitled in self-protection, I suppose, to hang him. Hang him at any rate we shall. But if we would prevent the future propagation of such distorted fiends, let us cease to plague our minds with futile efforts to divine the workings of such misshapen minds, and reserve our attention for careful and more profitable research into the social causes which favour their loathsome production.[5]

This is what the present study, in pointing out the significance of sexual tensions in the late nineteenth century, has attempted to provide. Cream's murders did not take place in a vacuum. They were structured by the problematical relations between the sexes and by what seemed to be a growing intensity of gender conflict, which misogynists played up.[6] This new intersexual violence emerged in a society marked by a jarring juxtaposition of bourgeois respectability on one hand and deviant sexuality, pornography, and criminality on the other.[7]

Cream's crimes and those of the Whitechapel murderer moreover revealed that this intersexual violence was emerging in a new environment, the nineteenth-century city, inhabited by a new type of potential victim, the young, relatively independent woman.[8] That the more vulnerable of them should have been cut down at a time of "moral panic" was more than a mere coincidence. When women seeking abortion were called killers, when prostitutes were portrayed as spreading disease, when women employing contraceptives to limit family size were charged with contributing to "race suicide," it is not altogether surprising that a murderous backlash should have been precipitated.

Having examined Cream and his crimes, what can be made of the response of the authorities to the challenges posed by nineteenth-century criminality? Upon investigation the new forms of policing and scientific theories of deviancy patently revealed themselves to be designed not simply to protect the innocent and punish the guilty. Degeneration theories and innovative policing techniques had as their chief function the defense of the social status quo. Authority was becoming less constrained, less content to wait and see who needed correction; it claimed to know in advance. Therefore, policing was made increasingly preventive, intrusive, and interventionist. Such changes increased the protection of some; others were put at risk.

Why did the serial murderer emerge just at a time when unprecedented attempts were being made to "moralize" the masses? Possibly because in a world in which secrets and surveillance had become increasingly important the lines between legitimate and illegitimate correction were blurred. The serial killer can be seen, in responding in his own particular fashion to the progressive's call to "discipline and punish" deviants and degenerates, as providing himself with a sense of "mission."[9]

America's first notorious serial killer was Herman Mudgett (also known as Harry Howard Holmes) of Chicago, who was executed in 1896. Although up to twenty-seven deaths were attributed to him, he only confessed to having killed two women who came seeking abortions.[10] The nineteenth-century European serial murderers we know most about, in addition to Cream and the Ripper, are Gruyo, of Vittoria, Spain, who in ten years strangled six prostitutes, and the two Frenchmen Joseph Philippe, who in the 1860s killed seven prostitutes, and Vacher the "ripper," who was tried in 1897 for the murder of two boys, five girls, and two women.[11] One should not be surprised that prostitutes emerged as the classic victims of the multiple murderer.[12] They were portrayed in medical literature as threats to the race. Police harassment forced them into transient lives cut off from community support and thus made them accessible to the murderer. A French prosecutor perceptively noted that Joseph Philippe had cold-bloodedly exploited the social exclusion these women suffered: "The isolation into which their abject profession drives them delivers them all the more easily into the hands of murderers."[13] Because the disappearance of a prostitute like Matilda Clover drew little public attention, Thomas Neill Cream was in effect *allowed* to become a serial killer.[14]

What are we to make of Cream's victims, the women? They were obviously victimized but by whom? Not simply by one man. They had already been victimized and marginalized by society and made available to Cream. At the same time the limits of the "victimization" interpretation have to be recognized. Even poor prostitutes rallied to protect themselves and played a crucial role in Cream's eventual capture. A review of the gains made by the women's movement in the 1880s and 1890s revealed that late-nineteenth-century Victorian women were far from passive. Disturbing reports that women were even seeking greater sexual pleasure raised the cry that manhood was "in danger."[15] Attacks on women were likely elicited at this particular time because of a backlash against what some regarded as the "revolt of women."

In reading the press accounts of the Cream case, one is repeatedly reminded of *Dracula* (1897). How, Bram Stoker asked, are one's women to be protected from the maniac? What if they are infected by his poisons? In the novel's most frightening scenes Mina Harker almost succumbs. For the Victorian reader the story mercifully ends, as it had to, with the monster destroyed and Mina's "successful restoration as subservient, faithful wife and mother."[16] This was the sort of reading the courts and newspapers would have liked to have made of the Cream affair, but facts proved more intractable than fictions. Cream died, but even the prostitutes who escaped him appeared to be beyond redemption. The thought that the extremes of male and female sexual evil were mutually destructive—the thought that like killed like—provided some solace.[17]

If this study has shed some light on the tensions created in the last decades of the 1800s by shifting gender boundaries, it will have accomplished its primary goal. Given the limits of our investigation, any attempt to use the Cream case to comment on the general phenomenon of modern serial killing is hazardous. The little that is known about the history of murder suggests, however, that serial killing was a creation of the later nineteenth century. Early modern England had higher levels of homicide than the nineteenth century; not infrequently whole families were killed off in what today would be called mass murders.[18] Closer to the modern serial killer were Burke and Hare, who in the 1820s suffocated victims to provide bodies for Edinburgh anatomists.[19] But "irrational," apparently motiveless, serial killing would appear to have first burst on the English-speaking world with Jack the Ripper. An enormous number of works have been devoted to the Ripper myth; unfortunately, most do no more than retell it.[20] The great advantage of looking at Cream is that one is dealing with a real individual whose motivations do not have to be based on mere speculation. We have his own disturbing words; more important, we have those of the society that created him.

AFTERWORD

Cream's most notorious murders were committed in Lambeth in 1891 and 1892. In the spring of 1990, with the vague idea of seeing London through Cream's eyes, I retraced the path he must have taken many times from the bustling Strand south across Waterloo Bridge to the dreary streets of Lambeth. As soon as I set out, I began to wonder if the expedition was not in fact rather foolish. South London is no longer the rough, working-class home of the costermongers, warehousemen, and prostitutes that it was in the 1890s. The Hayward Gallery and the National Theatre now flank the southern approaches to the new Waterloo Bridge, which was constructed in 1934. The demands of the automobile similarly led in the early twentieth century to the replacement of narrow, old Lambeth Bridge. Waterloo Station was rebuilt in 1922. A housing estate occupies the land once dominated by the Canterbury Arms Music Hall. The Church of St. Mary's at Lambeth in whose cemetery lies William Bligh, who died 7 December 1817 "beloved, respected and lamented," still stands but has been turned into a Museum of Garden History.

And yet some things have not changed. Lambeth still serves as a doormat for respectable London. The flat, featureless riverside lands which once invited the railway cuttings of the southern line are now crisscrossed by flyovers and motorways. Waterloo Station continues to disgorge its thousands of daily commuters, who make their way as rapidly as possible north over the bridge and into the city. Across from the station stands the ornate redbrick edifice of what was the Royal Waterloo Hospital for Children and Women (rebuilt in 1903) and is now some sort of college. Heading north leads one up Stamford Street. Here Alice Marsh and Emma Shrivell met their deaths. Many of the street's two-story terraced houses were torn down just before World War I; those remaining are now very much in the process of being gentrified. Retracing one's steps and moving south past Waterloo Station and down York Road, one is hemmed in by the ponderous bulk of faceless twentieth-century office blocks and the back of what was until recently London County Hall. A glimpse of the nineteenth century is finally offered by St. Thomas's Hospital stretching west from Westminster Bridge along the south bank of the Thames directly across the river from the House of Commons. Florence Nightingale is no longer at St. Thomas's, but her museum and school of nursing are, as well as the Nightingale Pub across the street.

Cream studied at St. Thomas's and lived most of the time he was in London directly opposite the hospital on Lambeth Palace Road. Lambeth Palace itself, the London residence of the archbishop of Canterbury, still stands where Lambeth Bridge leads back into Westminster, marking the eastern border of Cream's Lambeth. One can turn west, however, up Lambeth Road toward the Imperial War Museum housed in an imposing porticoed edifice which in Cream's time served as an insane asylum. At number 27 Lambeth Road lived another of Cream's victims, Matilda Clover, who may well have frequented the St. George's Public House, built in 1879 near St. George's Circus. The day of my visit the barman, with the aid of an 1872 ordinance map of the parish, sought in vain to locate Clover's lodgings. In the 1870s much of the south side of lower Lambeth Road was taken up by an Asylum for the Blind; in the twentieth century its occupants were displaced to make way for a new approach to Waterloo Station.

With its theaters, galleries, and museums Lambeth in 1990 was not the sort of place Cream knew in 1891. And yet the types of poverty which provided a context for his crimes had not disappeared. Beneath Waterloo Bridge a "cardboard city" existed vaguely reminiscent of something seen in television reports on South American barrios. On mattresses and in sleeping bags and refrigerator boxes, surrounded by torn plastic litter, bits of cardboard, and broken bottles, people seemed to have set up camp. One or two bag ladies tied and retied their possessions onto railway station baggage carts. Skinny dogs wandered about aimlessly. The commuters making their way briskly into the city were no doubt as oblivious to today's poor as their counterparts were to Cream's potential victims a century ago.

Gender roles had changed remarkably in a century. In 1891 women did not have the vote; in 1990 a woman was prime minister of the United Kingdom. Yet, in the liberated late twentieth century the idea that women "guilty" of aggressive behavior, of sexual indiscretions, deserve violent punishment—the idea that drove Cream—has yet to be expunged.[1] While this book was being written, Marc Lepine shot down in cold blood fourteen female Université de Montréal engineering students whom he regarded as feminists. In 1980, at the time of the discovery of the ninth victim of the "Yorkshire Ripper," the Kirklees coroner, in warning of the possibility of further murders, made the chilling comment: "There is no telling who it will be. Most of the victims in the past have been prostitutes, but it could be a completely innocent person."[2]

NOTES

INTRODUCTION

1. Thomas Stevenson, *The Principles and Practices of Medical Jurisprudence* (London: Churchill, 1883), 1:430.

2. Judith R. Walkowitz, *Prostitution and Victorian Society: Women, Class, and the State* (New York: Cambridge University Press, 1980).

3. Richard D. Altick, *Victorian Studies in Scarlet* (New York: Norton, 1970), p. 10.

4. A useful overview is provided by Clive Emsley, *Crime and Society in England, 1750–1900* (London: Longman, 1987).

5. Mary Hartman, *Victorian Murderesses* (New York: Schocken, 1977).

6. For the earlier period see Lincoln B. Faller, *Turned to Account: The Forms and Functions of Criminal Biography in Late Seventeenth and Eighteenth-Century England* (Cambridge: Cambridge University Press, 1987), pp. 21–41.

7. Elliott Leyton asserted in 1990 that "there are no recorded cases of female serial killers." In fact we know of some, such as Mary Cotton, mentioned in chap. 9. Since there have been so few, it is hazardous to generalize, but they seem to have been less geographically transient than their male counterparts and often fulfilled a nursing role. See Ann Jones, *Women Who Kill* (New York: Holt, Rinehart & Winston, 1980), pp. 129ff., 357; Pierre Bouchardon, *Hélène Jegado: L'empoisonneuse bretonne* (Paris: Albin Michel, 1937); Rupert Furnaux, *The Medical Murderer* (London: Elek Books, 1957), pp. 129ff.; Elliott Leyton, *Sole Survivor: Children Who Murder Their Families* (Toronto: Seal, 1990), p. 213.

8. The fact that serial murderers primarily kill women seems to have escaped the attention of Elliott Leyton, who, in his sensationalized account, resolutely ignores gender conflicts and unconvincingly insists on presenting

such murders as attacks made by a deprived individual on representatives of a superior class. Elliott Leyton, *Hunting Humans: The Rise of the Modern Multiple Murderer* (McClelland & Stewart, 1986).

9. D. J. West, *Sexual Crimes and Confrontations: A Study of Victims and Offenders* (Aldershot: Gower, 1987), 182; Robert K. Ressler, Ann W. Burgess, and John E. Douglas, *Sexual Homicide: Patterns and Motives* (Lexington, Mass.: Heath, 1988), pp. 16, 26, 34, 51–65.

10. Ronald M. Holmes and James De Burger, *Serial Murder* (Beverly Hills: Sage, 1988); Joel Norris and William J. Birnes, *Serial Killers: The Growing Menace* (New York: Dolphin, 1988); Colin Wilson and Donald Seaman, *The Serial Killers* (London: W. H. Allen, 1990); Donald J. Sears, *To Kill Again: The Motivation and Development of Serial Murder* (Wilmington: SR Books, 1991).

11. Philip Jenkins, *Contemporary Crises* 13 (1989): 195–96.

12. Natalie Zemon Davis, *The Return of Martin Guerre* (Cambridge, Mass.: Harvard University Press, 1983); *Fiction in the Archives: Pardon Tales and Their Tellers in Sixteenth-Century France* (Stanford: Stanford University Press, 1987), chap. 3.

CHAPTER 1

1. See such early accounts as James Greenwood, *The Wilds of London* (London: Chatto & Windus, 1874); Andrew Mearns, in Anthony S. Wohl, ed., *The Bitter Cry of Outcast London* (Leicester: Leicester University Press, 1978 [1883]).

2. In 1880 the idealistic young Oscar Wilde assisted the Lambeth poor who had been forced from their homes by the cresting of the Thames. Richard Ellman, *Oscar Wilde* (Harmondsworth: Penguin, 1987), p. 116.

3. H. P. White, *A Regional History of the Railways of Great Britain*, vol. 3: *Greater London* (Newton Abbot: David & Charles, 1963), p. 41. See also John R. Kellett, *The Impact of Railways on Victorian Cities* (London: Routledge & Kegan Paul, 1969), p. 259.

4. Sir Walter Besant, *London South of the Thames* (London: Adam & Charles Black, 1912), p. 92.

5. On the general impact of the displacement of the poor by nineteenth-century railroad construction, see H. J. Dyos, *Exploring the Urban Past: Essays in Urban History* (Cambridge: Cambridge University Press, 1982), pp. 101–28.

6. Francis Sheppard, *London, 1808–1870: The Infernal Wen* (London: Secker & Warburg, 1971), p. 134.

7. Charles Booth, *Life and Labour of the People in London*, 1st series: *Poverty* (London: Macmillan, 1902 [1889]), p. 278.

8. On slum clearances, see Anthony S. Wohl, *The Eternal Slum: Housing and Social Policy in Victorian London* (Montreal: McGill-Queens, 1977), pp. 133, 171, 180, 301, 324.

9. When most workers earned between 18s and 24s, the rent per week for three rooms would be about a third of their income; M. S. Pember Reeves, *Family Life on a Pound a Week*, Fabian Society Tract 162 (Fabian Society, 1912), pp. 2–3.

10. Charles Booth, *Life and Labour of the People in London*, 3d series: *Religious Influences*, 4: *Inner South London* (London: Macmillan, 1902), p. 49.

11. *South London Chronicle*, 18 November 1876.

12. Alexander Paterson, *Across the Bridges, or Life by the South London River-Side* (London: Edward Arnold, 1912), p. 7.

13. Booth, *Religious Influences*, pp. 9, 10. See also George R. Sims, *How the Poor Live* (London: Chatto & Windus, 1883).

14. Reeves, *Family Life*, p. 2.

15. Booth, *Religious Influences*, p. 54.

16. W. Somerset Maugham, *The Summing Up* (London: Heinemann, 1938), pp. vii–viii.

17. Gareth Stedman Jones, *Outcast London: A Study in the Relationships between Classes in Victorian Society* (Oxford: Clarendon, 1971), p. 299.

18. Jack London, *The People of the Abyss* (New York: Macmillan, 1903), pp. 124–25.

19. The Metropolitan Tabernacle of American evangelist Charles Spurgeon, the center of evangelical work in South London, was in 1892 in the course of splitting up into warring factions. *South London Chronicle*, 29 October 1892.

20. In April 1892 H. M. Hyndman was delivering the lecture "Why Socialism Is Inevitable" to the Peckham and Dulwich Radical Club. See *South London Mail*, 9 April 1892, p. 1.

21. Sheppard, *London*, pp. 162, 174; J. E. Martin, *Greater London: An Industrial Geography* (London: Bell, 1966), pp. 15–16.

22. Jones, *Outcast London*, p. 61.

23. Booth, *Poverty*, p. 275.

24. Until the half penny toll on Waterloo Bridge was removed in 1878 Lambeth laborers venturing north of the Thames had to go far out of their way via the Blackfriars or Westminster Bridges. David Owen, *The Government of Victorian London, 1855–1889* (Cambridge: Belknap Press, 1982), pp. 121–22.

25. Cecil Chapman, *The Poor Man's Court of Justice: Twenty-Five Years as a Metropolitan Magistrate* (London: Hodder & Stoughton, 1925), pp. 98, 31.

26. Henry Mayhew, *London Labour and the London Poor* (London: Griffin, 1861), 1:20.

27. Frederick Porter Wensley, *Detective Days* (London: Cassell, 1931), pp. 2–3.

28. George R. Sims, *My Life: Sixty Years' Recollections of Bohemian London* (London: Nash, 1917), p. 138.

29. *South London Mail*, 9 April 1892, p. 2; *South London Chronicle*, 16 April 1892.

30. Besant, *London South of the Thames*, p. 83. See also Edward Walford, *Old and New London* (London: Cassell, 1872–78), pp. 394–95.

31. John Hollingshead, *"Good Old Gaiety": A Histoirette and Remembrance* (London: Gaiety Theatre, 1903), p. 41.

32. Benny Green, ed., *The Last Empires: A Music Hall Companion* (London: Michael Joseph, 1986), p. 59.

33. Mayhew, *London Labour*, 3:159; Paterson, *Across the Bridges*, p. 28.

34. *Lloyd's Weekly London Newspaper*, 24 April 1892, p. 3. Local courts of-fered their own brand of "entertainment"; see Jean Davis, "'A Poor Man's System of Justice': The London Police Courts in the Second Half of the Nineteenth Century," *Historical Journal* 27 (1984): 309–35.

35. Besant, *London South of the Thames*, p. 81. On the shady practices of the Stamford Street Music Hall Agency see *Clarion*, 25 June 1892, p. 5.

36. The fate of the young women in what came to be known as the "Road to Ruin Case" was publicized by the moral purity activist Henry Labouchère. See *Times*, 30 July 1892, p. 10f.; *Penny Illustrated Paper*, 25 June 1892, p. 413.

37. Olive Anderson, *Suicide in Victorian and Edwardian England* (Oxford: Clarendon, 1987), p. 197.

38. London County Council, *Survey of London*, vol. 23: *Southbank and Vauxhall* (London: LCC, 1951), p. 25.

39. Walford, *Old and New London*, p. 349.

40. *Weekly Dispatch*, 4 October 1840, cited in Anna Clark, *Women's Silence, Men's Violence: Sexual Assault in England, 1770–1845* (London: Pandora, 1987), p. 123.

41. Hood cited in Eric Trudgill, *Madonnas and Magdalens: The Origins and Development of Victorian Sexual Attitudes* (London: Heinemann, 1976), p. 286. See also on river suicides, Anon., "A Night with the Thames Police," *Strand Magazine* 1 (1891): 124–31.

42. Booth, *Religious Influences*, p. 28.

43. James Greenwood, *Low-Life Deeps: An Account of the Strange Fish to Be Found There* (London: Chatto & Windus, 1875), p. 59.

CHAPTER 2
1. Elizabeth Masters Deposition: CRIM 1/38/1.

2. Elizabeth May Deposition: CRIM 1/38/1.

3. W. Teignmouth Shore, ed., *Trial of Thomas Neill Cream* (London: Hodge, 1923) (hereafter Shore), p. 188. The illiterate Annie Clements signed her deposition with a mark: CRIM 1/38/1.

4. Ernest Linnell Deposition: CRIM 1/38/1.

5. The illiterate Constance Linfield signed her deposition with a mark: CRIM 1/38/1.

6. The illiterate James Styles signed his deposition with a mark: CRIM 1/38/1.

7. Donworth Inquest, 16 and 23 October, 1891, MEPO 3 144.

8. John M. Johnson and Thomas Herbert Depositions: CRIM 1/38/1.

9. She was right to be worried. The *South London Chronicle* of 16 April 1892 carried a story of the death of a child of a similarly deserted mother who had to pay 2s 6d for rent out of the 6s to 7s a week she made charring and washing.

10. Emma Vowles Deposition: CRIM 1/38/1.

11. Lucy Rose Deposition: CRIM 1/38/1.

12. Rev. G. P. Merrick, *Work among the Fallen as Seen in the Prison Cells* (London: Ward, Lock, 1890), p. 29.

13. Clover was a member of the London and Manchester Club; see Robert Graham Deposition: CRIM 1/38/1.

14. The writer presumably found some humor in the cruel contrast of formally addressing her, as one might a lady, "Miss Clover" while reminding her of the drunken and impoverished state in which he had found her. This was Lucy Rose's recollection of the letter; the original disappeared. Lucy Rose Statement, 28 April 1892, MEPO 3 144.

15. Lucy Rose Deposition: CRIM 1/38/1. Lucy Rose Statement, 28 April 1892, MEPO 3 144.

16. Coppin later said that he thought Clover was having an epileptic fit. See Francis Coppin Deposition: CRIM 1/38/1; Coppin Evidence, 28 April 1892, MEPO 3 144.

17. Statement made at Clover's inquest, 22 June 1892. Clover's sister, Mrs. Swift, applied for the deceased's belongings. *Times,* 23 June 1892, p. 7d, and see also Shore, pp. 178–79.

18. "I knew at this time she was living the life of a prostitute," Mrs. Vowles (also known as Emma Philips) later admitted to the police. "I described her in the certificate as twenty-seven years of age and a charwoman and said I was present at her death." CRIM 1/38/1.

19. Shore, pp. 72–73.

20. Vowles reported that the child was subsequently adopted. Shore, p. 180.

21. Shore, p. 75.

22. Louisa Harris Deposition: CRIM 1/38/1.

23. James Lees-Milne, *Harold Nicolson, 1930–68* (London: Chatto & Windus, 1981), p. 230.

24. Kenneth Rose, *King George V* (London: Weideneld & Nicolson, 1983), pp. 21–23.

25. Besant, *London South of the Thames,* p. 81.

26. They were also described as "music hall singers waiting for engagements." *Reynolds Newspaper,* 17 April 1892, p. 5.

27. Shaw, cited in A. Maude Royden, ed., *Downward Paths: An Inquiry into the Causes Which Contribute to the Making of the Prostitute* (London: Bell, 1916), p. 180.

28. They had only been in London three weeks. Brighton Police to L Division, 13 April 1892, MEPO 3 144. Emma Stevens, Shrivell's aunt, later identified her; see *Lloyd's Weekly London Newspaper,* 17 April 1892, p. 11.

29. These were found by the police in their rooms. Alfred Ward Deposition: CRIM 1/38/1.

30. *Reynolds Newspaper,* 17 April 1892, p. 5; Charlotte Vogt Deposition: CRIM 1/38/1.

31. *Times,* 13 April 1892, p. 10d; Cuthbert Wyman Deposition: CRIM 1/38/1.

32. For the full account of Stevenson's investigations, see Shore, pp. 192–96.

CHAPTER 3

1. Shore, p. 125; L Division, George Comley Report, 14 April 1892, MEPO 3 144.

2. George Comley Deposition: CRIM 1/38/1.

3. The postcard, dated 11/4/92, read: "Sorry to disappoint you, but expect a letter tomorrow (Tuesday) for certain letting . . ." C.I.D., 21 April 1892, MEPO 3 144.

4. Shore, pp. 129, 192–96.

5. The letter is in Shore, pp. 97–98. Joseph Harper Deposition: CRIM 1/38/1.

6. The full letter is in Shore, p. 96. Henry John Clarke, who advertised under his father's name, received a letter on 4 May from "Murray" saying he would be contacted. Inspector Harvey left a package with Clarke for three weeks, but "Murray" never appeared. Henry John Clarke Deposition: CRIM 1/38/1; 23 May 1892, MEPO 3 144.

7. Shore, p. 96. Ernest Linnell lived with Donworth at 8 Duke Street.

8. Shore, p. 97; Alfred Dyke Acland Deposition: CRIM 1/38/1.

9. Shore, p. 10

10. Shore, p. 54

11. Shore, p. 55. On Horace Smith, see Cecil Chapman, *The Poor Man's Court of Justice: Twenty-Five Years as a Metropolitan Magistrate* (London: Hodder & Stoughton, 1925), p. 20.

12. Shore, pp. 65–66.

13. *Daily Chronicle*, 4 December 1891, p. 1.

14. The Russell divorce case was heard from 1 to 4 December and reported in the press from 2 to 5 December. Lady Russell showed the letter to her lawyer, George Lewis. She informed the Clover coroner's jury of its contents, but the actual letter was no longer in her possession. Shore, p. 188.

15. This was George Rich's recollection of the letter. Once handed over to Scotland Yard it was promptly lost. CRIM 1/38/1.

16. Russell cross-petitioned, claiming that his wife's language amounted to "legal cruelty." A minority in the House of Lords wanted to accept the notion that the impossibility of a relationship should be taken as a cause for divorce; the majority stuck to the older line that only an injury to health could warrant the designation "cruelty." To go further would open the floodgates. John M. Biggs, *The Concept of Matrimonial Cruelty* (London: Athlone Press, 1962), pp. 39–43; *Times*, 4 December 1891, p. 13f.

17. Frederick Smith, only twenty-three years of age, was elected M.P. for the Strand Division on 27 October 1891, replacing his father, W. H. Smith, who died 6 October 1891. See *Dictionary of National Biography* 18:565–68; *Dictionary of National Biography (1922–1930)*, pp. 791–92.

18. *Times*, 4 December 1891, p. 5f.; Sir Melville L. MacNaughton, *Days of My Years* (London: Edward Arnold, 1914), pp. 105, 116; Walter Broadbent, ed., *Selections from the Writings of Sir William Broadbent* (London: Froude, 1908).

19. Shore, p. 111.

153

20. See 27 April 1892, MEPO 3 144
21. Shore, pp. 109–10.
22. Horace Smith handed over the letters to Inspector Frank Thorpe, E Division, Kings Cross. Thorpe Deposition: CRIM 1/38/1.
23. L Division to Scotland Yard, 3 November, 23 November, 16 December 1891; MEPO 3 144; *Daily Chronicle,* 17 December 1891, p. 9; *Times,* 11 November 1891, p. 14b; 16 November 1891, p. 3e; 23 November 1891, p. 3f.; 17 December 1891, p. 6f.; 18 December 1891, p. 12a.
24. But Constable Comley stated that Slater was definitely not the man he saw leave 118 Stamford Street, 21 April 1892, MEPO 3 144.
25. Report on Joe Simpson, 21 April 1892, MEPO 3 144. The same report also cleared William Slater but advised that he be watched.
26. L Division to Scotland Yard, 12 April 1892, MEPO 3 144.
27. L Division, 16 April 1890 amended report, MEPO 3 144. J. Waring, a reporter, told the police he was acquainted with George Clifton. Clifton was known by the police to have used the name "Wilkes" and to have run a patent medicine store at 181 Queen Victoria Street; 9 May, 16 May 1892, MEPO 3 144. The press's mention of Chatham may have been responsible for the police receiving a letter from "E. Baxter" of Chatham, who claimed to know who the killer was; the Chatham constabulary determined that "Baxter" did not exist. Chatham Constabulary to Scotland Yard, 8 May, 23 May 1892, MEPO 3 144.
28. Shore, p. 100.
29. The arrests referred to were made in the Stamford Street "Road to Ruin Case" noted in chap. 1. Shore, p. 101; John Haynes Statement, 28 May 1892, MEPO 3 144.
30. George Comley and Alfred Ward Depositions: CRIM 1/38/1; Comley and Ward Reports, 16 May 1892, MEPO 3 144.
31. Shore, p. 99. For a slightly different and more graphic account, see John Patrick Haynes Statement, 23 May 1892, MEPO 3 144.
32. John Haynes Deposition: CRIM 1/38/1.
33. McIntyre agreed he was "connected with the dynamite explosions, following suspected persons in London." Shore, p. 107.
34. Shore, p. 106; Patrick McIntyre Report, 30 May 1892, MEPO 3 144; *British Medical Journal* 1 (7 May 1892): 974–75.
35. According to the *Oxford English Dictionary* the term "rip" referred to dissolute men and worn-out and useless women and horses. The "rip" of whom Neill spoke was Violet Beverley.
36. Shore, pp. 104–5; Patrick McIntyre Report, 24 May 1892, MEPO 3 144; Patrick McIntyre Deposition: CRIM 1/38/1. The police missed a crucial inconsistency. Neill told Haynes that he had sent the warning note to Marsh and Shrivell, but he told McIntyre that "Murray" had sent it.
37. "Towards the end of April the police came to me. Till the case was being inquired into at the inquest I did not know she had died of strychnine." Lucy Rose Deposition: CRIM 1/38/1.
38. Clover Report, 28 April 1892, MEPO 3 144.

39. See 7 May 1892, MEPO 3 144. Jessie Duncan, a prisoner in Holloway Prison, reported that she had seen Marsh with a thirty-year-old sailor; 18 May 1892, MEPO 3 144. Charles Burdett mentioned that Marsh had a "sea captain" friend; 6 May 1892, MEPO 3 144. Jack the Ripper's murders, which except for two were each spaced about a month apart, similarly suggested to the police that their perpetrator was only intermittently in London.

40. Harvey first heard of Clover's death on 28 April. He had never heard of the Broadbent letter describing her poisoning that Scotland Yard possessed. "It was never passed on to us at Lambeth. If referred to anyone it would have been referred to us first." George Harvey Deposition: CRIM 1/38/1.

41. See 5 May 1892, Clover Inquest, MEPO 3 144.

42. See Shore, appendix 6.

43. Thomas Stevenson used the strychnine on frogs because, he argued, "it does not give so much suffering as experimenting on a rabbit or a dog . . . As a rule we are not justified in resorting to experiments on animal life till we get some strong presumptive evidence justifying it, and giving good ground for thinking it desirable to do it." Shore, pp. 89–90. Stevenson's sensitivities were no doubt influenced in part by the vociferous antivivisection campaign led by Frances Power Cobbe.

44. Thomas Stevenson to Treasury, 23 May 1892, MEPO 3 144; Thomas Stevenson, *The Principles and Practices of Medical Jurisprudence* (London: Churchill, 1894), 1:453.

CHAPTER 4

1. Shore, p. 23. Scotland Yard Report, 19 May 1892, MEPO 3 144.

2. Scotland Yard Report, 23 May 1892, MEPO 3 144.

3. J. Braman, 23 May 1892, MEPO 3 144.

4. C.I.D., 28 May 1892, MEPO 3 144.

5. John McCarthy Reports, 26 May, 28 May 1892, MEPO 3 144.

6. The story was later put out that a small-time English criminal who had sometime earlier fled London, on accidently meeting Jarvis in New York and mistakenly believing that Scotland Yard had pursued him all the way to America, had turned himself in. See *South London Chronicle*, 29 October 1892.

7. On Gilmour, see *Dictionary of Canadian Biography* 12:366–67; *Quebec Directory for 1865–66* (Quebec: Charrier, 1866), p. 97. For photographs of Cream and information on his schooling see his file in the McGill University Archives.

8. *McGill Calendar*, 1876–77, p. 59; *Montreal Evening Star*, 31 March 1876, p. 2; 1 April 1876, p. 1; *Montreal Gazette*, 1 April 1876, p. 1; Frederick Jarvis Report, 30 June 1892, MEPO 3 144.

9. Frederick Jarvis Report, 4 July 1892, MEPO 3 144.

10. Miss Jane Porter, Cream's landlady between 1872 and 1876, remembered him as always being a gentleman. He appeared to have a macabre sense of humor, however; the firemen discovered a charred medical skeleton in his bed. Frederick Jarvis Report, 19 July 1892, MEPO 3 144.

11. L. H. Brooks was listed as proprietor of Brooks Hotel in Waterloo,

County of Shefford, in H. Belden and Co., *Illustrated Atlas of the Eastern Town-ships and S.W. Quebec* (Port Elgin, Ontario: Ross Cunning, 1872), p. 88. Brooks was a kinsman of Samuel Brooks, who sat with Alexander Galt (1817–93), the leading Anglo-Protestant politician in Quebec, on the board of the St. Lawrence and Atlantic Railway Company; see *Dictionary of Canadian* Biography, 12:349.

12. Rev. David Lindsay officiated at the private ceremony; C.I.D., 21 June, 7 July 1892, MEPO 3 144; *Waterloo Advertiser*, 15 September 1876.

13. Such postgraduate work in England was not uncommon; Herbert Lionel Reddy, who graduated with Cream from McGill in 1876, also went on to study at St. Thomas's. Reddy returned to Montreal, where he was affiliated for fifty years with the Women's General Hospital. In the 1940s it was renamed the Herbert Reddy Memorial Hospital. *McGill News* 27, no. 4 (1945–46): 26.

14. *South London Chronicle*, 23 September 1876.

15. *South London Chronicle*, 14 October, 4 November, 18 November, 23 December.

16. *South London Chronicle*, 7 October 1876.

17. Nightingale was unsympathetic to the movement in favor of qualifying women as doctors. Cecil Woodham-Smith, *Florence Nightingale, 1820–1910* (London: Constable, 1950), p. 485.

18. Not until 1883 did a woman gain the M.D. from the University of London. L. G. Anderson, *Louisa Garrett Anderson* (London: Faber & Faber, 1939), p. 224.

19. Arthur H. Nethercott, *The First Five Lives of Annie Besant* (Chicago, 1960), pp. 90ff.

20. *South London Chronicle*, 20 January, 21 April, 23 June 1877.

21. Rosanna Ledbetter, *A History of the Malthusian League, 1877–1927* (Columbus: Ohio State University Press, 1976).

22. Annie Besant, *The Law of Population* (London: Freethought Publishing, 1877); *An Autobiography* (London: Fisher Unwin, 1893), pp. 209–29.

23. *South London Chronicle*, 21 July 1877.

24. Frederick Jarvis Report, 7 July 1892, MEPO 3 144.

25. Given the vagaries of police spelling, Charlotte Louise Botteril was probably a relation of Quebec City shoe manufacturer John Henderson Botterell. *Dictionary of Canadian Biography* 12:126; William Buttle Testimony, 27 June 1892, MEPO 3 144.

26. *Waterloo Advertiser*, 12 August 1877.

27. Dr. Cornelius J. T. R. Phelan Testimony, reported by Frederick Jarvis, 7 July 1892, MEPO 3 144.

28. *Chicago Daily Tribune*, 23 August 1880, p. 2.

29. *Daily Advertiser*, 8 and 14 May 1879. Gardener died of the chloroform overdose; she had not been aborted. Frederick Jarvis Report, 14 July 1892, MEPO 3 144.

30. Birrell was likely a son of John Birrell (1815–75), London's leading merchant, whose family firm was worth over $300,000. *Dictionary of Canadian Biography* 10:68.

31. Edward Levy, who in 1892 was working as a Houndsditch victualler

and had known Cream in Chicago in 1880 and 1881, stated that Cream had admitted to having poisoned two women in Quebec between 1878 and 1880. This was possibly true, but Cream's time of medical practice in Canada between the summer of 1878 and the summer of 1879 was spent in Ontario and Inspector Frederick Jarvis was told by Canadian officials that no suspicious deaths had taken place while Cream was in Quebec. Edward Levy Statement, 14 July 1892, MEPO 3 144; Frederick Jarvis, 30 June 1892, MEPO 3 144; Shore, p. 190.

32. Joanne J. Meyerowitz, *Women Adrift: Independent Wage Earners in Chicago, 1880–1930* (Chicago: University of Chicago Press, 1988).

33. Mark Thomas Connelly, *The Response to Prostitution in the Progressive Era* (Chapel Hill: University of North Carolina Press, 1980), p. 92.

34. Vice Commission of Chicago, *The Social Evil in Chicago* (Chicago: Gunthorpe-Warren, 1911), pp. 70–71, 97; Walter C. Reckless, *Vice in Chicago* (Chicago: University of Chicago Press, 1933).

35. The *Chicago Tribune* provides a full account of the American phase of Cream's life, which Vincent Starrett used as the source for "The Chicago Career of Dr. Cream—1880," in Sewell P. Wright, ed., *Chicago Murders* (New York: Duell, Sloane & Pearce, 1945), pp. 14–44.

36. Inspector Frederick Jarvis stated that Cream was arrested 23 August 1880 for the death of "Julia Franklin"; Store gives her name as "Julia Faulkner." Jarvis probably confused Franklin with Faulkner, though it is possible that Julia Franklin was another of Cream's victims that only the Chicago police knew about; Jarvis Report, 11 July 1892, MEPO 3 144; *Chicago Tribune*, 22 August 1880, p. 3.

37. *Chicago Tribune*, 24 August 1880, p. 8.

38. *Chicago Tribune*, 22 August 1880, p. 3.

39. *Chicago Tribune*, 24 August 1880, p. 8; 26 August 1880, p. 8.

40. *Chicago Tribune*, 29 August 1880, p. 4. Later, investigators reported that of twenty midwives asked to perform an abortion twelve agreed and two provided the names of those who would. *Social Evil in Chicago*, pp. 225–26.

41. Judge Joseph S. Gary was to win notoriety in 1886 when, on the flimsiest of evidence, he sentenced to death seven anarchists for their purported participation in Chicago's Haymarket Square riots. Bessie Louise Pierce, *A History of Chicago* (Chicago: University of Chicago Press, 1957), 2:283; Paul Avrich, *The Haymarket Tragedy* (Princeton: Princeton University Press, 1984), pp. 252–53.

42. Alfred S. Trude was to become one of Chicago's most successful criminal attorneys. Pierce, *A History of Chicago*, 2:270; *Chicago Tribune*, 18 November 1880, p. 8; 19 November 1880, p. 10.

43. *Chicago Tribune*, 17 November 1880, p. 10.

44. Jarvis noted that Officer O'Hara testified that Cream was a "regular abortionist," but incorrectly reported that Cream was indicted 2 October 1880 and tried 16–18 October. See Frederick Jarvis Report, 14 July 1892, MEPO 3 144; *Chicago Tribune*, 20 November 1880, p. 16.

45. *Chicago Tribune*, 4 December 1880, p. 16.

46. HO 144/245 A 54360/13. These letters are in Mr. Justice Hawkins's trial notes, HO 144/245 A 54360/13.

47. Mr. Justice Hawkins's trial notes, HO 144/246 A 54360.

48. *Chicago Tribune*, 19 June 1881, p. 6.

49. Frederick Jarvis Report, 11 July 1892, MEPO 3 144.

50. *Chicago Tribune*, 22 September 1881, p. 5; 23 September 1881, p. 5. One curious aspect of the case was that Mr. Rayner, the druggist, hired an attorney to assist the prosecution. Frederick Jarvis Report, 11 and 14 July 1892, MEPO 3 144.

51. Billy the Kid's shooting on 15 July was only reported in the East two weeks later; *Chicago Tribune*, 27 July 1881, p. 1; 3 August 1881, p. 8.

52. Fuller, a prominent Republican, was a state senator (1878–82, 1888–92), circuit court judge (1897), and United States congressman (1902–26). See *Illinois State Historical Society Journal* 19 (1926): 278–79.

53. Julia Stott was supposed to stand trial as an accomplice on the second Monday of February 1882; there is no record of her ever being tried.

54. Frederick Jarvis Report, 11 July 1892, MEPO 3 144.

55. Prisoner's description; Frederick Jarvis Report, 29 July 1892, MEPO 3 144; Jay Robert Nash, *Murder, America* (New York: Simon & Schuster, 1980), pp. 116–17.

56. Thomas M. Beach, *Twenty-Five Years in the Secret Service: The Recollections of a Spy* (London: E.P. Publishing, 1974), p. 42. William Cream sent the wardens of Joliet two hundred dollars to use for his son as the authorities saw fit. Frederick Jarvis Report, 30 June 1892, MEPO 3 144.

57. William Cream, who died 12 May 1887 at Dansville, New York, at age sixty-four, was buried in Mount Heriman Cemetery, Quebec City, on 14 May. His estate was divided between his six children, Thomas receiving ten shares of Merchants Bank of Canada stock worth twelve hundred dollars each. C.I.D., 11 June 1892, MEPO 3 144. Daniel Cream interviewed by Frederick Jarvis, 30 June, 4 July 1892, MEPO 3 144.

58. Frank Murray to Robert Pinkerton, 12 June 1892, MEPO 3 144. See also in the same file a clipping from the *Chicago Herald*, June 1892.

59. Frederick Jarvis Report, 30 June 1892, MEPO 3 144. Fifer, a Republican, was elected in 1888 but defeated in 1892 by John Peter Altgeld, the first foreign-born governor of Illinois, who immediately freed the Haymarket martyrs. Robert P. Howard, *Illinois: A History of a Prairie State* (Grand Rapids, Mich.: Eerdmans, 1972), p. 385.

60. Cream's letters of 10 December 1890, 26 July 1891, and 8 August 1891 are referred to by Frank Murray in his letter to Robert Pinkerton, 12 June 1892; Robert Pinkerton to John Shore, C.I.D., 14 June 1892; MEPO 3 144. Cream was possibly inspired by Pinkerton agent Murray to call his fictitious detective "W. H. Murray."

61. Before leaving for England, Cream visited Mrs. Mary Aldous, a cousin (the daughter of his father's brother), in Brooklyn, New York, with whom he had corresponded while in prison. Frederick Jarvis Report, 4 July 1892, MEPO 3 144.

62. Emily Sleaper Deposition: CRIM 1/38/1.

63. *Illustrated Police News,* 19 November 1892, p. 4.

64. "Thomas Neill Cream: A Study of His Crimes by One Who Knew Him," *St. James's Gazette,* 24 October 1892, p. 9.

65. James Aitchinson Deposition: CRIM 1/38/1.

66. Strychnine was commonly employed in the 1890s; nux vomica and quinine (which Cream also ordered) were prescribed to alcoholics as a tonic. George Rendall of St. Thomas's later testified that Cream was not associated with the hospital in 1891–92; HO 144/246 A 54360.

67. Shore, pp. 67–68.

68. Shore, p. 118.

69. Emily Sleaper Deposition: CRIM 1/38/1.

70. Laura Sabbatini Deposition: CRIM 1/38/1. For Cream's letter thanking Sabbatini for promising to marry him, see *Lloyd's Weekly London Newspaper,* 30 October 1892, p. 2.

71. Shore, p. 185; HO 144/245 A54360/13. Cream was reported to have gone to Canada to collect a £3000 inheritance; see clipping from *Daily Chronicle,* 27 June 1892, MEPO 3 144.

72. C.I.D., 20 June 1892, statement of William Fisher, steward of the *Sarnia,* 22 July 1892, MEPO 3 144. Even the chaplain was not spared Cream's accounts of the women he had debauched; see, Robert Caswell Statement, 15 July 1892, MEPO 3 144.

73. Shore, p. 93.

74. Frederick Jarvis Report, 19 July 1892, MEPO 3 144; John Wilson McCulloch Deposition: CRIM 1/38/1.

75. George Francis Harvey, owner of the drug company, responded coolly to Cream's request to act as the firm's agent in the United Kingdom. Harvey remembered him as a "loose sort of man constantly talking about women and fond of reading smutty books." Frederick Jarvis Report, 21 July 1892, MEPO 3 144.

76. According to McIntyre's report Cream was in Liverpool on 5 April, stayed from 6 to 8 April at Edwards Hotel, Euston, in London with an unknown woman, with whom he registered under the names "Mr. and Mrs. Stanley." He returned to 103 Lambeth Palace Road on 10 April. These dates are obviously incorrect; 25 May 1892, MEPO 3 144.

77. The circular read:

ELLEN DONWORTH'S DEATH
To the Guests, of the Metropole Hotel
   Ladies and Gentlemen,
I hereby notify you that the person who poisoned Ellen Donworth on the 13th last October is today in the employ of the Metropole Hotel and that your lives are in danger as long as you remain in this Hotel.
Yours respectfully,
W. H. Murray
London April 1892

In March 1892 Cream drew up a draft of the circular and handed it over to Arthur Duggan, night editor of the *Quebec Morning Chronicle,* whom he had met the previous month at Blanchard's Hotel. Cream explained that the circular was to serve as a way of retaliating against a man who had insulted him in London. Duggan asked no more and had Mr. Drouin print up the circulars. Duggan sent them on to Cream at the Albion Hotel in Montreal. The name "W. H. Murray" also appeared on the letters sent to Clarke and Broadbent, 23 May, 3 June, 27 June 1892, MEPO 3 144.

78. For the same reason, Cream, who was traveling with Kingman, registered at the Albion Hotel as "Robert Neill of Waterloo." See *Montreal Gazette,* 22 March 1892, p. 3.

79. Shore, p. 17; Frederick Jarvis Report, 7 July 1892, MEPO 3 144.

80. Jarvis reported that Battersby gave copies of Cream's letter and the circular to the editor of the *Montreal Daily Star;* 4 and 7 July 1892, MEPO 3 144.

81. Laura Sabbatini Statement, 23 September 1892, MEPO 3 144.

82. Shore, p. 186. Emily Sleaper Deposition: CRIM 1/38/1; Emily Sleaper Testimony, 23 May 1892, MEPO 3 144.

83. Laura Sabbatini Deposition: CRIM 1/38/1.

84. Cream was also attempting to join the Masonic Lodge; Henry Robert Boyles Deposition: CRIM 1/38/1.

85. "Is Deeming Jack the Ripper?" *Illustrated Police News,* 16 April 1892, p. 1; *Times,* 2 May–30 May 1892.

86. Margaret Armstead Deposition: CRIM 1/38/1.

87. In late April when Cream went down to Berkhamstead he gave Emily Sleaper his notebooks for safekeeping. On 16 May, seeing that the house was being watched, he destroyed them. CRIM 1/38/1.

88. J. B. Tunbridge Report, 29 May 1892, MEPO 3 144.

89. See 23 May 1892, MEPO 3 144.

90. Apparently, the question of Cream's pornographic pictures was raised as well, because he assured the officers he had destroyed them. Patrick McIntyre Report, 30 May 1892, MEPO 3 144.

91. The two were Lucy Rose and Ida St. Houstine; Patrick McIntyre Report, 24 May 1892, MEPO 3 144. Tunbridge did arrange for Cream to walk by Lucy Rose a few days later, but she did not recognize him. J. B. Tunbridge Report, 29 May 1892, MEPO 3 144.

92. J. E. Waters and T. W. Bryan, solicitors, 26 and 27 May 1892; Patrick McIntyre Report, 30 May 1892, MEPO 3 144.

93. Cream had provided McIntyre with a specimen of his handwriting on this notepaper; C.I.D., 3 June 1892, MEPO 3 144.

94. C.I.D., 3 June 1892, MEPO 3 144.

95. J. Braman to Home Office, 4 June 1892, MEPO 3 144.

96. Robert Anderson to Home Office, 4 June 1892, MEPO 3 144. Lucy Rose, Constance Linfield, and the owner of the Prince of Wales Hotel all failed to identify Cream as either "Fred" or "George Clifton." C.I.D., 11 June 1892, MEPO 3 144.

160
Notes to Pages 49–53

CHAPTER 5

1. For the notes on his elaborate tests, see Shore, pp. 197–207; Thomas Stevenson, *The Principles and Practices of Medical Jurisprudence* (London: J. A. Churchill, 1894), 1:453. See also Arthur P. Luff, *Text-Book of Forensic Medicine and Toxicology* (London: Longmans, Green, 1895), pp. 273–77.

2. Laura Sabbatini was visited by the police and her specimens of Cream's writing compared to the Broadbent letter of 28 November 1891; when Cream's room was searched, one of Alice Marsh and Emma Shrivell's notes giving their address was found; Marsh's sister, Mrs. Taylor, identified Cream as having been seen with Marsh. C.I.D., 6, 7, and 11 June 1892, MEPO 3 144.

3. Identification Parade, 25 June 1892, MEPO 3, 144.

4. *Daily Telegraph*, 23–25 June 1892; Clover Inquest, 8 July 1892, MEPO 3 144.

5. The Broadbent letter had apparently been lost at Scotland Yard. Tunbridge finally retrieved it and recognized the writing as Cream's. John Tunbridge Report, 6 June 1892, MEPO 3 144.

6. For the inquest, see *Times*, 23, 24, 25, and 27 June; 8 and 14 July 1892.

7. C.I.D., 4 and 13 July 1892, MEPO 3 144.

8. Later, Lou Harvey (Louisa Harris) said the hotel was on Garrick Street.

9. Shore, pp. 28–29. In her deposition Harris mentioned another peculiarity; the night they slept together Cream never took off his spectacles. Louisa Harris Deposition: CRIM 1/38/1.

10. Louisa Harris Deposition: CRIM 1/38/1.

11. The coroner read to the jury on 13 July an amazing letter he had received that claimed that the crimes had been carried out by the author disguised as Cream and that if the doctor were not released "trouble" would ensue. It was signed "Juan Pollen, alias Jack the Ripper, Beware all. I warn but once." This sounds like one of Cream's concoctions, but the *Times* reported the letter was received with "laughter, in which Neill heartily joined." *Times*, 14 July 1892, p. 12d.

12. *Lloyd's Weekly London Newspaper*, 30 October 1892, p. 2. For copies of Cream's letters to Sabbatini of 4 and 14 July and 5 August, see HO 144/246 A 54360.

13. Joanna Richardson, *The Pre-Eminent Victorian: A Study of Tennyson* (London: Cape, 1962), p. 264.

14. A "true bill" was a bill of indictment endorsed by a grand jury as being sustained by evidence; C.I.D., 14 September 1892, MEPO 3 144.

15. Forgetting Hawkins's dedication to his terrier "Jack," one defense counsel was so carried away in making his closing address that he made the mistake of saying that the crown had not produced enough evidence "to hang a dog." An enraged Hawkins interrupted to demand how much would be required. "That would depend, my Lord," replied the now cautious counsel, "to whom the dog belonged." Albert Crew, *The Old Bailey* (London: Nicolson & Watson, 1933), p. 70; *Dictionary of National Biography (1901–1911)*, pp. 228–30. On the Penge case, which also involved conspiracy to murder, see J. B. Atlay, ed., *Trial of the Stauntons* (London: Hodge, 1911).

16. Cecil Chapman recalled being shocked by the ferocious five-year sentence handed down by Hawkins to a seventeen-year-old boy for an "act of immorality" which would have likely gone unreported in a public school. Sir Edward Clarke simply called Hawkins "a wicked judge and a wicked man." Cecil Chapman, *The Poor Man's Court of Justice: Twenty-Five Years as a Metropolitan Magistrate* (London: Hodder & Stoughton, 1925), p. 14; A. W. B. Simpson, ed., *Biographical Dictionary of the Common Law* (London: Butterworths, 1984), pp. 229–30.

17. George R. Sims, *My Life: Sixty Years' Recollections of Bohemian London* (London: Nash, 1917), p. 143.

18. Russell was assisted by Bernard Coleridge, Q.C., M.P., Henry Sutton, and Charles Frederick Gill. On Russell, a Liberal Ulster Catholic, see *Who Was Who (1897–1916)*, pp. 617–18; Richard Barry O'Brien, *Life and Letters of Lord Russell of Killowen* (London: Nelson, 1901).

19. Geoghegan was assisted by H. Warburton, Clifford Luxmoore Drew, and W. Howel Scratton and was instructed by the solicitor John E. Waters of Waters and Bryan. On the career of Geoghegan, who committed suicide in 1902, see Martin L. Friedland, *The Trial of Israel Lipski* (London: Macmillan, 1984), pp. 23, 30; Brian Simpson, *Cannibalism and the Common Law: The Story of the Tragic Last Voyage of the Mignonette and the Strange Legal Proceedings to Which It Gave Rise* (Chicago: University of Chicago Press, 1984), p. 257.

20. *Montreal Gazette*, 22 October 1892, p. 1.

21. See Shore, p. 119, for the authorities cited by the crown counsel on the admissibility of such evidence. These were poison cases in which the deceased had lived in the same house as the murderer and were thus qualitatively different from Cream's case. For a trial in which 120 witnesses were required to establish the accused's guilt see Eric R. Watson, ed., *Trial of Joseph Smith* (London: Hodge, 1923).

22. For the judge's account of the trial, witness by witness, see HO 144/246 A 54360. An abbreviated, printed version which provides the witnesses' testimony but not the counsels' addresses is found in PCOM 1 143: Session Papers 1892, 1417–60.

23. The prosecution was so anxious to have McCulloch testify that it offered him first-class passage to England, two hundred dollars a month, and a pound a day subsistence. His employer, Alexander Jardine, not the most civic-minded of businessmen, also wanted to be remunerated for any loss of business incurred by McCulloch's absence. C.I.D., 10, 11, 12, 16, and 27 August 1892, MEPO 3 144.

24. Shore, pp. 80–81.

25. Walter de Grey Birch made some blunders. He originally told the police that the letter sent to Wyatt was by Cream; in fact Laura Sabbatini wrote it. The police had also employed the services of George Smith Inglis, another handwriting expert. Inglis also identified as being in Cream's hand letters prepared by Sabbatini. He was warned by the police and redid his report for the Treasury. See Walter de Grey Birch Deposition: CRIM 1/38/1; George Smith Inglis Report, 22 June 1892, MEPO 3 144.

26. For copies of the Wyatt, Broadbent, Smith, and Harper letters see HO 144/245 A 54360/13

27. *Penny Illustrated Paper*, 2 July 1892, p. 8.

28. For these letters in full see *Lloyd's Weekly London Newspaper*, 23 October 1892, p. 4.

29. Conservative judges like Mr. Justice Hawkins were even opposed to prisoners' being provided with counsel at public expense. See Graham Parker, "The Prisoner in the Box: The Making of the Criminal Evidence Act, 1898," in J. A. Guy and H. G. Beale, eds., *Legal and Social Change in British History* (London: Royal Historical Society, 1984), pp. 156–75.

30. Shore, p. 78.

31. Shore, pp. 142–43.

32. Constance Linfield Deposition: CRIM 1/38/1; Shore, p. 55.

33. *Penny Illustrated Paper*, 25 June 1892, p. 413.

34. McCulloch claimed that, though not bothered by Cream's references to abortion and prostitution, he shunned the doctor after being shocked at his suggestion of poisoning an American to obtain two thousand dollars. Shore, p. 96.

35. Shore, p. 134.

36. *Lancet*, 29 October 1892, p. 1003.

37. Nigel Walker, *Crime and Insanity in England* (Edinburgh: Edinburgh University Press, 1968), pp. 86–87.

38. At mid-century about one-seventh of murderers were found unfit or acquitted as insane; by the early twentieth century about one-third. Forbes Winslow, *The Plea of Insanity in Criminal Cases* (London: Renshaw, 1843), p. 75; Roger Smith, *Trial by Medicine: Insanity and Responsibility in Victorian Trials* (Edinburgh: Edinburgh University Press, 1981), pp. 14–16; Martin J. Wiener, *Reconstructing the Criminal: Culture, Law and Policy in England, 1830–1914* (Cambridge: Cambridge University Press, 1990), p. 279.

39. *British Medical Journal* 1 (10 June 1893): 1234.

40. *British Medical Journal* 2 (9 July 1892): 83–85; *Times*, 5 April 1892, p. 10c; 15 April 1892, p. 5d.

41. The press noted that Louis Riel, leader of the unsuccessful 1885 Métis rebellion in Canada, despite clear signs of insanity, had also been executed. *Times*, 3 May 1892, p. 10a.

42. *Times*, 24 October 1892, p. 8a; *British Medical Journal* 2 (29 October 1892): 963.

43. The Cream case was reminiscent of the December 1881 trial of G. H. Lamson, an American doctor who used aconite to poison his Wimbledon brother-in-law. Dr. Stevenson was the expert witness and Mr. Justice Hawkins the judge. Lamson also tried to plead insanity to avoid execution, but failed. *Illustrated Police News*, 12 November 1892, p. 2.

44. Frederick Jarvis Report, 30 June 1892, MEPO 3 144.

45. *Illustrated Police News*, 19 November 1892, p. 2.

46. HO 144/246 A 54360/23.

47. *Illustrated Police News*, 19 November 1892, p. 2.

48. Frederick Jarvis Report, 4 July 1892, MEPO 3 144.

49. HO 144/246 A 54360/13.

50. Frederick Jarvis Report, 2 September 1892, MEPO 3 144.

51. Frederick Jarvis Report, 4 July 1892, MEPO 3 144.

52. *Pall Mall Gazette*, 22 October 1892, p. 1; 24 October 1892, p. 2.

53. The report was necessarily brief; the Holloway medical staff was obliged to provide insanity examinations for about a thousand inmates each year. See Olive Anderson, *Suicide in Victorian and Edwardian England* (Oxford: Clarendon, 1987), p. 391.

54. HO 144/245 A 54360/10A; C.I.D., 12 November 1892, MEPO 3 144. See also *British Medical Journal* 2 (29 October 1892): 263; *Lancet*, 19 November 1892, pp. 1179–80. According to Shore, once Cream's fate was sealed, "It was stated that he acknowledged to his gaolers the justice of his sentence and admitted that he had murdered many other women." Shore, p. 36. Thomas Holdstock of Buffalo, New York, wrote the Home Office referring to other crimes committed by Cream in the United States. HO 144/246 A 54360/21.

55. *Illustrated Police News*, 12 November 1892, p. 4.

56. On 6 August 1890, a New York convict by the name of Kemmler suffered the United States' first electrocution. See *British Medical Journal* 2 (8 August 1890): 354; *Lancet*, 16 August 1890, pp. 345–46; 11 July 1891, p. 86; 5 March 1892, p. 544.

57. Leon Radzinowicz, *A History of Criminal Law and Its Administration from 1750* (London: Stevens & Son, 1968), 4:352. It was the custom to build the gallows on Sunday and carry out the execution on Monday. With that peculiar Victorian respect for the Sabbath, after 1859 the gallows were erected on Monday and the executions held on Tuesday.

58. *Toronto Globe*, 16 November 1892, p. 1.

59. *Pall Mall Gazette*, 15 November 1892, pp. 4–5.

60. The most accessible source on the Cream trial remains the account provided in the "Notable British Trial Series," W. Teignmouth Shore, ed., *Trial of Thomas Neill Cream* (London: William Hodge, 1923). A fictionalized "autobiography" is provided in John Cashman, *The Gentleman from Chicago: Being an Account of the Doings of Thomas Neill Cream, M.D. (McGill), 1850–1892* (New York: Harper & Row, 1973). Cream's murderous activities were not bizarre enough for his Canadian chroniclers. Donald Bell argues, in "'Jack the Ripper'—The Final Solution," *Criminologist* 9 (1974): 40–51, that Cream was also the Whitechapel serial killer. In Chris Scott's novel *Jack* (Toronto: Macmillan, 1988), Cream is given multiple personalities—those of Cream the murderer, G. Wentworth Bell-Smith, a Canadian missionary among London prostitutes, and an Irish detective called Malone. David Fennario, in his play *Dr. Neill Cream* (reviewed in the *Toronto Star*, 4 November 1988, and the *Toronto Globe and Mail*, 5 November 1988, p. C11), depicts Cream as having served the Montreal Anglo elite by running a high-class brothel and providing bodies for Dr. William Osler to dissect at the McGill Medical School.

61. *Reynold's Newspaper*, 30 October 1892, p. 5.

PART 2

1. Pieter Spierenburg, *The Spectacle of Suffering: Executions and the Evolution of Repression from a Preindustrial Metropolis to the European Experience* (Cambridge: Cambridge University Press, 1984).

2. *Lloyd's Weekly London Newspaper,* 30 October 1892, p. 2; *Halifax Herald,* 16 November 1892, p. 5.

3. Charles Rosenberg, *The Trial of the Assassin Guiteau* (Chicago: University of Chicago Press, 1978), pp. 257–58.

CHAPTER 6

1. MEPO 3 140; W. J. Fishman, *East End 1888: A Year in a London Borough among the Labouring Poor* (London: Duckworth, 1988), pp. 206–29.

2. MEPO 3 143; *Times,* 14 February 1891, p. 12c; 16 February 1891, p. 12a.

3. On Europe, see Jill Harsin, *Policing Prostitution in Nineteenth-Century France* (Princeton: Princeton University Press, 1985); Alain Corbin, *Women for Hire: Prostitution in Nineteenth-Century France* (Cambridge, Mass:, Harvard University Press, 1990); Mary Gibson, *Prostitution and the State in Italy, 1860–1915* (Rutgers: Rutgers University Press, 1986).

4. Alexandre Parent-Duchâtelet, *De la prostitution dans la ville de Paris* (Paris, Baillière, 1836), 1:7, cited in Charles Bernheimer, *Figures of Ill Repute: Representing Prostitution in Nineteenth-Century France* (Cambridge, Mass.: Harvard University Press, 1989), p. 15.

5. *Times,* 4 January 1858, p. 4e; 7 January 1858, p. 10d; 16 January 1858, p. 10d; 4 February 1858, p. 12f; 11 February 1858, p. 9e; 24 February 1858, p. 12d.

6. *Times,* 9 March 1858, p. 12d; 9 April 1858, pp. 8ef, 9a; 10 April 1858, p. 11b; "The Purity of the Press," *Saturday Review,* 26 June 1858, pp. 656–57.

7. As late as 1891, 1,500 men out of 196,000 were reported as unfit. See *British Medical Journal* 2 (26 August 1893): 481.

8. Judith Walkowitz, *Prostitution and Victorian Society: Women, Class and the State* (Cambridge: Cambridge University Press, 1980).

9. William Acton, *Prostitution, Considered in Its Moral, Social, and Sanitary Aspects* (London: Churchill, 1857). For the argument that prostitution prevented the far worse crime of adultery, see William Lecky, *A History of European Morals* (London: Longmans, 1869), 2:380–85.

10. The traditional cure—massive doses of mercury, which resulted in the loss of teeth, bowel ruptures, and so on—was as bad as the disease. *Lancet,* 6 June 1891, pp. 1255–56; Allan M. Brandt, *No Magic Bullet: A Social History of Venereal Disease in the United States since 1880* (New York: Oxford University Press, 1985), pp. 9–17.

11. On doctors opposed to the Acts, see Benjamin Scott, *A State Iniquity: Its Rise, Extension, and Overthrow* (London: Kegan Paul, 1890), pp. 116, 119, 217.

12. Josephine Butler, *Personal Reminiscences of a Great Crusade* (London: Marshall, 1896); Paul McHugh, *Prostitution and Victorian Social Reform* (London: Croom Helm, 1980).

13. W. Douglas Morrison, *Crime and Its Causes* (London: Swan Sonnenschein, 1908), p. 6.

14. Even without the Contagious Diseases Acts the police and philanthropic groups through vagrancy laws and refuges retained a variety of means to control the movements of prostitutes. See Linda Mahood, *The Magdalenes: Prostitution in the Nineteenth Century* (London: Routledge, 1990).

15. G. P. Merrick, *Work among the Fallen as Seen in the Prison Cells* (London: Ward, Lock, 1890), p. 34.

16. An early-twentieth-century inquiry found that overcrowded homes, incest, low wages, and unemployment on one hand and a desire for some zest on the other provided the backdrop for the entry into prostitution. A. Maude Royden, ed., *Downward Paths: An Inquiry into the Causes Which Contribute to the Making of the Prostitute* (London: Bell, 1916), pp. 4, 14, 24–27, 142.

17. Deborah Gorham, "The 'Maiden Tribute of Modern Babylon' Reexamined: Child Prostitution and the Idea of Childhood in Late-Victorian England," *Victorian Studies* 21 (1978): 353–79.

18. J. W. Robertson Scott, *The Life and Death of a Newspaper* (London: Methuen, 1952), pp. 125–33.

19. Conservatives attacked the "filth" published by Stead while the socialist Ernest E. Williams devoted one of the articles in his series "Nineteenth-Century Humbug" to Stead and the "Prostitution Crusade." See William McGlashan, *England on Her Defence!* (London: Barnes, 1888); *Justice*, 12 March 1892.

20. *Fourth Report of the London Committee for the Suppression of That Traffic, Six Years Labour and Sorrow: In Reference to the Traffic in the Souls and Bodies of British Girls, 1885* (London: Dyer, 1885), pp. 83ff.

21. The Labouchère clause in the 1885 act also had the effect of criminalizing homosexuals. Jeffrey Weeks, *Coming Out: Homosexual Politics in Britain from the Nineteenth Century to the Present* (London: Quartet, 1977), pp. 18–20.

22. The Indecent Advertisements Act of 1889 made "any advertisement relating to syphilis, gonorrhea, nervous debility, or other complaint or infirmity arising from or relating to sexual intercourse" an indecent publication; 52 & 53 Vict. c. 18. See also Edward Bristow, *Vice and Vigilance: Purity Movements in Britain since 1700* (Totowa, N.J.: Roman & Littlefield, 1977); Frank Mort, *Dangerous Sexualities: Medico-Moral Politics in England since 1830* (London: Routledge & Kegan Paul, 1987), pp. 95–109.

23. *Daily Chronicle*, 5 November 1891, p. 2.

24. On the activities of the Charing Cross Vigilance and Rescue Committee, see *Lancet*, 26 July 1890, p. 187. On similar campaigns by American progressives, see Ruth Rosen, *The Lost Sisterhood: Prostitution in America, 1900–1918* (Baltimore: Johns Hopkins University Press, 1982).

25. Cited in Patricia Stubbs, *Women and Fiction: Feminism and the Novel, 1880–1920* (New York: Barnes & Noble, 1979), p. 55.

26. Merrick, *Work among the Fallen*, p. 48.

27. In nineteenth-century Ontario such offenses accounted for 87.7 percent of all female crime in 1865 and 63.0 percent in 1895. Only the occasional male brothel keeper or "frequenter" was prosecuted. Constance B. Backhouse, "Nineteenth-Century Canadian Prostitution Law: Reflection of a Discriminatory Society," *Histoire sociale/Social History* 18 (1985): 397–99. The

situation was not much different in the twentieth century; see Andrée Lévesque, *La norme et les déviances: Des femmes au Québec pendant l'entre deux guerres* (Montreal: Les éditions du remue-ménage, 1989), p. 94.

28. James Greenwood, *The Seven Curses of London* (London: Rivers, 1869), p. 275; E. M. Sigsworth and T. S. Wyke, "A Study of Victorian Prostitution and Venereal Disease," in Martha Vicinus, ed., *Suffer and Be Still: Women in the Victorian Age* (Bloomington: Indiana University Press, 1972), p. 79.

29. Shore, p. 93.

30. L Division, Eversfield Report, 13 April 1892, MEPO 3 144.

31. Shore, p. 73.

32. Emma Vowles Statement, 28 April 1892, MEPO 3 144.

33. Merrick, *Work among the Fallen*, pp. 14, 23, 25.

34. And on the high infant mortality rate of their children, see Merrick, *Work among the Fallen*, pp. 31, 34.

35. L Division to Scotland Yard, 16 April 1892, MEPO 3 144.

36. C.I.D., 21 April 1892, MEPO 3 144.

37. Charles Burdett, a member of the "theatrical profession," had heard of Marsh's seafaring friend two years previous when she lived on York Road. The description Burdett provided of the "sea captain"—5 feet 8 inches tall, forty to forty-five years of age, moustache, nose pincers, and high silk hat— sounded very much like Cream. Burdett Testimony, 6 May 1892, MEPO 3 144. Burdett, who lived at 79 Stamford Street, did not in fact identify Cream when he first saw him; two weeks later he did, and for this reason the police regarded his testimony as unsatisfactory; 19 May 1892, MEPO 3 144.

38. For an insightful discussion of this issue see Luise White, "Prostitutes, Reformers and Historians," *Criminal Justice History* 6 (1985): 207–11.

39. Ernest Linnell Deposition: CRIM 1/38/1.

40. Donworth Inquest, 16 October 1891, MEPO 3 144.

41. Shore, p. 123.

42. Charles Harvey Deposition: CRIM 1/38/1.

43. Donworth Inquest, 23 October 1891, MEPO 3 144.

44. Thomas Holmes, *Pictures and Problems from London Police Courts* (London: Edward Arnold, 1900), p. 25.

45. C.I.D., 14 October 1892, MEPO 3 144.

46. Frances Finnegan, *Poverty and Prostitution: A Study of Victorian Prostitutes in York* (Cambridge: Cambridge University Press, 1979), p. 53.

47. *Times*, 23 June 1892, p. 7d.

48. Edward J. Bristow, *Prostitutes and Prejudice: The Jewish Fight against White Slavery, 1870–1939* (Oxford: Clarendon, 1982), pp. 204–6.

49. Brighton Police to L Division, 9 and 13 April 1892, MEPO 3 144.

50. Lizzie Sullivan Statement, 26 May 1892, MEPO 3 144.

51. *Lloyd's Weekly London Newspaper*, 30 October 1892, p. 2.

52. Brighton Police to Scotland Yard, 21 April 1892, MEPO 3 144.

53. M. R. D. Foot and H. C. G. Matthew, eds., *The Gladstone Diaries* (Oxford: Clarendon, 1974), 3:xliv–xlviii.

54. *Pall Mall Gazette*, 21 October 1892, p. 1.

55. *Illustrated Police News*, 12 November 1892, p. 4.

56. For reports of a woman "who was leading an immoral life" having her throat cut and of another "of the unfortunate class" who was stabbed to death, see *Times*, 28 July 1890, p. 4d; *Lancet*, 21 March 1891, p. 690.

57. *Pall Mall Gazette*, 4 November 1889, p. 3.

58. *Montreal Daily Star*, 15 November 1892, p. 2.

59. *Lloyd's Weekly London Newspaper*, 30 October 1892, p. 2.

60. *St. James's Gazette*, 22 October 1892, p. 3.

61. Shore, p. 45.

62. Shore, p. 48.

63. Shore, p. 140.

64. Shore, p. 147.

65. *British Medical Journal* 2 (29 October 1892): 962. One is reminded that the Victorian reader of Bram Stoker's *Dracula* (1897) found the three deadly but alluring female vampires far more frightening than the count himself.

66. Holmes, *Pictures and Problems*, p. 25.

67. William Acton, *Prostitution Considered in Its Moral, Social, and Sanitary Aspects* (London: Churchill, 1857), pp. 126, 140; and on the "icon" of the prostitute see Sander Gilman, *Sexuality: An Illustrated History* (New York: John Wiley, 1989), pp. 231–49.

68. D. G. Halsted, *Doctor in the Nineties* (London: Christopher Johnson, 1959), p. 56. Deeming, according to Marshall Hall, murdered women because he believed they spread disease. Edward Marjoribanks, *The Life of Sir Edward Marshal Hall* (London: Gollancz, 1929), pp. 49–50.

69. Lucy Rose's secondhand report of Matilda Clover's dying statement was not offered as evidence in court. Lucy Rose Report, 29 April 1892, MEPO 3 144.

70. Only in the twentieth century would sympathetic portraits of prostitutes that viewed them as victims of circumstance appear. See Royden, *Downward Paths;* Mrs. Cecil Chesterton [née Ada Jones], *In Darkest London* (London: Stanley Paul, 1926).

71. On the risks of death run by prostitutes outside Britain, see Harsin, *Policing Prostitution*, pp. 166–67; Anne M. Butler, *Daughters of Joy, Sisters of Mercy* (Urbana: University of Illinois Press, 1985), p. 110; Barbara Meil Hobson, *Uneasy Virtue: The Politics of Prostitution and the American Reform Tradition* (New York: Basic Books, 1987), pp. 72–73.

72. Robert Anderson, *Criminals and Crime: Some Facts and Suggestions* (London: Nisbet, 1907), cited in Richard Whittington-Egan, *A Casebook on Jack the Ripper* (London: Wildly, 1975), p. 4.

CHAPTER 7

1. The *Lancet* regarded it as a "grim irony" that Mrs. McConville, who also sold abortifacients, thought she could avoid a conflict with the law by keeping accurate accounts of her profits for the benefit of the income tax commissioners. *Lancet*, 19 September 1896, p. 829.

2. Similar ploys were tried elsewhere. "Old Dr. Gordon's Pearls of Health,

or Female Regulators" came with the warning, "Not to be taken during first four months of pregnancy." *Victoria Daily Times,* 24 October 1892, p. 2.

3. The Medical Defense Union was in February 1892 preparing to press charges against Alfred Harcourt, the purveyor of Widow Winslow's Female Pills, but insisted that it would not lodge a prosecution unless any subsequent fines were paid to it to cover costs. Unqualified Practitioners, MEPO 3 149.

4. *Times,* 20 and 21 November 1899; CRIM 6: Madame Frain Trial; CRIM 9: Calendar of Prisoners; Madame Frain Trial; *British Medical Journal* 2 (2 December 1899): 1583–84; *Chemist and Druggist,* 23 October 1897, pp. 663–64.

5. Louisa Rebecca Fenn sold an apparently effective abortifacient mixture of aloes and iron on almost as large a scale as "Madame Frain." In 1897 the police found at her premises "hundreds of letters testifying to her [Fenn's] cure, or stating that the medicine had no effect, whilst in other letters people complained that they had no medicine. Counterfoils of two cheque-books showed that £600 had been paid to newspaper proprietors for advertisements during six months." *Chemist and Druggist,* 26 June 1897, p. 1004. See also ibid., 24 December 1898, p. 1011.

6. Joseph A. Banks, *Prosperity and Parenthood: A Study of Family Planning among the Victorian Middle Classes* (London: Routledge & Kegan Paul, 1954).

7. Curiously enough, the discussion of contraception was considered more shocking than many criminal acts. In France, which had the lowest birthrate in Europe, the "ladies covered their faces" when in open court a man denied paternity and stated, "I had taken precautions." Joëlle Guillais, *Crimes of Passion: Dramas of Private Life in Nineteenth-Century France,* Jane Dunnett, trans. (New York: Routledge, 1990), p. 124.

8. Rosanna Ledbetter, *A History of the Malthusian League, 1877–1927* (Columbus: Ohio State University Press, 1976).

9. *Clarion,* 13 February 1892, p. 4.

10. *Chemist and Druggist,* 10 July 1897, p. 64; Angus McLaren, *Birth Control in Nineteenth Century England* (London: Croom Helm, 1978), pp. 222–26.

11. MEPO 2 399: Infant Life Protection Act. Report of 27 April 1896 on Dead Bodies (Infants) for Year 1895.

12. Single pregnant women were particularly isolated. Those who continued their pregnancies and left their babies at the Thomas Coram Foundling Hospital frequently spoke of their lovers as either disappearing or attempting to force them to take abortifacients. John Gillis, *For Better, for Worse: British Marriages, 1600 to the Present* (New York: Oxford University Press, 1985), p. 238; Françoise Barret-Ducrocq, *L'amour sous Victoria: Sexualité et classes populaires à Londres au XIXe siècle* (Paris: Plon, 1989), pp. 170–73.

13. The handful of British doctors who supported birth control were listed in Charles R. Drysdale, *The Population Question* (London: Standring, 1892), pp. 74–84.

14. Jukes de Styrap, *The Young Practitioner* (London: H. K. Lewis, 1890), p. 52. See also John W. Taylor, *On the Diminishing Birth Rate* (London: British Gynaecological Society, 1904).

15. *Toronto Globe,* 29 October 1892, p. 1; *Montreal Daily Star,* 28 October 1892, p. 6.

16. Carl N. Degler, *At Odds: Women and the Family in America from the Revolution to the Present* (New York: Oxford, 1980), pp. 227–48.

17. Norman Barnesby, *Medical Chaos and Crime* (London: Mitchell Kennerley, 1910), pp. 222–23.

18. Angus McLaren, "Women's Work and the Regulation of Family Size: The Question of Abortion in the Nineteenth Century," *History Workshop* 4 (1977): 70–81.

19. *Lancet*, 1 January 1881, p. 15. See also Barbara Brookes, *Abortion in England, 1900–1967* (London: Croom Helm, 1988), 51–67.

20. Sir George Clark, *A History of the Royal College of Physicians of London* (Oxford: Clarendon, 1964–72), pp. 980–81.

21. *Lancet*, 29 March 1884, p. 578.

22. James Mohr, *Abortion in America: The Origins and Evolution of National Policy, 1800–1900* (New York: Oxford University Press, 1978); Carroll Smith-Rosenberg, "The Abortion Movement and the A.M.A., 1850–1880," in Carroll Smith-Rosenberg, ed., *Disorderly Conduct: Visions of Gender in Victorian America* New York: Knopf, 1985), pp. 217–44; John Keown, *Abortion, Doctors and the Law: Some Aspects of the Legal Regulation of Abortion in England from 1803 to 1982* (Cambridge: Cambridge University Press, 1988).

23. Kristin Luker, *Abortion and the Politics of Motherhood* (Berkeley: University of California Press, 1984), p. 39.

24. Angus McLaren, *Reproductive Rituals: The Perception of Fertility in England from the Sixteenth to the Nineteenth Century* (London: Methuen, 1984), pp. 113–44.

25. Mohr, *Abortion in América*, pp. 78–82.

26. Gerald Geoghegan, Cream's attorney, had in 1891 unsuccessfully defended a young man for attempting to procure a miscarriage. See *Times*, 19 December 1891, p. 12b.

27. Marsall Hall could be seen as indirectly responsible for his wife's death inasmuch as their deed of separation stipulated that she was only to receive maintenance as long as she led a chaste and virtuous life; *Times*, 12 June 1890, p. 4e; 11 July 1890, p. 13c. Edward Marjoribanks, *For the Defence: The Life of Sir Edward Marshall Hall* (New York: Macmillan, 1930), pp. 68–69.

28. Robert Roberts, *The Classic Slum: Salford Life in the First Quarter of the Century* (Manchester: Manchester University Press, 1971), p. 100.

29. "Quacks and Abortion: A Critical and Analytical Inquiry," *Lancet*, 10 December 1898, pp. 1570–71. See also "Report from the Joint Committee on Lotteries and Indecent Advertisements," *Parliamentary Papers* 9 (1908): 410–15, 457, 475.

30. *Chicago Tribune*, 29 August 1880, p. 4.

31. *Lancet*, 11 July 1891, pp. 80–81; *East London Advertiser*, 24 September 1898, p. 1; *Times*, 10 December 1898, p. 8d.

32. *Lancet*, 21 February 1891, pp. 463–64; *Times*, 13 November 1891, p. 9e; 28 March 1892, p. 7d; 16 May 1893, p. 3f; 25 November 1893, p. 11d.

33. *Times*, 7 December 1893, p. 9e; Lionel Rose, *The Massacre of the Innocents: Infanticide in Britain, 1800–1939* (London: Routledge & Kegan Paul, 1986), p. 87.

34. Gerald Geoghegan, Cream's counsel, defended in December 1892 Dr. George Francis, charged with an abortion-related death. *Times,* 5 December 1892, p. 14a.

35. Shore, p. 93; Frederick Jarvis Report, 19 July 1892, MEPO 3 144; John Wilson McCulloch Deposition: CRIM 1/38/1.

36. *Illustrated Police News,* 26 November 1892, p. 2.

37. Bertrand Russell and Patricia Russell, eds., *The Amberley Papers* (London: Hogarth, 1937), pp. 168–249.

38. Shore, p. 50.

39. Shore, pp. 54–55.

40. Shore, p. 130. See also *Pall Mall Gazette,* 20 October 1892.

41. The jury recommended mercy, but the judge insisted on the death penalty. *Lancet,* 15 July 1893, pp. 153–54.

42. Sir Sydney Smith, *Taylor's Principles and Practices of Medical Jurisprudence* (London: Churchill, 1951), 2:611.

43. Donald Rumbelow, *The Complete Jack the Ripper* (London: W. H. Allen, 1975), p. 227.

44. MEPO 3 140; and for an account of another woman's death from an illegal operation which a coroner's inquest ruled "willful murder by some person or persons unknown" see *Times,* 16 April 1891, p. 6d.

45. Sylvanus Stall, *What a Young Man Ought to Know* (Toronto: Briggs, 1897), p. 198.

46. George Napheys, *Physical Life of Women* (London: Homeopathic Publishing Co., 1869), p. 93; *The Transmission of Life: Counsels on the Nature and Hygiene of the Masculine Function* (Philadelphia: Fergus, 1872), p. 195.

47. Hugh H. Hodge, *Foeticide, or Criminal Abortion* (Philadelphia, Lindsay & Blackiston, 1869), p. 38.

48. William B. Ryan, *Infanticide: Its Law, Prevalence, Prevention and History* (London: Churchill, 1862), p. 152.

49. Thomas Radford, *The Value of the Embryonic and Foetal Life, Legally, Socially, and Obstetrically Considered* (London: British Record of Obstetrics, 1848), p. 10.

50. P. H. Chavasse, *Advice to a Wife* (Toronto: Musson, 1879), 1:119.

51. Mohr, *Abortion in America,* p. 105.

52. H. S. Pomeroy, *The Ethics of Marriage* (New York: Funk & Wagnalls, 1888), pp. 36, 65–69. The American antiabortion movement was spearheaded by Professor H. R. Storer, who in 1866 won the American Medical Association gold medal for an essay opposed to abortion entitled "Why Not? A book for Every Woman," which later appeared in expanded form as *On Criminal Abortion: Its Nature, Its Evidence, and Its Law* (Boston: Little, Brown, 1868). John Todd, *Serpents in the Dove's Nest* (Boston: Lee & Shepard, 1867), kept up the attack. See G. J. Barker-Benfield, *The Horrors of the Half-Known Life: Male Attitudes towards Women and Sexuality in Nineteenth Century America* (New York: Harper, 1976), pp. 203–5.

53. Emma F. Angell Drake, *What a Young Wife Ought to Know* (Toronto: Vir Publishing, 1908), pp. 123–24.

54. John Cowan, *The Science of the New Life* (New York: Cowan & Co., 1874), p. 109.

55. Augustus K. Gardner, *Conjugal Sins against the Laws of Life and Health* (New York: Stringer, 1874), pp. 180–81; Mervin N. Olasky, *The Press and Abortion, 1838–1988* (London: Erlbaum, 1988), pp. 24–32.

56. *Canadian Medical Association Journal* 12 (1922): 166.

57. Radford, *The Value of the Embryonic and Foetal Life*, p. 11.

58. *Canada Lancet*, December 1871, pp. 185–86; March 1889, pp. 217–18.

59. On earlier suspicions of obstetrics, see Roy Porter, "A Touch of Danger: The Man Midwife as Sexual Predator," in G. S. Rousseau and Roy Porter, eds., *Sexual Underworlds of the Enlightenment* (Manchester: Manchester University Press, 1987), pp. 206–32.

60. Ornella Moscucci, *The Science of Woman: Gynecology and Gender in England, 1800–1929* (Cambridge: Cambridge University Press, 1990), p. 134.

61. Elizabeth Blackwell, *The Human Element in Sex* (London: Churchill, 1885), pp. 15, 30, 56; and on the linked themes of the secrets of nature being unveiled and the woman dissected, see Ludmilla Jordanova, *Sexual Visions: Images of Gender in Science and Medicine between the Eighteenth and Twentieth Centuries* (Madison: University of Wisconsin Press, 1989), p. 99.

62. Some gynecologists believed that even women's mental problems could be surgically treated. See I. S. Stone, "Can the Gynaecologist Aid the Alienist?" *British Gynaecological Journal* 7 (1891–92): 272–82; and on excessive surgery in general, see Ann Dally, *Women under the Knife* (London: Radius, 1991).

63. By the turn of the century the Home Office was aware that incest was common. See Victor Bailey and Sheila Blackburn, "The Punishment of Incest Act, 1908: A Case Study of Law Creation," *Criminal Law Review* 1979:708–18.

64. C. H. F. Routh, "On the Etiology and Diagnosis, Considered Specially from a Medico-Legal Point of View, of Those Cases of Nymphomania Which Lead Women to Make False Charges against Their Medical Attendants," *British Gynaecological Journal* 2 (1887): 490.

65. Routh, "Nymphomania," p. 501.

66. Routh, "Nymphomania," p. 501. In 1864 Sir William Wilde, father of Oscar Wilde, was charged by Mary Travers with having given her chloroform and then raping her. Richard Ellmann, *Oscar Wilde* (Harmondsworth: Penguin, 1987), pp. 13–15. On the profession's fear that "naturally pure-minded women" when under anesthesia had "unfounded dreams" of being molested by their doctors, see Frederick J. Smith, *Lectures on Medical Jurisprudence and Toxicology* (London: Churchill, 1900), pp. 187–88.

67. Tait's chief work was *Diseases of Women and Abdominal Surgery* (Leicester: Richardson, 1889).

68. Tait actually cited a hundred cases despite the title of his published report. Lawson Tait, "An Analysis of the Evidence in 70 Consecutive Cases of Charges Made under the New Criminal Law Amendment Act," *Provincial Medical Journal*, 1 May 1894, p. 236. On Freud and continental discussions of

incest and child rape, see Jeffrey Moussaieff Masson, *The Assault on Truth: Freud's Suppression of the Seduction Theory* (New York: Viking, 1985).

69. A nurse's declaration that Tait was her child's father helped destroy his career. Was he thinking of his own problems when, in the midst of his essay on child rape, he told the story of a nurse who sought to blackmail a doctor by threatening to claim that he had seduced and then aborted her with ergot of rye? Tait, "An Analysis," p. 228; I. Harvey Flack, *Lawson Tait* (London: Heinemann, 1949), p. 114.

70. On the argument that the new nineteenth-century belief in the incommensurability of the sexes underlay the belief that the testicles were sacrosanct but that failed femininity should be surgically attacked, see Thomas Laqueur, *Making Sex: Body and Gender from the Greeks to Freud* (Cambridge, Mass.: Harvard University Press, 1990), pp. 175–76.

71. Wilkie Collins described Dr. Downward, the fictional abortionist, as follows: "If the expression may be pardoned, he was one of those carefully-constructed physicians, in whom the public—especially the female public—implicitly trust. He had the necessary bald head, the necessary double eyeglass, the necessary blandness of manner, all complete. His voice was soothing, his ways were deliberate, his smile was confidential. What particular branch of his profession Doctor Downward followed, was not indicated on his door-plate— but he had utterly mistaken his profession, if he was not a ladies' medical man." Wilkie Collins, *Armadale* (London: Dover, 1960 [1865]), p. 300. On America, see Barker-Benfield, *The Horrors of the Half-Known Life*, pp. 83–90.

72. Interestingly enough, the childless Tait, a devotee of blue Persian cats, was a fervent supporter of the antivivisection movement. See Lawson Tait, *The Uselessness of Vivisection* (London: Victoria Street Society, 1882); Richard D. French, *Antivivisection and Medical Science in Victorian Society* (Princeton: Princeton University Press, 1975); Mary Ann Elston, "Women and Antivivisection in Victorian England, 1870–1900," in Nicolas Rupke, ed., *Vivisection in Historical Perspective* (London: Croom Helm, 1987), pp. 259–94.

73. Cora Lansbury, "Gynecology, Pornography and Antivivisection," *Victorian Studies* 28 (1985): 424.

74. H. G. Wells provided the classic depiction of the experimental physiologist as torturer in *The Island of Dr. Moreau* (London: Heinemann, 1896), while George Bernard Shaw likened the vivisectors to contemporary terrorists; both destroyed while claiming to care. George Bernard Shaw, "The Dynamitards of Science," (1900) cited in Barbara Arnett Melchiori, *Terrorism in the Late Victorian Novel* (London: Croom Helm, 1985), p. 245; Coral Lansbury, *The Old Brown Dog: Women, Workers and Vivisection in Edwardian England* (Madison: University of Wisconsin Press, 1985), p. 142.

75. Richard D. Altick, *Victorian Studies in Scarlet* (New York: Norton, 1970), pp. 146–74.

76. Elaine Showalter, *The Female Malady: Women, Madness and English Culture, 1830–1980* (New York: Pantheon, 1985), p. 78.

77. J. M. P. Munaret, *Du médecin des villes et du médecin de campagne* (Paris: Baillière, 1840), p. 427.

78. Jukes de Styrap, *The Young Practitioner* (London: H. K. Lewis, 1890), p. 50.

79. John Reese, *Text-Book of Medical Jurisprudence and Toxicology* (Philadelphia: Blakiston, 1906), p. 214.

80. Professional confidentiality provided a warrant for doctors' toleration of lies of omission, for example, not warning a woman that her prospective spouse suffered from a venereal disease. See H. Montgomery Hyde, *A Tangled Web: Sex Scandals in British Politics and Society* (London: Constable, 1986), pp. 101–5; Gail Savage, "The Willful Communication of a Loathsome Disease: Marital Conflict and Venereal Disease in Victorian England," *Victorian Studies* 34 (1990): 35–54; Jill Harsin, "Syphilis, Wives and Physicians: Medical Ethics and the Family in Late Nineteenth-Century France," *French Historical Studies* 16 (1989): 72–95.

81. But some magistrates were. In one case a doctor, when approached by a couple seeking abortifacients, immediately alerted the police. On their advice he provided a useless drug. Upon taking it, they were arrested for committing a felony and at the trial had to face the doctor, who appeared as both an informer and a medical expert. The presiding judge found such entrapment disquieting; in his opinion it was not the doctor's duty to act as a detective. A. S. Taylor, *A Manual of Medical Jurisprudence* (New York: Lea, 1897), p. 552. Similarly Mr. Justice Henry Hawkins made it clear in *Kitson v. Playfair* (1896) that medical men were not bound to provide evidence given in confidence. *Times*, 26 March 1896, p. 13d; Stanley B. Atkinson, *The Law in General Practice: Some Chapters in Every-Day Forensic Medicine* (London: Froude, 1908), pp. 97–98.

82. It was not so much what was done as who decided that was significant. Take the case of the doctor who performed surgery on an unmarried woman, discovered her to be pregnant, and in the "natural course" of the operation terminated the pregnancy but never told her. Such a scenario was envisaged by one expert in medical jurisprudence who cautioned the young doctor, "He must decline to relieve, under anaesthetic, a wedding-ringless young woman of the shame as yet unknown to herself." Atkinson, *The Law in General Practice*, p. 147.

83. A number of other nineteenth-century murderers were involved in abortion. When such an operation was forced underground, it could obviously be exploited by those who wished to kill. In 1879 Rev. Anthony Hayden was accused of giving his pregnant servant Mary Stannard arsenic, which he claimed was "quick medicine." Dr. William Palmer, the famous poisoner executed in 1856, recommended abortion to a friend. Dr. Edward Pritchard, in 1865 the last man to be executed in public in Scotland, induced a miscarriage in a seduced servant girl. Dr. Thomas Smethurst, tried in 1859 for murdering his six- to seven-weeks-pregnant mistress, had probably given her an overdose of some poison meant to abort. John Christie, the most infamous of the post–World War II English serial murderers, ultimately charged with six murders, was known as the "local abortionist" and used his purported expertise to lure women to his home. Colin Wilson and Patricia Pitman, *Encyclopedia*

of Murder (London: Barker, 1961), pp. 267–68; George H. Knott, ed., *Trial of William Palmer* (London: Hodge, 1912), p. 14; William Roughead, ed., *Trial of Dr. Pritchard* (London: Hodge, 1906), p. 102; Leonard A. Parry, ed., *Trial of Dr. Smethurst* (Toronto: Canada Law Book Co., 1931), pp. 23–24; F. Tennyson Jesse, ed., *Trials of Timothy John Evans and John Reginald Halliday Christie* (London: Hodge, 1957), pp. 62–66.

CHAPTER 8

1. A sense of the emotional nature of the trial can be gained by comparing the disdainful dismissal of the claims of the "slaughterman of Wagga Wagga" in Ernest H. Coleridge, *Life and Correspondence of John, Duke Lord Coleridge* (London: Heinemann, 1904), 2:178–98, with Dr. E. V. Kenealey, *The Trial at Bar of Sir Roger C. D. Tichborne* (London: "Englishman" Office, 1875).

2. Another of Mayer's dodges was to offer to set the woman up in a flat in St. John's Wood. The most incredible aspect of this case was that Adolph Beck, an innocent but slow-witted man who bore some resemblance to Mayer, served two prison terms for the latter's crimes. See MEPO 3 154/155; Eric R. Watson, ed., *Adolph Beck, 1877–1904* (Edinburgh: Hodge, 1925).

3. Self-interested deception is about all that links the infinite forms of fraud. See Frederick Moncrief, *A Treatise on the Law Relating to Fraud and Misrepresentation* (London: Stevens & Sons, 1891); Sydney Edward Williams, *Kerr on Fraud and Mistake* (London: Sweet & Maxwell, 1929).

4. Dickens, Thackeray, and Trollope all provided fictional portrayals of shady businessmen. See Norman Russell, *The Novelist and Mammon: Literary Responses to the World of Commerce in the Nineteenth Century* (Oxford: Clarendon, 1986).

5. Robert Sindall, "Middle-Class Crime in Nineteenth-Century England," *Criminal Justice History* 4 (1983): 23–40; Karen Halttunen, *Confidence Men and Painted Women: A Study of Middle-Class Culture in America, 1830–1870* (New Haven: Yale University Press, 1982), pp. 206–10.

6. MEPO 3 157.

7. Buckland claimed to have seen a letter regarding the boys' activities written by the Earl de la Warr.

8. Sarah Rachel Leverson, who in the 1860s ran an establishment that was part Mayfair beauty salon, part house of assignation, was perhaps the most notorious nineteenth-century female blackmailer. See William Roughead, *Bad Companions* (Edinburgh: Green, 1930), pp. 33–73; Elizabeth Jenkins, *Six Criminal Women* (London: Pan, 1949), pp. 9–33; Kellow Chesney, *The Anti-Society: An Account of the Victorian Underworld* (Boston: Gambit, 1970), pp. 239–41.

9. Frank Pimm Interview, 21 April 1892, MEPO 3 144. In some of the police reports his name appears as "Pymm."

10. Leonore Davidoff, *The Best Circles: Society, Etiquette and the Season* (London: Croom Helm, 1973).

11. Leon Radzinowicz, *A History of English Criminal Law* (London: Steven, 1978), 1:73–74, 308, 641.

12. Mike Hepworth, *Blackmail: Publicity and Secrecy in Everyday Life* (London: Routledge & Kegan Paul, 1975), pp. 7, 14, 16; Randolph Trumbach,

"London's Sodomites: Homosexual Behavior and Western Culture in the Eighteenth Century," *Journal of Social History* 2 (1977): 20–21.

13. For eighteenth-century attempts to extort money with the threat of using a sodomy charge, see Randolph Trumbach, ed., *Sodomy Trials: Seven Documents* (New York: Garland, 1986).

14. In the eighteenth century blackmail was only a misdemeanor punishable by seven years of transportation (deportation to the American colonies); in the nineteenth it was punished severely with up to a life sentence and whipping. The Libel Act of 1843 recognized the dangers posed by those publishing, "or threatening to publish, or proposing to abstain or prevent from publishing, a libel in order to extort money or some other valuable thing." The Larceny Act of 1916 pulled together the collection of statutes dealing with "threats" and "menaces," but in fact no crime officially known as "blackmail" existed until the 1968 Theft Act. See W. H. D. Winder, "The Development of Blackmail," *Modern Law Review* 5 (1941): 21–49.

15. Arthur Conan Doyle, "Charles Augustus Milverton," in *The Penguin Complete Sherlock Holmes* (Harmondsworth: Penguin, 1981), p. 581. Conan Doyle was much influenced by Emile Gaboriau (1832–73), the father of French detective fiction, who wrote *Le dossier no 113*, translated into English as *The Blackmailers*. See Roger Bonniot, *Emile Gaboriau, ou la naissance du roman policier* (Paris: Vrin, 1985).

16. Coincidentally Pigott, while in London, stayed as Cream would do in Anderton's Hotel, Fleet Street. The *Times*, in order to establish that Parnell was indeed the author of the forged letters, enlisted the support of George Smith Inglis, the Home Office's handwriting expert, who also participated in the Cream investigation in June 1892. *The History of the "Times": The Twentieth Century Test, 1884–1912* (London: Times, 1977), 3:43–79.

17. *Times*, 14 December 1905, p. 3. The blackmail theme was first exploited in Nathaniel Hawthorne, *The Scarlet Letter* (1850), and taken up in Wilkie Collins, *The Woman in White* (1860), Anthony Trollope, *Castle Richmond* (1860), Mary Elizabeth Braddon's two novels, *Lady Audley's Secret* (1862) and *Aurora Floyd* (1863), and several of George Eliot's works. See Alexander Welsh, *George Eliot and Blackmail* (Cambridge, Mass.: Harvard University Press, 1985).

18. Quoted by George Ives, who attacked the new puritanical laws as creating blackmailers and pointed out that since only the unsuccessful were exposed the vast majority escaped detection; the higher the position in society enjoyed by the victim, the more strenuous would be their attempts to keep scandal hidden. Ives, born illegitimately in Germany in 1867, was the leader of a homosexual society—the Order of Chaeronea—and a friend of Oscar Wilde, Lord Alfred Douglas, and Edward Carpenter. See George Ives, *A History of Penal Methods* (London: Stanley Paul, 1914), pp. 353–56; Jeffrey Weeks, *Coming Out: Homosexual Politics in Britain from the Nineteenth Century to the Present* (London: Quartet, 1977), pp. 118–24.

19. But even in France the classic ruse of the criminal claiming his victim was a pederast was common. See Eugen Weber, *France, Fin-de-siècle* (Cambridge, Mass.: Harvard University Press, 1988), p. 37, n. 34.

20. One might have expected Labouchère to have been more sensitive to

invasions of privacy. Living unmarried with the actress Henrietta Hodson, he was greeted during the 1868 election campaign by the cry, "'Ows 'Enrietta?" See Eric Trudgill, *Madonnas and Magdalens: The Origins and Development of Victorian Sexual Attitudes* (London: Heinemann, 1976), p. 199.

21. See *Times*, 6 August 1886, p. 7e.

22. This was still the case in the twentieth century. A study carried out by the German sexologist Magnus Hirschfeld found that three thousand of ten thousand homosexuals had been victimized by blackmailers. Of seventy-one cases of blackmail reported to the police in England and Wales in the 1950–53 period, thirty-two related to homosexual activities. See Charlotte Wolfe, *Magnus Hirschfeld: A Portrait of a Pioneer in Sexology* (London: Quartet Books, 1986), pp. 63–67; Havelock Ellis, *Studies in the Psychology of Sex* (New York: Random House, 1936), 2:91; Charles Berg, *Fear, Punishment, Anxiety and the Wolfenden Report* (London: George Allen, 1959), p. 26.

23. H. Montgomery Hyde, *The Cleveland Street Scandal* (London: Allen, 1976); James Lees-Milne, *Harold Nicolson, 1930–68* (London: Chatto & Windus, 1981), 2:231.

24. Richard Ellmann, *Oscar Wilde* (Harmondsworth: Penguin, 1987), pp. 362, 367, 416, 420, 426–27, 432.

25. *Times*, 8 May 1895, p. 4f.

26. MEPO 3 152.

27. MEPO 3 152.

28. For a fuller account of the Chrimes case see *Times*, 17 December 1898, p. 14e; 19 December 1898, p. 14b; 20 December 1898, p. 9d; 21 December 1898, p. 12c; Angus McLaren, *Birth Control in Nineteenth Century England* (London: Croom Helm, 1978), pp. 231–40.

29. The Indecent Advertisements Act of 1889 made "any advertisement relating to syphilis, gonorrhea, nervous debility, or other complaint or infirmity arising from or relating to sexual intercourse" an indecent publication. Samuel Hynes, *The Edwardian Turn of Mind* (Princeton: Princeton University Press, 1968), p. 256.

30. The classic French treatise on the subject was Paul Brouardel, *Le secret médical* (Paris: Baillière, 1887).

31. Cited in Welsh, *George Eliot and Blackmail*, p. 73.

32. Is the landlord who threatens to throw the tenant out unless the rent is paid or the doctor who withholds services until higher fees are offered an extortionist? No, because in a capitalist system what they are doing is legal. On the question of whether capitalism is itself a form of blackmail see Jeffrey G. Murphy, "Blackmail: A Preliminary Inquiry," *Monist* 63 (1980): 156–71; Eric Mack, "In Defense of Blackmail," *Philosophical Studies* 41 (1982): 273–8.

33. On Inspector Tunbridge's entrapment of a Blanchard Street seller of obscene prints, see *Times*, 5 November 1891, p. 4b; on the general problem, see Edwin M. Schur, *Our Criminal Society* (Englewood Cliffs: Prentice-Hall, 1969), pp. 192–96; Schur, *Crimes without Victims* (Englewood Cliffs: Prentice-Hall, 1965).

34. D. J. D. Perrin, "Thomas Neill Cream," *St. Thomas's Hospital Gazette* 47 (1949): 229–32.

35. Among the first problems discussed by the British Society for the Study of Sex Psychology (organized in 1914) was "the wide-spread existence of blackmail which takes criminal advantage of the law as it now stands." Hynes, *The Edwardian Turn of Mind,* p. 160.

CHAPTER 9

1. Straight was mistaken; the last jury of matrons was struck in the 1879 trial of Catherine Webster.

2. *Pall Mall Gazette,* 24 October 1892, p. 2. See also James C. Oldham, "On Pleading the Belly: A History of the Jury of Matrons," *Criminal Justice History* 6 (1985): 1–64.

3. John Laurence, *A History of Capital Punishment* (London: Sampson Low, 1963), p. 24.

4. Raymond Villey, *Histoire du secret médical* (Paris: Seghers, 1986).

5. Shore, p. 133.

6. Francis Coppin's father had previously owned the practice that Dr. McCarthy took over; *Times,* 24 June 1892, p. 12a.

7. Because of his "good character," Graham was apparently not prosecuted for furnishing Matilda Clover's faulty death certificate. See *Lancet,* 21 January 1893, pp. 153–54; Shore, pp. 77–79.

8. See 15 March 1893, 19 June 1893, MEPO 3 149.

9. Robert Forbes, *Sixty Years of Medical Defense* (London: Medical Defense Union, 1948), pp. 1–16.

10. See 2 March 1893, 23 March 1893, 21 June 1893, MEPO 3 149. Dr. Henry Slade, a spiritualist medium, was prosecuted in 1876; *South London Chronicle,* 28 October 1876.

11. See 17 April 1893, 13 March 1894, 12 January 1897, MEPO 3 149.

12. "Unqualified Medical Practitioners," MEPO 3 149.

13. Shore, p. 48.

14. William Roughead, ed., *Trial of Dr. Pritchard* (London: Hodge, 1906), p. 148.

15. *British Medical Journal* 2 (9 September 1893): 593.

16. Virginia Berridge, "Morality and Medical Science: Concepts of Narcotic Addiction in Britain, 1820–1926," *Annals of Science* 36 (1979): 67–85; *British Medical Journal* 2 (15 July 1893): 142.

17. *British Medical Journal* 2 (7 December 1893): 802.

18. *Lancet,* 7 May 1892, pp. 1040–41; 20 May 1893, pp. 1213–14. On Freud's use of cocaine, see Eugen Weber, *France, Fin-de-siècle* (Cambridge, Mass.: Harvard University Press, 1989), p. 32.

19. Virginia Berridge and Griffith Edwards, *Opium and the People: Opiate Use in Nineteenth-Century England* (London: Allen Lane, 1981); Terry M. Parssinen, *Secret Passion, Secret Remedies: Narcotic Drugs in British Society, 1820–1930* (Philadelphia: I.S.H.I., 1983).

20. Shore, p. 83; Frederick Jarvis Report, 19 July 1892, MEPO 3 144.

21. *Pall Mall Gazette,* 22 October 1892, p. 2; George H. Knott, ed., *Trial of William Palmer* (London: Hodge, 1912); *Times,* 15–28 March 1856.

22. G. Lantham Browne and C. G. Stewart, *Reports of Trials for Murder by Poisoning* (London: Stevens, 1883); and on the decline of poisonings, see Jean-Claude Chesnais, *Histoire de la violence en Occident de 1800 à nos jours* (Paris: Laffont, 1981), p. 93.

23. Norbert Kohl, *Oscar Wilde: The Works of a Conformist Rebel* (Cambridge: Cambridge University Press, 1989), pp. 116–19. See also Thomas de Quincey, "On Murder Considered as One of the Fine Arts," in *Collected Writings* (Edinburgh: Adam & Charles Black, 1889–90), 13:9–64.

24. Oscar Wilde, "Pen, Pencil and Poison," in H. Montgomery Hyde, ed., *The Annotated Oscar Wilde* (London: Orbis, 1982), p. 396.

25. Sherlock Holmes was introduced to the reading public in a tale in which a professor's lecture on poisons inspires the culprit; Arthur Conan Doyle, *A Study in Scarlet* (1887).

26. Marshall Hall also claimed that he once defended Cream against a charge of bigamy and years later came to the conclusion that Cream had a double. But Hall could not have defended such a case; he was only admitted to the bar in 1883, by which time Cream was in Joliet State Prison. Edward Marjoribanks, *The Life of Sir Edward Marshall Hall* (London: Gollancz, 1929), pp. 20, 47.

27. *Reg. v. Silas Barlow, alias Silas Smith,* CCC November 1876.

28. Shore, p. 87.

29. Given the fact that household cleansers were often toxic, that many patent medicines contained morphine, chloroform, and other hazardous ingredients, and that patent medicines were often improperly labeled, it was inevitable that numerous accidental and self-administered poisonings would also result. See Olive Anderson, *Suicide and Edwardian England* (Oxford: Clarendon, 1987), pp. 362–67.

30. The vast majority of poisonings were accidental. The 1891 annual report of the Registrar for England and Wales noted that only 5 of 876 poisoning deaths were classed as homicides. *British Medical Journal* 1 (28 January 1893): 191–92.

31. C.I.D., 6 September 1892, MEPO 3 144.

32. Frederick Jarvis Report, 12 September 1892, MEPO 3 144.

33. Scotland was more advanced. See M. Anne Crowther and Brenda White, *On Soul and Conscience: The Medical Expert: One Hundred and Fifty Years of Forensic Medicine in Glasgow* (Aberdeen: Aberdeen University Press, 1988).

34. J. D. J. Harvard, *The Detection of Secret Homicide* (London: Macmillan, 1960), pp. 38–48.

35. *British Medical Journal* 1 (26 March 1892): 669–70; 1 (11 February 1893): 310.

36. The medically trained, such as Charles Lyddon, a Canterbury medical student who in 1890 poisoned his step-brother Dr. William Lyddon, presumably knew more than most about how such noxious substances might be surreptitiously administered. *Times,* 24 December 1890, p. 4f.

37. Leonard A. Parry, ed., *Trial of Dr. Smethurst* (Toronto: Canada Law Book Co., 1931).

38. William Roughead, ed., *Trial of Dr. Pritchard* (Glasgow: Hodge, 1906), p. 149.

39. *Times,* 9 October 1891, p. 10f.

40. Thirty-nine of the fifty-five criminal poisonings committed in the Department of the Seine in the 1870s were carried out by women. See Joelle Guillais, *Crimes of Passion: Dramas of Private Life in Nineteenth-Century France* (New York: Routledge, 1990), p. 16; A. Lacassagne, "Notes statistiques sur l'empoisonnement criminel en France," *Archives d'anthropologie criminelles et sciences pénale* 1 (1886): 260–64.

41. A spate of poisonings in the late 1840s led to legislation in 1850 restricting the sale of arsenic; Thomas Forbes, *Surgeons at the Bailey: English Forensic Medicine to 1878* (New Haven: Yale University Press, 1985), p. 131. For an attempt by pharmacists to use the Cream trial to push for further restrictions on the sales of poisons see *Pharmaceutical Journal,* 22 October 1892, pp. 300, 309, 327.

42. Mary S. Hartman, *Victorian Murderesses* (New York; Schocken, 1977), pp. 5–6; Patrick Wilson, *Murderess* (London: Michael Joseph, 1971).

43. Richard S. Lambert, *When Justice Failed: A Study of Nine Peculiar Murder Trials* (London: Methuen, 1935), pp. 113–36.

44. *Cox's Criminal Law Cases* 15 (1884): 403.

45. Only enormous public sympathy saved her from execution; Hartman, *Victorian Murderesses,* pp. 286–90.

46. *Times,* 27 February 1890, p. 5f.

47. *Times,* 26 September 1891, p. 6a; 21 December 1891, p. 10e.

CHAPTER 10

1. Carlo Ginzberg, "Morelli, Freud and Sherlock Holmes: Clues and Scientific Method," *History Workshop Journal* 9 (1980): 7–36.

2. Julian Symons, *Bloody Murder: From the Detective Story to the Crime Novel* (London: Penguin, 1974); Ian Ousby, *Bloodhounds of Heaven: The Detective in English Fiction from Godwin to Doyle* (Cambridge, Mass.: Harvard University Press, 1976); D. H. Miller, *The Novel and the Police* (Berkeley: University of California Press, 1988).

3. W. H. Smith was purportedly earning forty thousand pounds a year in the 1870s. The firm's refusal to stock titles it found objectionable won it, in the twentieth century, *Private Eye*'s sobriquet of "W. H. Smug." See *South London Chronicle,* 30 September 1876; Colin Watson, *Snobbery with Violence: Crime Stories and Their Audience* (New York: St. Martins, 1971).

4. N. H. Avison, "Criminal Statistics as Social Indicators," in A. Schonfield and S. Shaw, eds., *Social Indicators and Social Policy* (London: Heinemann, 1972), pp. 33–52.

5. Richard D. Altick, *Victorian Studies in Scarlet* (New York: Norton, 1970), p. 10; and for a contemporary lament that in the colorless and monoto-

nous nineteenth century even murders were becoming passionless, see Leslie Stephen, "The Decay of Murder," *Cornhill Magazine* 20 (1869): 722–33.

6. Roland Marx, *Jack L'Eventreur et les fanatasmes victoriens* (Paris: Editions complexe, 1988); Mary Kilbourne Matossian, "Death in London," *Journal of Interdisciplinary History* 16 (1985): 195.

7. On the role of such literature in depoliticizing crime, see David Ray Papke, *Framing the Criminal: Crime, Cultural Work and the Loss of Critical Perspective, 1830–1900* (New York: Archon, 1987).

8. Jennifer Davis, "The London Garotting Panic of 1862: A Moral Panic and the Creation of a Criminal Class in Mid-Victorian England," in V. A. C. Gatrell, B. Lenman, and G. Parker, eds., *Crime and the Law: The Social History of Crime in Western Europe since 1500* (London: Europa, 1980), pp. 190–213.

9. Stanley H. Palmer, *Police and Protest in England and Ireland, 1780–1850* (Cambridge: Cambridge University Press, 1988).

10. Christopher Andrew, *Secret Service: The Making of the British Intelligence Community* (London: Heinemann, 1985), p. 16.

11. Andrew Landsowne, *A Life's Reminiscences of Scotland Yard* (London: Leadenhall, 1890), p. 13; T. A. Critchley, *A History of the Police in England and Wales, 900–1966* (London: Constable, 1967), p. 161.

12. S. H. Jeyes and F. D. How, *The Life of Sir Howard Vincent* (London: George Allen, 1912), pp. 53–67.

13. *Times*, 25 November 1880, p. 11e.

14. *Times*, 13 December 1880, p. 4a.

15. *Times*, 17 December 1880, p. 9b.

16. *Times*, 18 December 1880, p. 12a.

17. *Times*, 14 December 1880, p. 9a.

18. The precedent to which Harcourt referred was the conviction in 1871 of Charles de Badderley and his wife, Sarah, for supplying ergot of rye with the intent to cause miscarriage. A woman was sent by the Detective Department of Scotland Yard to say her niece required an abortion. A letter from the "niece" was prepared by an inspector. Madame de Badderley's ingenious idea of posing as a clairvoyant and giving her advice while in a trance failed to protect her from prosecution. *Times*, 17 June 1871, p. 12b; 23 June 1871, p. 11d; 17 July 1871, p. 13b.

19. During the 1897 trial of Louisa Fenn, the press carried the disconcerting report that "Sergeant Crooke, who had posed as Miss Florence Bluett, a person in the family way, was the purchaser of the medicines and gave evidence." Presumably the sergeant did not go in drag but merely corresponded with Fenn; whether he sought Home Office approval was not stated. *Chemist and Druggist*, 26 June 1897, p. 1004.

20. *Parliamentary Debates* 257 (11 January 1881): 442–444; *Times*, 12 January 1881, p. 6b. On poor communications between the Home Office and Scotland Yard during the Ripper investigations, see William Vincent, "The Whitechapel Murders," *Police Review*, 6 January 1978, pp. 16–17.

21. *Times*, 14 March 1881, p. 9c.

22. David A. T. Stafford, "Spies and Gentlemen: The Birth of the British Spy Novel, 1893–1914," *Victorian Studies* 24 (1981): 489–509.

23. K. R. M. Short, *The Dynamite War: Irish Bombers in Victorian Britain* (Atlantic Hylands, N.J.: Humanities Press, 1979), p. 23.

24. Bernard Porter, *The Origins of the Vigilant State: The London Metropolitan Police Special Branch before the First World War* (London: Weidenfeld & Nicolson, 1987).

25. Lieutenant-Colonel Leon Vohl had served with the "Voltigeurs de Quebec" Ninth Battalion Rifles. See *The Militia List of the Dominion of Canada* (Ottawa: Queens Printer, 1891).

26. Cream reciprocated by sending Vohl some neckties from his favorite Holborn shop. Frederick Jarvis Report, 29 July 1892, MEPO 3 144.

27. *Pall Mall Gazette*, 19 October 1892.

28. Thomas M. Beach, *Twenty-Five Years in the Secret Service: The Recollections of a Spy* (London: E.P. Publishing, 1974 [1893]). Beach later completed his medical studies in Detroit and practiced medicine in Wilmington, Illinois.

29. Le Caron, in betraying the Fenian's plan for an 1870 invasion of Canada, communicated with the Canadian chief commissioner of police, Gilbert McMicken. See *Dictionary of Canadian Biography* 12:675–79. See also Robert Anderson, *The Lighter Side of My Official Life* (London: Hodder & Stoughton, 1910), pp. 95–96.

30. F. S. L. Lyons, *Charles Stewart Parnell* (London: Collins, 1977), pp. 155–56, 415–16.

31. J. A. Cole, *Prince of Spies: Henri Le Caron* (London: Faber & Faber, 1984), p. 176. The *Times* provided a pension for Le Caron in return for his revealing himself; after testifying, he once again went underground, dying five years later.

32. Littlechild was used to dealing with police spies, or "narks," such as Haynes. See John George Littlechild, *The Reminiscences of Chief Inspector Littlechild* (London: Leadenhall Press, 1894), p. 96.

33. Scotland Yard, 19 May 1892, MEPO 3 144. See also J. B. Tunbridge Report, 28 May 1892, MEPO 3 144.

34. C.I.D., 26 September 1892, MEPO 3 144.

35. Treasury to C.I.D., 28 June 1892, MEPO 3 144.

36. *Reynold's Newspaper*, 10 February 1895, p. 5.

37. Rupert Allason, *The Branch: A History of the Metropolitan Police Special Branch, 1883–1983* (London: Secker & Warburg, 1983), pp. 10–12. See also John Sweeney, *At Scotland Yard* (London: Grant Richards, 1904), pp. 127–29.

38. Bernard Porter, *Origins of Britain's Political Police*, Warick Working Paper in Social History, no. 3 (1985): 20.

39. Hermia Oliver, *The International Anarchist Movement in Late Victorian England* (London: Croom Helm, 1983), p. 75.

40. *Times*, 1, 2, 4, 5, 21, 27 April, 7 May 1892; John Quayle, *The Slow Burning Fuse: The Lost History of British Anarchists* (London: Paladin, 1978), pp. 103–43; Laurence Thompson, *The Enthusiasts: A Biography of John and Katherine Bruce Glasier* (London: Gollancz, 1971), pp. 50–51.

41. On the "providential" nature of the Walsall plot, see Bernard Porter, *Plots and Paranoia: A History of Political Espionage in Britain, 1790–1988* (London: Unwin & Hyman, 1989), pp. 113–14.

42. Chief Inspector Littlechild led the raid. See *Commonweal*, 27 February, 5 March, 2 April, 9 April, 16 April, 23 April 1892.

43. *Reynolds Newspaper*, 24 April 1892, p. 5. William Morris, who had withdrawn from the Socialist League and *Commonweal* in 1890, privately stated that D. J. Nicoll's article was a stupid invitation for police retaliation. J. W. Mackail, *The Life of William Morris* (London: Longmans, 1899), 2:237.

44. Paul Avrich, *Anarchist Portraits* (Princeton: Princeton University Press, 1988), pp. 153–61; and for pictures of Mowbray and Nicoll, see *Penny Illustrated Paper*, 7 May 1892, p. 294.

45. McIntyre's series appeared in *Reynolds Newspaper* between 3 March and 26 May 1895.

46. *Lloyd's Weekly London Newspaper*, 22 May 1892, p. 1.

47. *Clarion*, 2 July 1892, p. 5.

48. But the theme of anarchist attacks was also exploited by Jack London and Robert Louis Stephenson. See Barbara Arnett Melchiori, *Terrorism in the Late Victorian Novel* (London: Croom Helm, 1985).

49. Phyllis Grosskurth, *Havelock Ellis: A Biography* (Toronto: McClelland & Stewart, 1980), pp. 191–94.

50. Sweeney had also participated in the arrest of Nicoll in 1892. See Sweeney, *At Scotland Yard*, pp. 176–88; Oliver, *The International Anarchist Movement*, p. 145.

51. Andrew, *Secret Service*, p. 20; Vincent Brome, *Havelock Ellis, Philosopher of Sex: A Biography* (London: Routledge & Kegan Paul, 1979), pp. 101–2.

52. Bernard Porter, *The Origins of the Vigilant State* (London: Weidenfeld & Nicolson, 1989).

53. Israel Zangwill, in presenting an ex-detective as a diabolically skilled murderer, reflected this dawning suspicion of authority. See *The Big Ben Mystery* (London: Heinemann, 1913 [1903]); Beth Kalikoff, *Murder and Moral Decay in Victorian Popular Literature* (Ann Arbor: UMI, 1986), pp. 161–63.

54. The grudging respect police and professional criminals had for each other was noted by the head of Scotland Yard; by a "good burglar" the police meant a successful one. This same line of reasoning explains why a picture of Cream's execution in the *Illustrated Police News* was entitled, "Closing Scenes in the Career of a Great Criminal." Robert Anderson, *Criminals and Crime: Some Facts and Suggestions* (London: Nisbet, 1907), p. vi; *Illustrated Police News*, 19 November 1892, p. 1.

CHAPTER 11

1. John D. Davies, *Phrenology: Fad and Science: A Nineteenth-Century American Crusade* (New Haven: Yale University Press, 1955), p. 98.

2. On Fowler, see Roger Cooter, ed., *Phrenology in the British Isles: An Annotated, Historical Bibliography and Index* (Metuchen, N.J.: Scarecrow Press, 1989).

3. Despite the fact that every London police court missionary—a sort of early social worker—had had his head measured by a phrenologist, the police turned down both requests and were particularly unsympathetic to Thorburn, whom they labeled an "advertising quack." See HO 144/246 A 54360/13, 18; Thomas Holmes, *Pictures and Problems from London Police Courts* (London: Edward Arnold, 1900), p. 1. But such phrenological charts of famous criminals were common. A cast of Dr. Pritchard's head was taken immediately after his execution in 1865, and charts were done of Guiteau, who in 1881 murdered President James Garfield. See William Roughead, ed., *Trial of Dr. Pritchard* (Glasgow: Hodge, 1906), p. 45; Charles E. Rosenberg, *The Trial of the Assassin Guiteau* (Chicago: University of Chicago Press, 1978), frontispiece.

4. Wells was perhaps thinking of the essay by Havelock Ellis, "The Ear of the Criminal," *Lancet*, 25 January 1890, p. 189; H. G. Wells, *Mankind in the Making* (London: Chapman & Hall, 1903), p. 53.

5. For similar developments in France, see Robert A. Nye, Crime, *Madness and Politics in Modern France: The Medical Concept of National Decline* (Princeton: Princeton University Press, 1984).

6. Michael Ignatieff, *A Just Measure of Pain: The Penitentiary in the Industrial Revolution, 1750–1850* (New York: Pantheon, 1978).

7. J. E. Thomas, *The English Prison Officer since 1850: A Study in Conflict* (London: Routledge & Kegan Paul, 1972).

8. Bruce Thompson, "The Hereditary Nature of Crime," *Journal of Mental Science* 15 (1870): 487–95.

9. E. Ray Lankester, *Degeneration: A Chapter in Darwinism* (London: Macmillan, 1880), pp. 58ff.

10. B. A. Morel, *Traité des dégénérescences physiques, intellectuelles et morales de l'espèce humaine* (Paris: Baillière, 1857); Ruth Harris, *Murders and Madness: Medicine, Law and Society in the Fin de Siècle* (Oxford: Clarendon, 1989), p. 40; Pierre Darmon, *Médecins et assassins à la belle époque* (Paris: Seuil, 1989).

11. In the United States the argument was also made that lawyers had "failed" to end crime; it was now the doctors' turn to try. Larry K. Hartsfield, *The American Response to Professional Crime, 1870–1917* (Westport, Conn.: Greenwood Press, 1985), pp. 162–73.

12. Cesare Lombroso, cited in Nye, *Crime*, pp. 99–100.

13. David Garland, "British Criminology before 1935," in Paul Rock, ed., *A History of British Criminology* (Oxford: Clarendon, 1988), pp. 1–17.

14. Martin J. Wiener, *Reconstructing the Criminal: Culture, Law and Policy in England, 1830–1914* (Cambridge: Cambridge University Press, 1990), pp. 232–34.

15. William Osler, "On the Brains of Criminals," *Canadian Medical Association Journal* 10 (1882): 385; and on the measuring of Deeming's head, see *Times*, 13 April 1892, p. 10d.

16. Henry Maudsley, *Responsibility in Mental Disease* (London: Henry S. King, 1874), pp. 123, 229; *The Pathology of Mind* (London: Macmillan, 1879), p. 333.

17. Maudsley, *Responsibility in Mental Disease*, p. 163.

18. D. W. Forrest, *Francis Galton: The Life and Work of a Victorian Genius* (London: Paul Elek, 1974).

19. Francis Galton, *Inquiries into Human Faculty and Its Development* (London: Macmillan, 1883), p. 17n; Richard Soloway, *Demography and Degeneration: Eugenics and the Declining Birthrate in Twentieth-Century Britain* (Chapel Hill: University of North Carolina Press, 1990), pp. 18–37.

20. Galton, *Inquiries*, 62–63. See also Robert Fletcher, M.D., "The New School of Criminal Anthropology," *American Anthropologist* 4 (July 1891): 214–15.

21. Galton's interest in the subject led to his recommendation of finger-printing as a means of identification. *Lancet*, 29 August 1891, pp. 494–95; "Identification of Habitual Criminals: Report," *Parliamentary Papers* 72 (1893–94): 233, 264–68. Francis Galton, "Criminal Anthropology," *Nature*, 22 May 1890, pp. 75–76.

22. In 1894 Galton helped to establish the Evolution Committee of the Royal Society, where he was joined by the statistician Karl Pearson. Between 1891 and 1906 Pearson created the science of biometry—the study of stature, cephalic index, eye color, fertility, and longevity. The intent was to prove statistically the significance of inherited traits. Galton provided the funds in 1904 to establish a Eugenics Record Office, which was ultimately run by Pearson. In his various studies of "deterioration" Pearson remained true to the argument that crime was a cause, not an effect, of mental defect and called for prisons, asylums, and reformatories to become laboratories for the study of degeneration. E. S. Pearson, "Karl Pearson: An Appreciation of Some Aspects of His Life and Work," *Biometrika* 28 (1936): 193–257.

23. Some, like Maudsley, who in the 1870s supported the notion of degeneration, were turning away from it in the 1880s. Hyslop, for example, though accepting the notion of hereditary "predispositions," argued that "genius" was a social, not a psychological, concept. Theo. B. Hyslop, *Mental Physiology* (London: Churchill, 1895), pp. 416–19; and see Garland, "British Criminology," pp. 1–17.

24. T. S. Clouston, *The Hygiene of Mind* (London: Methuen, 1906), p. 56.

25. Havelock Ellis, *The Criminal* (London: Scot, 1890), pp. 51, 63–64, 74, 108, 126, 139, 143–44.

26. Enrico Ferri, *Criminal Sociology* (London: Fisher Unwin, 1895).

27. William Douglas Morrison, *Crime and Its Causes* (London: Swan Sonnenschein, 1908 [1891]), pp. vii, 112–14. See also Henry Smith, *A Plea for the Unborn* (London: Watts, 1897), pp. 2–30; J. W. Horsley, *Prisons and Prisoners* (London: Pearson, 1898), pp. 21–30.

28. L. Gordon Rylands, *Crime: Its Cause and Remedy* (London: Fisher Unwin, 1889), pp. 30–37; Wiener, *Reconstructing the Criminal*, pp. 236–37.

29. Robert Anderson, *Criminals and Crime: Some Facts and Suggestions* (London: Nisbet, 1907), p. 86.

30. Arnold White, *The Problems of a Great City* (London: Remington, 1886), pp. 47, 57–63. See also Arnold White, *Efficiency and Empire* (Brighton: Harvester Press, 1973 [1901]); W. A. Chapple, *The Fertility of the Unfit* (Melbourne: Whitcombe & Tombs, 1904), pp. x, 107.

31. John Berry Haycraft, *Darwinism and Race Progress* (London: Swan Sonnenschein, 1895), p. 108.

32. Angus McLaren, *Birth Control in Nineteenth-Century England* (London: Croom Helm, 1978), p. 148.

33. Robert Wilson McClaughry (1839–1920) edited an English translation of Adolphe Bertillon's anthropometrical identification system entitled *Signaletic Instruction* (Chicago: Werner, 1896).

34. Henry M. Boies, *Prisoners and Paupers: A Study* (New York: Putnam's, 1893), pp. 182, 266, 267, 270.

35. David Nicolson, deputy superintendent of Broadmoor and accordingly someone well qualified to comment on the criminal mind, was an outspoken critic of hereditarian theories. Convicts were, he argued, no more irrational than the grocer who adulterated tea or the businessman who forged bills; *Journal of Mental Science* 24 (1878): 1–25, 249–73; 41 (1895): 567–91.

36. Peter Norton, *The Vital Science: Biology and the Literary Imagination, 1860–1900* (London: George Allen, 1984), pp. 136–40.

37. Martin Richman, *Alfred Russell Wallace* (Boston: Twayne, 1981), p. 140; Grant Allen, *Falling in Love* (London: Smith Elder, 1891), pp. 11–12, 328.

38. Wells, *Mankind in the Making*, pp. 53–54.

39. Not only did the Home Office provide Galton with photographs of criminals to make his famous composite portraits of the criminal type; it also allowed him to read the letters sent by the female prisoners of the Princess Mary Village Homes to their children. The women, no doubt suspecting such surveillance, were naturally guarded in their communications. Galton had the effrontery, while carrying out such snooping, to cite the prevailing tone of alarm and suspicion in the letters as evidence of the female criminals' emotional instability. Galton, *Inquiries*, pp. 214, 343.

40. Cesar Lombroso and William Ferrero, *The Female Offender* (New York: Appleton, 1899), pp. 17, 57, 74, 187; *Lancet*, 22 April 1893, p. 941. Havelock Ellis lamented the fact that prudery led the English translator of Lombroso and Ferrero's work to omit much of their discussion of female sexuality; *Journal of Mental Science* 41 (1895): 720–21.

41. Karl Pearson, *The Life of Francis Galton* (Cambridge: Cambridge University Press, 1914–30), 2:111.

42. Mrs. E. Lynn Linton, "The Wild Women as Social Insurgents," *Nineteenth Century* 30 (1891): 592–605; 31 (1892): 455–64. On the fictional representations of "odd women" and "new women," see Elaine Showalter, *Sexual Anarchy: Gender and Culture at the Fin de Siècle* (New York: Viking, 1990).

43. Walter Heape, *Sex Antagonisms* (London: Constable, 1913), pp. 207–10.

44. McLaren, *Birth Control in Nineteenth-Century England*, pp. 146–47; Galton, *Inquiries*, p. 318.

45. The idea that modern literature itself was "degenerate" was voiced by Lombroso's friend, the physician, Zionist, and novelist Max Nordau, in *Degeneration* (London: Heinemann, 1895).

46. Ed Block, Jr., "James Sully, Evolutionist Psychology and Late Victorian Gothic Fiction," *Victorian Studies* 25 (1982): 443–69.

47. Robert Louis Stevenson, *Strange Case of Dr. Jekyll and Mr. Hyde* (Lon-

don: Longmans, 1886), p. 60; and on the novel's half-hidden sexual pre-occupations, see Stephen Heath, "Psychopathia Sexualis: Stevenson's Strange Case," *Critical Quarterly* 28 (1986): 93–108.

48. Bram Stoker, *Dracula* (London: Constable, 1897), pp. 17–18; and on fictions of degeneration generally, see Daniel Pick, *Faces of Degeneration: A European Disorder, c. 1848–c. 1918* (Cambridge: Cambridge University Press, 1989).

49. A. Conan Doyle, "The Final Problem," *The Penguin Complete Sherlock Holmes* (Harmondsworth: Penguin, 1981), p. 470.

50. A. Conan Doyle, "The Empty House," *The Penguin Complete Sherlock Holmes*, p. 494.

51. *Chicago Tribune*, 17 November 1880, p. 10.

52. *Chicago Tribune*, 22 September 1881, p. 5.

53. See the descriptions of Cream given in the *St. James's Gazette*, 22 October 1892, p. 3; 24 October 1892, p. 9.

54. *Illustrated Police News*, 5 November 1892, p. 1.

55. W. Douglas Morrison, Introduction to Lombroso and Ferrero, *The Female Offender*, p. xvi.

56. Robert Reid Rentoul, *Proposed Sterilization of Certain Mental and Physical Degenerates* (London: Walter Scott, 1903), p. 17.

57. On degeneration theory's role in absolving alienists for their inability to cure, see S. E. D. Shortt, *Victorian Lunacy: Richard M. Bucke and the Practice of Late Nineteenth-Century Psychiatry* (Cambridge: Cambridge University Press, 1986), pp. 101–4.

58. Charles Goring's work is usually presented as having provided the final refutation of criminal anthropology's idea of a specific "criminal type." But Goring followed Karl Pearson's eugenic and statistical approach, which, while undermining Lombroso's belief in physical stigmata, sought to highlight the importance of feeblemindedness as a cause of crime. "Defective intelligence," argued Goring, underlay a "constitutional proclivity" of some to crime. If education failed to counter such dispositions, the restriction of the reproduction of the feebleminded, the insane, the epileptic, and those with a defective social instinct would be required. Charles Goring, *The English Convict* (London: Darling, 1913). See also Sir Bryan Donkin, "Notes on Mental Defect in Criminals," *Journal of Mental Science* 63 (1917): 16–35; William Healey, *The Individual Delinquent* (Boston: Little, Brown, 1922); Edwin D. Driver, "Charles Buchman Goring," in Edward Glover, ed., *Pioneers in Criminology* (London: Stevens, 1960), pp. 335–48.

59. On the relation of degeneration fears to law reform, see Leon Radzinowicz and Roger Hood, "Incapacitating the Habitual Criminal: The English Experience," *Michigan Law Review* 78 (1980): 1305–89.

CHAPTER 12

1. *South London Chronicle*, 29 October 1892.

2. Shore, p. 169.

3. Shore, p. 111.

4. Was the man Mrs. Vowles remembered coming to 27 Lambeth Road

saying he was from the *New York Herald* possibly Cream? Mr. Blumenfeld and Mrs. Vowles Statements, 30 September 1892, MEPO 3 144.

5. L Division to Scotland Yard, 23 October 1891, MEPO 3 144.

6. L Division to Scotland Yard, 16 April 1892, MEPO 3 144.

7. L Division to Scotland Yard, 12 April, 13 April, 28 April 1892, MEPO 3 144.

8. See 9 May, 18 May, 24 May 1892, MEPO 3 144. To be fair it should be noted that tainted canned salmon had caused deaths in London. In 1892 special precautions were taken by the navy to prevent future poisonings. See *Times*, 2 July 1891, p. 12c; *British Medical Journal* 1 (7 May 1892): 981.

9. Robert Anderson to Home Office, 4 June 1892, MEPO 3 144.

10. James Greenwood, *The Seven Curses of London* (London: Rivers, 1869), pp. 289, 323.

11. Robert D. Storch, "Police Control of Street Prostitution in Victorian London: A Study in Contexts of Police Action," in David H. Bailey, ed., *Police and Society* (Beverly Hills: Sage, 1977), pp. 52–62; Edward J. Bristow, *Vice and Vigilance: Purity Movements in Britain since 1700* (London: Gill & Macmillan, 1977), pp. 154–66.

12. Alice Marsh's sister, Mrs. Fanny Taylor, of 37 St. Paul Street, Lewes Road, Brighton, testified that her sister's writing was on paper possessed by Cream. Shore, p. 98.

13. C.I.D., 28 April 1892, MEPO 3 144.

14. C.I.D., 16 May, 19 May 1892, MEPO 3 144.

15. Lizzie Sullivan Testimony, 19 May, 23 May, 26 May 1892, MEPO 3 144.

16. Violet Beverley and Ida St. Houstine Statements, 23 May 1892, MEPO 3 144.

17. Patrick McIntyre Report, 24 May 1892, MEPO 3 144.

18. George Comley and Alfred Ward Report, 16 May 1892, MEPO 3 144.

19. Shore, p. 23. Scotland Yard Report, 19 May 1892, MEPO 3 144.

20. Patrick McIntyre Report, 20 May 1892, MEPO 3 144. Beverley made an official statement 23 May.

21. The official record does not make clear whether they came forward voluntarily or were sought by the police.

22. Charles Harvey Deposition: CRIM 1/38/1

23. Louisa Harris Deposition: CRIM 1/38/1.

24. Identification Parade, 25 June 1892, MEPO 3 144.

25. R. F. Quinton, *Crime and Criminals, 1876–1910* (London: Longmans, Green, 1910), p. 42.

26. Louisa Harris Deposition: CRIM 1/38/1.

27. Clement Scott, cited in Raymond Mander and Joe Mitchenson, *The Lost Theatres of London* (New York: Taplinger, 1968), p. 213. The Wesleyan Methodists bought the Royal Aquarium in 1902 and hence put an end to such risqué goings-on.

28. Strychnine was sometimes passed off as quinine in order to explain the bitter taste. See Thomas Stevenson, *The Principles and Practices of Medical Jurisprudence* (London: Churchill, 1883), 1:430.

29. Frederick Jarvis Report, 29 August 1892, MEPO 3 144.

30. Anna Clark, *Women's Silence, Man's Violence* (London: Pandora, 1987), p. 110.

31. *Montreal Gazette,* 20 October 1892, p. 1.

32. *Lloyd's Weekly London Newspaper,* 17 April 1892, p. 8.

33. Pat Thane, "Late Victorian Women," in T. R. Gourvish and Alan O'Day, eds., *Later Victorian Britain, 1867–1900* (London: Macmillan, 1988), pp. 188–92.

34. *Lloyd's Weekly London Newspaper,* 1 May 1892, p. 8.

35. Lee Holcombe, *Wives and Property: Reform of the Married Women's Property Law in Nineteenth-Century England* (Toronto: University of Toronto Press, 1983); Mary Lyndon Shanley, *Feminism, Marriage and the Law in Victorian England, 1850–1895* (Princeton: Princeton University Press, 1989).

36. Ellen Ross, "Fierce Questions and Taunts: Married Life in Working-Class London, 1870–1914," *Feminist Studies* 8 (1982): 575–602.

37. John Cordy Jeafferson, *Brides and Bridals* (London: Hurst & Blackett, 1872), 1:320–21, 336; Lawrence Stone, *Road to Divorce, 1530–1987* (Oxford: Oxford University Press, 1990), p. 389.

38. Margaret May, "Violence in the Family: An Historical Perspective," in J. P. Martin, ed., *Violence and the Family* (Chichester: John Wiley, 1978), pp. 139–48.

39. Iris Minor, "Working-Class Women and Matrimonial Law Reform, 1890–1914," in David E. Martin and David Rubinstein, eds., *Ideology and the Labour Movement* (London: Croom Helm, 1979), pp. 103–24.

40. H. Montgomery Hyde, *Carson: The Life of Sir Edward Carson, Lord Carson of Duncairn* (London: Heinemann, 1953), pp. 164–66; Allen Horstman, *Victorian Divorce* (London: Croom Helm, 1985), p. 147.

41. Edmund Haughton Jackson, *The True Story of the Clitheroe Abduction; or, Why I Ran Away with My Wife* (Blackburn, N. E. Lancashire Publishing, 1891).

42. 1 *Queen's Bench Division,* 671–86. Asking if a man could be charged with stealing his own spoons, the opponents of Mrs. Jackson praised her husband as a "young Lochinear" and damned her supporters as the "shrieking sisterhood." *Lancashire Evening News,* 9 March 1891, p. 2; 10 March 1891, p. 3; 23 March 1891, p. 3.

43. David Bernstein, *Before the Suffragettes: Women's Emancipation in the 1890s* (Brighton: Harvester, 1986), pp. 54–58.

44. Regina v. Clarence (1888), 22 *Queen's Bench Division,* 52.

45. Angus McLaren, *A History of Contraception: From Antiquity to the Present Day* (Oxford: Basil Blackwell, 1990), pp. 193–207.

46. Edith Lanchester was a real live "Woman Who Did." Refusing to marry the man with whom she planned to live, she was committed by her family to an asylum. The Legitimation League's defense of her actions brought about the police scrutiny mentioned above in chap. 10.

47. Samuel Hynes, *The Edwardian Turn of Mind* (Princeton: Princeton University Press, 1968), pp. 160–79; Peter Keating, *The Haunted Study: A Social History of the English Novel, 1875–1914* (London: Secker & Warburg, 1989), pp. 182–95.

48. Martha Vicinus, *Independent Women: Work and Community for Single Women, 1850–1920* (Chicago: University of Chicago Press, 1985); Pat Jalland, *Women, Marriage and Politics: 1860–1914* (Oxford: Clarendon, 1986), pp. 280–87.

49. Carroll Smith-Rosenberg, *Disorderly Conduct: Visions of Gender in Victorian America* (New York: Knopf, 1985), pp. 245–96; Sheila Jeffreys, *The Spinster and Her Enemies: Feminism and Sexuality, 1880–1930* (London: Pandora, 1985); Bram Dijkstra, *Idols of Perversity: Fantasies of Feminine Evil in Fin-de-siècle Culture* (New York: Oxford University Press, 1986).

50. For a similar reading of the Jack the Ripper hysteria, see Judith R. Walkowitz, "Jack the Ripper and the Myth of Male Violence," *Feminist Studies* 8 (1982): 543–75; Christopher Frayling, "The House That Jack Built: Some Stereotypes of the Rapist in the History of Popular Culture," in Sylvana Tomaselli and Roy Porter, eds., *Rape* (Oxford: Blackwell, 1986), pp. 174–215.

51. Commissioner, Scotland Yard, November 1892, MEPO 3 144.

52. Doctors were as self-centered as the police. One medical writer concluded his account of the Neill affair by extending his journal's sympathy, not to the prostitutes but to the blackmailed doctors who had suffered notoriety, "the waiting in police courts . . . the loss of time and money." *British Medical Journal* 1 (25 June 1892): 1369.

CONCLUSION

1. *Times*, 12 September 1888, cited in Richard Whittington-Egan, *A Casebook on Jack the Ripper* (London: Wildy, 1975), p. 9; A. Thiénard, *L'assassinat* (Paris: Girard and Brière, 1892), pp. 89–92.

2. *British Medical Journal* 1 (14 May 1892): 1042. The notion of such an "epidemic" was strengthened when James Slater was reported to have declared, while attacking his wife with a knife, that "he was going to have a game of Deeming." *Times*, 24 August 1892, p. 11b.

3. Edward Shorter, "On Writing the History of Rape," *Signs* 3 (1977–78): 475.

4. Twenty-two death sentences were levied against twenty men and two women. Eighteen men were executed; two men and two women were sentenced to penal servitude for life. *British Sessional Papers* 103 (1893–94): 38.

5. "The Motives of Murderers," *Clarion*, 29 October 1892, p. 6. A contributor to the Social Democratic Federation's journal concurred. "Every respectable member of society has been grinding his teeth for the past fortnight over a wretched congenital criminal, and gloating over the prospect of his being strangled by the myrmidons of the law." The writer went on to argue that the slum landlords of London, responsible as they were for the scarlet fever deaths of countless children, were far more destructive and pernicious than Cream. *Justice*, 19 November 1892, p. 1.

6. The point has been made: "Sexism is structural; it is not simply the result of inherent biological or psychological differences between the sexes, or of superficial socialization processes." Lorenne Clark and Debra Lewis, *Rape: The Price of Coercive Sexuality* (Toronto: Women's Press, 1977), p. 176.

7. Thomas Boyle, *Black Swine in the Sewers of Hampstead: Beneath the Surface of Victorian Sensationalism* (New York: Viking, 1989).

8. If England was the "home" of the serial killer, it was soon surpassed. Germany had a bloody wave of serial killings in the 1920s and 1930s; America's surge in such murders began in the 1970s. What such outbursts tell us about their respective societies awaits investigation. See Philip Jenkins, "Serial Murder in England, 1940–1985," *Journal of Criminal Justice* 16 (1988): 1–16; "Serial Murder in the United States, 1900–1940: A Historical Perspective," *Journal of Criminal Justice* 17 (1989): 377–92.

9. Michel Foucault, *Discipline and Punish: The Birth of the Prison* (New York: Vintage, 1979).

10. *New York Times*, 8 May 1896, pp. 1–2; David Franke, *The Torture Doctor* (New York: Hawthorn Books, 1975); Charles Boswell and Lewis Thompson, *The Girls in Nightmare House* (Manchester: Fawcett, 1955); Patterson Smith, "Books on the American Serial Killer," *Bookman's Yearbook*, 1989–90, pp. 9–18.

11. Cesar Lombroso, *L'homme criminel* (Paris: Alcan, 1895), 2:36, 96; Richard von Krafft-Ebing, *Psychopathia Sexualis* (New York: Putnams, 1965 [1886]), pp. 117–27; Alexandre Lacassagne, *Vacher l'éventreur et les crimes sadiques* (Lyon: Storck, 1899).

12. On French examples, see Dr. Paul Aubry, *La contagion du meutre* (Paris: Baillière, 1896), pp. 152–53.

13. *Gazette des Tribunaux*, 27 June 1866, p. 615.

14. Early-twentieth-century English killers of prostitutes included Frederick Field, Frederick Murphy, and Robert Dixon; Douglas G. Browne and E. V. Tullett, *Bernard Spilling: His Life and Cases* (London: Penguin, 1955), pp. 370–74.

15. Peter Gay, *The Bourgeois Experience, Victoria to Freud: The Education of the Senses* (New York: Oxford University Press, 1984), p. 88.

16. Daniel Pick, *Faces of Degeneration: A European Disorder, c. 1848–c. 1918* (Cambridge: Cambridge University Press, 1989), p. 175. See also Andrea Trudd, *Domestic Crime and the Victorian Novel* (New York: St. Martins, 1989).

17. For such a reading of the Whitechapel murders, see Sander Gilman, *Sexuality: An Illustrated History* (New York: John Wiley, 1989), pp. 232–49.

18. For the debate over long-term patterns of English homicide, see Lawrence Stone, "Interpersonal Violence in English Society, 1300–1980," *Past and Present* 101 (1983): 206–15; J. A. Sharpe, "The History of Violence in England: Some Observations," *Past and Present* 108 (1985): 206–15; J. M. Beattie, "Violence and Society in Early Modern England," in A. N. Doob and E. L. Greenjean, eds., *Perspectives in Criminal Law* (Aurora, Ontario: Canada Law Book, 1985), pp. 36–60; J. S. Cockburn, "Patterns of Violence in English Society: Homicide in Kent, 1560–1985," *Past and Present* 130 (1990): 70–106; Frank McLynn, *Crime and Punishment in Eighteenth-Century England* (New York: Routledge, 1989).

19. Burke and Hare were tried for the murders of at least ten people whose bodies they sold to an Edinburgh anatomy school. Hare turned king's

evidence; only Burke was hanged. In London the body snatchers Bishop and Williams were executed in December 1831 for killing three vagrants; Ruth Richardson, *Death, Dissection and the Destitute* (London: Routledge & Kegan Paul, 1987), pp. 132–33, 196–97.

20. For a bibliographical account of the many variants, see Alexander Kelly, *Jack the Ripper* (London: Association of Assistant Librarians, 1984).

AFTERWORD

1. On contemporary feminist interpretations of violence, see Deborah Cameron and Elizabeth Frazer, *The Lust to Kill: A Feminist Investigation of Sexual Murder* (London: Polity, 1987); Jane Caputi, *The Age of Sex Crime* (London: Women's Press, 1987); Joan Smith, *Misogynies* (London: Faber & Faber, 1989).

2. Helen Roberts, "Trap the Ripper," *New Society*, 6 April 1978, p. 11. See also Nicole Ward Jouve, *"The Street Cleaner:" The Yorkshire Ripper on Trial* (London: Martin Boyars, 1982).

SELECT BIBLIOGRAPHY

UNPUBLISHED SOURCES

PUBLIC RECORD OFFICE PAPERS
CRIM 1/38/1 (Cream Trial Depositions)
CRIM 6 (Madame Frain Trial)
CRIM 9 (Calendar of Prisoners; Madame Frain Trial)
HO 144/245-246 (Mr. Justice Henry Hawkins's Trial Notes)
MEPO 2 399 (Infant Life Protection Act. Report of 27 April 1896 on Dead
    Bodies [Infants] for Year 1895)
MEPO 3 144 (Cream Trial Police Investigation)
MEPO 3 149 (Unqualified Medical Practitioners)
MEPO 3 152 (Arthur Lewis Pointing)
MEPO 3 154/155 (Adolph Beck)
MEPO 3 157 (Horatio Buckland)
PCOM 1 143 (Session Papers 1892)

McGILL UNIVERSITY ARCHIVES
Thomas Neill Cream File

PERIODICALS, SERIALS, AND NEWSPAPERS
American Anthropologist
Archives d'anthropologie criminelles et sciences pénales
British Gynaecological Journal
British Medical Journal
Canada Lancet
Canadian Medical Association Journal

Chemist and Druggist
Chicago Tribune
Clarion
Commonweal
Cornhill Magazine
Daily Chronicle
Daily Telegraph
East London Advertiser
Gazette des Tribunaux
Illustrated Police News
Joliet Daily News
Journal of Mental Science
Justice
Lancet
Lloyd's Weekly London Newspaper
Montreal Daily Star
Montreal Gazette
Nature
Nineteenth Century
Pall Mall Gazette
Penny Illustrated Paper
Pharmaceutical Journal
Provincial Medical Journal
Reynolds Newspaper
St. James's Gazette
South London Chronicle
South London Mail
Times
Toronto Globe
Waterloo Advertiser

BOOKS AND ARTICLES

Acton, William. *Prostitution, Considered in Its Moral, Social, and Sanitary Aspects.* London: Churchill, 1857.

Allason, Rupert. *The Branch: A History of the Metropolitan Police Special Branch, 1883–1983.* London: Secker & Warburg, 1983.

Allen, Grant. *Falling in Love.* London: Smith Elder, 1891.

Altick, Richard D. *Victorian Studies in Scarlet.* New York: Norton, 1970.

Anderson, L. G. *Louisa Garrett Anderson.* London: Faber & Faber, 1939.

Anderson, Olive. *Suicide in Victorian and Edwardian England.* Oxford: Clarendon, 1987.

Anderson, Robert. *Criminals and Crime: Some Facts and Suggestions.* London: Nisbet, 1907.

———. *The Lighter Side of My Official Life.* London: Hodder & Stoughton, 1910.

Andrew, Christopher. *Secret Service: The Making of the British Intelligence Community.* London: Heinemann, 1985.

Anonymous. *The History of the "Times,"* vol. 3: *The Twentieth Century Test, 1884–1912.* London: Times, 1977.

Atkinson, Stanley B. *The Law in General Practice: Some Chapters in Every-Day Forensic Medicine.* London: Froude, 1908.

Atlay, J. B., ed. *Trial of the Stauntons.* London: Hodge, 1911.

Aubry, Dr. Paul. *La contagion du meutre.* Paris: Baillière, 1896.

Avison, N. H. "Criminal Statistics as Social Indicators." In *Social Indicators and Social Policy,* A. Schonfield and S. Shaw, eds., pp. 33–52. London: Heinemann, 1972.

Avrich, Paul. *Anarchist Portraits.* Princeton: Princeton University Press, 1988.

———. *The Haymarket Tragedy.* Princeton: Princeton University Press, 1984.

Backhouse, Constance B. "Nineteenth-Century Canadian Prostitution Law: Reflection of a Discriminatory Society." *Histoire sociale/Social History* 18 (1985): 397–99.

Bailey, Victor, and Blackburn, Sheila. "The Punishment of Incest Act, 1908: A Case Study of Law Creation." *Criminal Law Review,* 1979, pp. 708–18.

Banks, Joseph A. *Prosperity and Parenthood: A Study of Family Planning among the Victorian Middle Classes.* London: Routledge & Kegan Paul, 1954.

Barker-Benfield, G. J. *The Horrors of the Half-Known Life: Male Attitudes towards Women and Sexuality in Nineteenth Century America.* New York: Harper, 1976.

Barnsby, Norman. *Medical Chaos and Crime.* London: Mitchell Kennerley, 1910.

Barret-Ducrocq, Françoise. *L'amour sous Victoria: Sexualité et classes populaires à Londres au XIXe siècle.* Paris: Plon, 1989.

Beach, Thomas M. *Twenty-Five Years in the Secret Service: The Recollections of a Spy.* London: E. P. Publishing, 1974 [1893].

Beattie, J. M. "Violence and Society in Early Modern England." In *Perspectives in Criminal Law,* A. N. Doob and E. L. Greenjean, eds., pp. 36–60. Aurora, Ontario: Canada Law Book, 1985.

Belden, H., and Co. *Illustrated Atlas of the Eastern Townships and S. W. Quebec.* Port Elgin, Ontario: Ross Cunning, 1872.

Bell, Donald. "Jack the Ripper—The Final Solution." *Criminologist* 9 (1974): 40–51.

Berg, Charles. *Fear, Punishment, Anxiety and the Wolfenden Report.* London: George Allen, 1959.

Bernheimer, Charles. *Figures of Ill Repute: Representing Prostitution in Nineteenth-Century France.* Cambridge, Mass.: Harvard University Press, 1989.

Bernstein, David. *Before the Suffragettes: Women's Emancipation in the 1890s.* Brighton: Harvester, 1986.

Berridge, Virginia. "Morality and Medical Science: Concepts of Narcotic Addiction in Britain, 1820–1926." *Annals of Science* 36 (1979): 67–85.

Berridge, Virginia, and Edwards, Griffith. *Opium and the People: Opiate Use in Nineteenth-Century England.* London: Allen Lane, 1981.

Besant, Annie. *An Autobiography.* London: Fisher Unwin, 1893.

———. *The Law of Population.* London: Freethought Publishing, 1877.

Besant, Walter. *London South of the Thames.* London: Adam & Charles Black, 1912.

Biggs, John M. *The Concept of Matrimonial Cruelty.* London: Athlone Press, 1962.

Blackwell, Elizabeth. *The Human Element in Sex.* London: Churchill, 1885.

Block, Ed, Jr. "James Sully, Evolutionist Psychology and Late Victorian Gothic Fiction." *Victorian Studies* 25 (1982): 443–69.

Boies, Henry M. *Prisoners and Paupers: A Study.* New York: Putnam's, 1893.

Bonniot, Roger. *Emile Gaboriau, ou la naissance du roman policier.* Paris: Vrin, 1985.

Booth, Charles. *Life and Labour of the People in London,* 1st series: *Poverty.* London: Macmillan, 1902 [1889].

———. *Life and Labour of the People in London,* 3d series: *Religious Influences,* 4: *Inner South London.* London: Macmillan, 1902.

Boswell, Charles, and Thompson, Lewis. *The Girls in Nightmare House.* Manchester: Fawcett, 1955.

Boyle, Thomas. *Black Swine in the Sewers of Hampstead: Beneath the Surface of Victorian Sensationalism.* New York: Viking, 1989.

Brandt, Allan M. *No Magic Bullet: A Social History of Venereal Disease in the United States since 1880.* New York: Oxford University Press, 1985.

Bristow, Edward J. *Prostitutes and Prejudice: The Jewish Fight against White Slavery, 1870–1939.* Oxford: Clarendon, 1982.

———. *Vice and Vigilance: Purity Movements in Britain since 1700.* London: Gill & Macmillan, 1977.

Broadbent, Walter, ed. *Selections from the Writings of Sir William Broadbent.* London: Froude, 1908.

Brome, Vincent. *Havelock Ellis, Philosopher of Sex: A Biography.* London: Routledge & Kegan Paul, 1979.

Brookes, Barbara. *Abortion in England, 1900–1967.* London: Croom Helm, 1988.

Brouardel, Paul. *Le secret médical.* Paris: Baillière, 1887.

Browne, Douglas G., and Tullett, E. V. *Bernard Spilling: His Life and Cases.* London: Penguin, 1955.

Browne, G. Lantham, and Stewart, C. G. *Reports of Trials for Murder by Poisoning.* London: Stevens, 1883.

Butler, Anne M. *Daughters of Joy, Sisters of Mercy: Prostitutes in the American West.* Urbana: University of Illinois Press, 1985.

Butler, Josephine. *Personal Reminiscences of a Great Crusade.* London: Marshall, 1896.

Cameron, Deborah, and Frazer, Elizabeth. *The Lust to Kill: A Feminist Investigation of Sexual Murder.* London: Polity, 1987.

Caputi, Jane. *The Age of Sex Crime.* London: Women's Press, 1987.

Cashman, John. *The Gentleman from Chicago: Being an Account of the Doings of Thomas Neill Cream, M.D. (McGill), 1850–1892.* New York: Harper & Row, 1973.

Chapman, Cecil. *The Poor Man's Court of Justice: Twenty-Five Years as a Metropolitan Magistrate.* London: Hodder & Stoughton, 1925.

Chapple, W. A. *The Fertility of the Unfit.* Melbourne: Whitcombe & Tombs, 1904.

Chavasse, P. H. *Advice to a Wife*. Toronto: Musson, 1879.

Chesnais, Jean-Claude. *Histoire de la violence en Occident de 1800 à nos jours*. Paris: Laffont, 1981.

Chesney, Kellow. *The Anti-Society: An Account of the Victorian Underworld*. Boston: Gambit, 1970.

Chesterton, Ada [Mrs. Cecil Chesterton]. *In Darkest London*. London: Stanley Paul, 1926.

Clark, Anna. *Women's Silence, Man's Violence: Sexual Assault in England, 1770–1845*. London: Pandora, 1987.

Clark, George. *A History of the Royal College of Physicians of London*. Oxford: Clarendon, 1964–72.

Clark, Lorenne, and Lewis, Debra. *Rape: The Price of Coercive Sexuality*. Toronto: Women's Press, 1977.

Clouston, T. S. *The Hygiene of Mind*. London: Methuen, 1906.

Cockburn, J. S. "Patterns of Violence in English Society: Homicide in Kent, 1560–1985." *Past and Present* 130 (1990): 70–106.

Cole, J. A. *Prince of Spies: Henri Le Caron*. London: Faber & Faber, 1984.

Coleridge, Ernest H. *Life and Correspondence of John, Duke Lord Coleridge*. London: Heinemann, 1904.

Collins, Wilkie. *Armadale*. London: Dover, 1980.

Connelly, Mark Thomas. *The Response to Prostitution in the Progressive Era*. Chapel Hill: University of North Carolina Press, 1980.

Cooter, Roger, ed. *Phrenology in the British Isles: An Annotated, Historical Bibliography and Index*. Metuchen, N.J.: Scarecrow Press, 1989.

Corbin, Alain. *Women for Hire: Prostitution in Nineteenth-Century France*. Cambridge, Mass.: Harvard University Press, 1990.

Cowan, John. *The Science of the New Life*. New York: Cowan & Co., 1874.

Crew, Albert, *The Old Bailey*. London: Nicolson & Watson, 1933.

Critchley, T. A. *A History of the Police in England and Wales, 900–1966*. London: Constable, 1967.

Crowther, M. Anne, and White, Brenda. *On Soul and Conscience: The Medical Expert: One Hundred and Fifty Years of Forensic Medicine in Glasgow*. Aberdeen: Aberdeen University Press, 1988.

Dally, Ann. *Women under the Knife*. London: Radius, 1991.

Darmon, Pierre. *Médecins et assassins à la belle époque*. Paris: Seuil, 1989.

Davidoff, Leonore. *The Best Circles: Society, Etiquette and the Season*. London: Croom Helm, 1973.

Davies, John D. *Phrenology: Fad and Science: A Nineteenth-Century American Crusade*. New Haven: Yale University Press, 1955.

Davis, Jean. "'A Poor Man's System of Justice:' The London Police Courts in the Second Half of the Nineteenth Century." *Historical Journal* 27 (1984): 309–35.

Davis, Jennifer. "The London Garotting Panic of 1862: A Moral Panic and the Creation of a Criminal Class in Mid-Victorian England." In *Crime and the Law: The Social History of Crime in Western Europe since 1500*, V. A. C. Gatrell, B. Lenman, and G. Parker, eds., pp. 190–213. London: Europa, 1980.

Davis, Natalie Zemon. *Fiction in the Archives: Pardon Tales and Their Tellers in Sixteenth-Century France*. Stanford: Stanford University Press, 1987.

———. *The Return of Martin Guerre*. Cambridge, Mass.: Harvard University Press, 1983.

Degler, Carl N. *At Odds: Women and the Family in America from the Revolution to the Present*. New York: Oxford, 1980.

Dijkstra, Bram. *Idols of Perversity: Fantasies of Feminine Evil in Fin-de-siècle Culture*. New York: Oxford University Press, 1986.

Doyle, Arthur Conan. *The Complete Sherlock Holmes*. 2 vols. Harmondsworth: Penguin, 1981.

Drake, Emma F. Angell. *What a Young Wife Ought to Know*. Toronto: Vir Publishing, 1908.

Driver, Edwin D. "Charles Buchman Goring." In *Pioneers in Criminology*, Edward Glover, ed., pp. 335–48. London: Stevens, 1960.

Drysdale, Charles R. *The Population Question*. London: Standring, 1892.

Dyos, H. J. *Exploring the Urban Past: Essays in Urban History*. Cambridge: Cambridge University Press, 1982.

Ellis, Havelock. *The Criminal*. London: Scot, 1890.

———. *Studies in the Psychology of Sex*. 4 vols. New York: Random House, 1936.

Ellmann, Richard. *Oscar Wilde*. Harmondsworth: Penguin, 1987.

Elston, Mary Ann. "Women and Antivivisection in Victorian England, 1870–1900." In *Vivisection in Historical Perspective*, Nicolas Rupke, ed., pp. 259–94. London: Croom Helm, 1987.

Emsley, Clive. *Crime and Society in England, 1750–1900*. London: Longman, 1987.

Faller, Lincoln B. *Turned to Account: The Forms and Functions of Criminal Biography in Late Seventeenth and Eighteenth-Century England*. Cambridge: Cambridge University Press, 1987.

Ferri, Enrico. *Criminal Sociology*. London: Fisher Unwin, 1895.

Flack, I. Harvey. *Lawson Tait*. London: Heinemann, 1949.

Foot, M. R. D., and Matthew, H. C. G., eds., *The Gladstone Diaries*. 11 vols. Oxford: Clarendon, 1974.

Forbes, Robert. *Sixty Years of Medical Defense*. London: Medical Defense Union, 1948.

Forbes, Thomas. *Surgeons at the Bailey: English Forensic Medicine to 1878*. New Haven: Yale University Press, 1985.

Forrest, D. W. *Francis Galton: The Life and Work of a Victorian Genius*. London: Paul Elek, 1974.

Foucault, Michel. *Discipline and Punish: The Birth of the Prison*. New York: Vintage, 1979.

Franke, David. *The Torture Doctor*. New York: Hawthorn Books, 1975.

Frayling, Christopher. "The House That Jack Built: Some Stereotypes of the Rapist in the History of Popular Culture." In *Rape*, Sylvana Tomaselli and Roy Porter, eds., pp. 174–215. Oxford: Blackwell, 1986.

French, Richard D. *Antivivisection and Medical Science in Victorian Society*. Princeton: Princeton University Press, 1975.

Friedland, Martin L. *The Trial of Israel Lipski.* London: Macmillan, 1984.

Furnaux, Rupert. *The Medical Murderer.* London: Elek Books, 1957.

Galton, Francis. *Inquiries into Human Faculty and Its Development.* London: Macmillan, 1883.

Gardner, Augustus K. *Conjugal Sins against the Laws of Life and Health.* New York: Stringer, 1874.

Garland, David. "British Criminology before 1935." In *A History of British Criminology,* Paul Rock, ed., pp. 1–17. Oxford: Clarendon, 1988.

Gay, Peter. *The Bourgeois Experience, Victoria to Freud: The Education of the Senses.* New York: Oxford University Press, 1984.

Gibson, Mary. *Prostitution and the State in Italy, 1860–1915* Rutgers: Rutgers University Press, 1986.

Gillis, John. *For Better, for Worse: British Marriages, 1600 to the Present.* New York: Oxford University Press, 1985.

Gilman, Sander. *Sexuality: An Illustrated History.* New York: John Wiley, 1989.

Ginzberg, Carlo. "Morelli, Freud and Sherlock Holmes: Clues and Scientific Method." *History Workshop Journal* 9 (1980): 7–36.

Gorham, Deborah. "The 'Maiden Tribute of Modern Babylon' Re-examined: Child Prostitution and the Idea of Childhood in Late-Victorian England." *Victorian Studies* 21 (1978): 353–79.

Goring, Charles. *The English Convict.* London: Darling, 1913.

Green, Benny, ed. *The Last Empires: A Music Hall Companion.* London: Michael Joseph, 1986.

Greenwood, James. *Low-Life Deeps: An Account of the Strange Fish to Be Found There.* London: Chatto & Windus, 1875.

———. *The Seven Curses of London.* London: Rivers, 1869.

———. *The Wilds of London.* London: Chatto & Windus, 1874.

Grosskurth, Phyllis. *Havelock Ellis: A Biography.* Toronto: McClelland & Stewart, 1980.

Guillais, Joëlle. *Crimes of Passion: Dramas of Private Life in Nineteenth Century France.* Jane Dunnett, trans. New York: Routledge, 1990.

Halsted, D. G. *Doctor in the Nineties.* London: Christopher Johnson, 1959.

Halttunen, Karen. *Confidence Men and Painted Women: A Study of Middle-Class Culture in America, 1830–1870.* New Haven: Yale University Press, 1982.

Harris, Ruth. *Murders and Madness: Medicine, Law and Society in the Fin de Siècle.* Oxford: Clarendon, 1989.

Harsin, Jill. *Policing Prostitution in Nineteenth-Century France.* Princeton: Princeton University Press, 1985.

———. "Syphilis, Wives and Physicians: Medical Ethics and the Family in Late Nineteenth-Century France." *French Historical Studies* 16 (1989): 72–95.

Hartman, Mary S. *Victorian Murderesses.* New York; Schocken, 1977.

Hartsfield, Larry K. *The American Response to Professional Crime, 1870–1917.* Westport, Conn.: Greenwood Press, 1985.

Harvard, J. D. J. *The Detection of Secret Homicide.* London: Macmillan, 1960.

Haycraft, John Berry. *Darwinism and Race Progress.* London: Swan Sonnenschein, 1895.

Healey, William. *The Individual Delinquent.* Boston: Little, Brown, 1922.

Heape, Walter. *Sex Antagonisms.* London: Constable, 1913.

Heath, Stephen. "Psychopathia Sexualis: Stevenson's Strange Case." *Critical Quarterly* 28 (1986): 93–108.

Hepworth, Mike. *Blackmail: Publicity and Secrecy in Everyday Life.* London: Routledge & Kegan Paul, 1975.

Hobson, Barbara Meil. *Uneasy Virtue: The Politics of Prostitution and the American Reform Tradition.* New York: Basic Books, 1987.

Hodge, Hugh H. *Foeticide, or Criminal Abortion.* Philadelphia: Lindsay & Blackiston, 1869.

Holcombe, Lee. *Wives and Property: Reform of the Married Women's Property Law in Nineteenth-Century England.* Toronto: University of Toronto Press, 1983.

Holmes, Thomas. *Pictures and Problems from London Police Courts.* London: Edward Arnold, 1900.

Horsley, J. W. *Prisons and Prisoners.* London: Pearson, 1898.

Horstman, Allen. *Victorian Divorce.* London: Croom Helm, 1985.

Howard, Robert P. *Illinois: A History of a Prairie State.* Grand Rapids: Eerdmans, 1972.

Hyde, H. Montgomery. *Carson: The Life of Sir Edward Carson, Lord Carson of Duncairn.* London: Heinemann, 1953.

———. *The Cleveland Street Scandal.* London: Allen, 1976.

———. *A Tangled Web: Sex Scandals in British Politics and Society.* London: Constable, 1986.

Hynes, Samuel. *The Edwardian Turn of Mind.* Princeton: Princeton University Press, 1968.

Hyslop, Theo. B. *Mental Physiology.* London: Churchill, 1895.

Ignatieff, Michael. *A Just Measure of Pain: The Penitentiary in the Industrial Revolution, 1750–1850.* New York: Pantheon, 1978.

Ives, George. *A History of Penal Methods.* London: Stanley Paul, 1914.

Jackson, Edmund Haughton. *The True Story of the Clitheroe Abduction; or, Why I Ran Away with My Wife.* Blackburn, N. E. Lancashire Publishing, 1891.

Jalland, Pat. *Women, Marriage and Politics, 1860–1914.* Oxford: Clarendon, 1986.

Jeafferson, John Cordy. *Brides and Bridals.* 2 vols. London: Hurst & Blackett, 1872.

Jeffreys, Sheila. *The Spinster and Her Enemies: Feminism and Sexuality, 1880–1930.* London: Pandora, 1985.

Jenkins, Elizabeth. *Six Criminal Women.* London: Pan, 1949.

Jenkins, Philip. "Serial Murder in England, 1940–1985." *Journal of Criminal Justice* 16 (1988): 1–16.

———. "Serial Murder in the United States, 1900–1940: A Historical Perspective." *Journal of Criminal Justice* 17 (1989): 377–92.

Jesse, F. Tennyson, ed. *Trials of Timothy John Evans and John Reginald Halliday Christie.* London: Hodge, 1957.

Jeyes, S. H. and How, F. D. *The Life of Sir Howard Vincent.* London: George Allen, 1912.

Jones, Gareth Stedman. *Outcast London: A Study in the Relationships between Classes in Victorian Society*. Oxford: Clarendon, 1971.

Jordanova, Ludmilla. *Sexual Visions: Images of Gender in Science and Medicine between the Eighteenth and Twentieth Centuries*. Madison: University of Wisconsin Press, 1989.

Jouve, Nicole Ward. *"The Street Cleaner:" The Yorkshire Ripper on Trial*. London: Martin Boyars, 1982.

Kalikoff, Beth. *Murder and Moral Decay in Victorian Popular Literature*. Ann Arbor: OUI, 1986.

Keating, Peter. *The Haunted Study: A Social History of the English Novel, 1875–1914*. London: Secker & Warburg, 1989.

Kellett, John R. *The Impact of Railways on Victorian Cities*. London: Routledge & Kegan Paul, 1969.

Kelly, Alexander. *Jack the Ripper*. London: Association of Assistant Librarians, 1984.

Kenealey, E. V. *The Trial at Bar of Sir Roger C. D. Tichborne*. London: "Englishman" Office, 1875.

Keown, John. *Abortion, Doctors and the Law: Some Aspects of the Legal Regulation of Abortion in England from 1803 to 1982*. Cambridge: Cambridge University Press, 1988.

Knott, George H., ed. *Trial of William Palmer*. London: Hodge, 1912.

Kohl, Norbert. *Oscar Wilde: The Works of a Conformist Rebel*. Cambridge: Cambridge University Press, 1989.

Krafft-Ebing, Richard von. *Psychopathia Sexualis*. New York: Putnams, 1965 [1886].

Lacassagne, Alexandre. *Vacher l'éventreur et les crimes sadiques*. Lyon: Storck, 1899.

Lambert, Richard S. *When Justice Failed: A Study of Nine Peculiar Murder Trials*. London: Methuen, 1935.

Lankester, E. Ray. *Degeneration: A Chapter in Darwinism*. London: Macmillan, 1880.

Lansbury, Cora. "Gynaecology, Pornography and Antivivisection." *Victorian Studies* 28 (1985): 413–37.

———. *The Old Brown Dog: Women, Workers and Vivisection in Edwardian England*. Madison: University of Wisconsin Press, 1985.

Lansdowne, Andrew. *A Life's Reminiscences of Scotland Yard*. London: Leadenhall, 1890.

Laqueur, Thomas. *Making Sex: Body and Gender from the Greeks to Freud*. Cambridge, Mass.: Harvard University Press, 1990.

Laurence, John. *A History of Capital Punishment*. London: Sampson Low, 1932.

Lecky, William. *A History of European Morals*. 2 vols. London: Longmans, 1869.

Ledbetter, Rosanna. *A History of the Malthusian League, 1877–1927*. Columbus: Ohio State University Press, 1976.

Lees-Milne, James. *Harold Nicolson, 1930–68*. London: Chatto & Windus, 1981.

Lévesque, Andrée. *La norme et les déviances: Des femmes au Quebec pendant l'entre deux guerres.* Montreal: Les éditions du remue-ménage, 1989.

Leyton, Elliott. *Hunting Humans: The Rise of the Modern Multiple Murderer.* Toronto: McClelland & Stewart, 1986.

———. *Sole Survivor: Children Who Murder Their Families.* Toronto: Seal, 1990.

Littlechild, John George. *The Reminiscences of Chief Inspector Littlechild.* London: Leadenhall Press, 1894.

Lombroso, Cesar, *L'homme criminel.* 3 vols. Paris: Alcan, 1895.

Lombroso, Cesar, and Ferrero, William. *The Female Offender.* New York: Appleton, 1899.

London, Jack. *The People of the Abyss.* New York: Macmillan, 1903.

London Committee for Suppression of That Traffic. *Six Years Labour and Sorrow: In Reference to the Traffic in the Souls and Bodies of British Girls, 1885.* London: Dyer, 1885.

Luff, Arthur P. *Text-Book of Forensic Medicine and Toxicology.* London: Longmans, Green, 1895.

Luker, Kristin. *Abortion and the Politics of Motherhood.* Berkeley: University of California Press, 1984.

Lyons, F. S. L. *Charles Stewart Parnell.* London: Collins, 1977.

McClaughry, Robert Wilson. *Signaletic Instruction.* Chicago: Werner, 1896.

McHugh, Paul. *Prostitution and Victorian Social Reform.* London: Croom Helm, 1980.

Mack, Eric. "In Defense of Blackmail." *Philosophical Studies* 41 (1982): 273–78.

Mackail, J. W. *The Life of William Morris.* 2 vols. London: Longmans, 1899.

McLaren, Angus. *Birth Control in Nineteenth Century England.* London: Croom Helm, 1978.

———. *A History of Contraception: From Antiquity to the Present Day.* Oxford: Basil Blackwell, 1990.

———. *Reproductive Rituals: The Perception of Fertility in England from the Sixteenth to the Nineteenth Century.* London: Methuen, 1984.

———. "Women's Work and the Regulation of Family Size: The Question of Abortion in the Nineteenth Century." *History Workshop* 4 (1977): 70–81.

McLynn, Frank. *Crime and Punishment in Eighteenth-Century England.* New York: Routledge, 1989.

MacNaughton, Melville L. *Days of My Years.* London: Edward Arnold, 1914.

Mahood, Linda. *The Magdalenes: Prostitution in the Nineteenth Century.* London: Routledge, 1990.

Mander, Raymond, and Mitchenson, Joe. *The Lost Theatres of London.* New York: Taplinger, 1968.

Marjoribanks, Edward. *The Life of Sir Edward Marshall Hall.* London: Gollancz, 1929.

Martin, J. E. *Greater London: An Industrial Geography.* London: Bell, 1966.

Marx, Roland. *Jack L'Eventreur et les fanatasmes victoriens.* Paris, Editions complexe, 1988.

Masson, Jeffrey Moussaieff. *The Assault on Truth: Freud's Suppression of the Seduction Theory.* New York: Viking, 1985.

Matossian, Mary Kilbourne. "Death in London," *Journal of Interdisciplinary History* 16 (1985): 183–97.

Maudsley, Henry. *The Pathology of Mind*. London: Macmillan, 1879.

———. *Responsibility in Mental Disease*. London: Henry S. King, 1874.

Maugham, W. Somerset. *The Summing Up*. London: Heinemann, 1938.

May, Margaret. "Violence in the Family: An Historical Perspective." In *Violence and the Family*, J. P. Martin, ed., pp. 139–48. Chichester: John Wiley, 1978.

Mayhew, Henry. *London Labour and the London Poor*. 2 vols. London: Griffin, 1861.

Mearns, Andrew. *The Bitter Cry of Outcast London*. Anthony S. Wohl, ed. Leicester: Leicester University Press, 1978 [1883].

Melchiori, Barbara Arnett. *Terrorism in the Late Victorian Novel*. London: Croom Helm, 1985.

Merrick, G. P. *Work among the Fallen as Seen in the Prison Cells*. London: Ward, Lock, 1890.

Meyerowitz, Joanne J. *Women Adrift: Independent Wage Earners in Chicago, 1880–1930*. Chicago: University of Chicago Press, 1988.

Miller, D. H. *The Novel and the Police*. Berkeley: University of California Press, 1988.

Minor, Iris. "Working-Class Women and Matrimonial Law Reform, 1890–1914." In *Ideology and the Labour Movement*, David E. Martin and David Rubinstein, eds., pp. 103–24. London: Croom Helm, 1979.

Mohr, James. *Abortion in America: The Origins and Evolution of National Policy, 1800–1900*. New York: Oxford University Press, 1978.

Moncrief, Frederick. *A Treatise on the Law Relating to Fraud and Misrepresentation*. London: Stevens & Sons, 1891.

Morel, B. A. *Traité des dégénérescences physiques, intellectuelles et morales de l'èspece humaine*. Paris: Baillière, 1857.

Morrison, William Douglas. *Crime and Its Causes*. London: Swan Sonnenschein, 1908 [1891].

Mort, Frank. *Dangerous Sexualities: Medico-Moral Politics in England since 1830*. London: Routledge & Kegan Paul, 1987.

Moscucci, Ornella. *The Science of Woman: Gynaecology and Gender in England, 1800–1929*. Cambridge: Cambridge University Press, 1990.

Munaret, J. M. P. *Du médecin des villes et du médecin de campagne*. Paris: Baillière, 1840.

Murphy, Jeffrie G. "Blackmail: A Preliminary Inquiry." *Monist* 63 (1980): 156–71.

Napheys, George. *Physical Life of Women*. London: Homeopathic Publishing Co., 1869.

———. *The Transmission of Life: Counsels on the Nature and Hygiene of the Masculine Function*. Philadelphia: Fergus, 1872.

Nethercott, Arthur H. *The First Five Lives of Annie Besant*. Chicago: University of Chicago Press, 1960.

Nordau, Max. *Degeneration*. London: Heinemann, 1895.

Norris, Joel, and Birnes, William J. *Serial Murder*. Beverly Hills: Sage, 1988.
Norton, Peter. *The Vital Science: Biology and the Literary Imagination, 1860–1900*. London: George Allen, 1984.
Nye, Robert A. *Crime, Madness and Politics in Modern France: The Medical Concept of National Decline*. Princeton: Princeton University Press, 1984.
O'Brien, Richard Barry. *Life and Letters of Lord Russell of Killowen*. London: Nelson, 1901.
Olasky, Mervin N. *The Press and Abortion, 1838–1988*. London: Erlbaum, 1988.
Oldham, James C. "On Pleading the Belly: A History of the Jury of Matrons." *Criminal Justice History* 6 (1985): 1–64.
Oliver, Hermia. *The International Anarchist Movement in Late Victorian England*. London: Croom Helm, 1983.
Ousby, Ian. *Bloodhounds of Heaven: The Detective in English Fiction from Godwin to Doyle*. Cambridge, Mass.: Harvard University Press, 1976.
Owen, David. *The Government of Victorian London, 1855–1889*. Cambridge: Belknap Press, 1982.
Palmer, Stanley H. *Police and Protest in England and Ireland, 1780–1850*. Cambridge: Cambridge University Press, 1988.
Papke, David Ray. *Framing the Criminal: Crime, Cultural Work and the Loss of Critical Perspective, 1830–1900*. New York: Archon, 1987.
Parent-Duchâtelet, Alexandre. *De la prostitution dans la ville de Paris*. Paris: Baillière, 1836.
Parker, Graham. "The Prisoner in the Box: The Making of the Criminal Evidence Act, 1898." In *Legal and Social Change in British History*, J. A. Guy and H. G. Beale, eds., pp. 156–75. London: Royal Historical Society, 1984.
Parry, Leonard A., ed. *Trial of Dr. Smethurst*. Toronto: Canada Law Book Co., 1931.
Parssinen, Terry M. *Secret Passion, Secret Remedies: Narcotic Drugs in British Society, 1820–1930*. Philadelphia: Institute for the Study of Human Issues, 1983.
Paterson, Alexander. *Across the Bridges, or Life by the South London River-Side*. London: Edward Arnold, 1912.
Pearson, E. S. "Karl Pearson: An Appreciation of Some Aspects of His Life and Work." *Biometrika* 28 (1936): 193–257.
Pearson, Karl. *The Life of Francis Galton*. 4 vols. Cambridge: Cambridge University Press, 1914–30.
Perrin, D. J. D. "Thomas Neill Cream." *St. Thomas's Hospital Gazette* 47 (1949): 229–32.
Pick, Daniel. *Faces of Degeneration: A European Disorder, c. 1848–c. 1918*. Cambridge: Cambridge University Press, 1989.
Pierce, Bessie Louise. *A History of Chicago*. 2 vols. Chicago: University of Chicago Press, 1957.
Pomeroy, H. S. *The Ethics of Marriage*. New York: Funk & Wagnalls, 1888.
Porter, Bernard. "Origins of Britain's Political Police." *Warwick Working Paper in Social History* 3 (1985).

————. *The Origins of the Vigilant State: The London Metropolitan Police Special Branch before the First World War*. London: Weidenfeld & Nicolson, 1987.

————. *Plots and Paranoia: A History of Political Espionage in Britain, 1790–1988*. London: Unwin & Hyman, 1989.

Porter, Roy. "A Touch of Danger: The Man Midwife as Sexual Predator." In *Sexual Underworlds of the Enlightenment*, G. S. Rousseau and Roy Porter, eds., pp. 206–232. Manchester: Manchester University Press, 1987.

Quayle, John. *The Slow Burning Fuse: The Lost History of British Anarchists*. London: Paladin, 1978.

Quinton, R. F. *Crime and Criminals, 1876–1910*. London: Longmans, Green, 1910.

Radford, Thomas. *The Value of Embryonic and Foetal Life, Legally, Socially, and Obstetrically Considered*. London: British Record of Obstetrics, 1848.

Radzinowicz, Leon. *A History of English Criminal Law*. 5 vols. London: Steven, 1978.

Radzinowicz, Leon, and Hood, Roger. "Incapacitating the Habitual Criminal: The English Experience." *Michigan Law Review* 78 (1980): 1305–89.

Reckless, Walter C. *Vice in Chicago*. Chicago: University of Chicago Press, 1933.

Reese, John. *Text-Book of Medical Jurisprudence and Toxicology*. Philadelphia: Blakiston, 1906.

Reeves, M. S. Pember. *Family Life on a Pound a Week*. London: Fabian Society Tract 162, 1912.

Rentoul, Robert Reid. *Proposed Sterilization of Certain Mental and Physical Degenerates*. London: Walter Scott, 1903.

Ressler, Robert K., Burgess, Ann W., and Douglas, John E. *Sexual Homicide: Patterns and Motives*. Lexington: Heath, 1988.

Richardson, Joanna. *The Pre-Eminent Victorian: A Study of Tennyson*. London: Cape, 1962.

Richardson, Ruth. *Death, Dissection and the Destitute*. London: Routledge & Kegan Paul, 1987.

Richman, Martin. *Alfred Russell Wallace*. Boston: Twayne, 1981.

Roberts, Helen. "Trap the Ripper." *New Society* (6 April 1978): 11–12.

Roberts, Robert. *The Classic Slum: Salford Life in the First Quarter of the Century*. Manchester: Manchester University Press, 1971.

Rose, Kenneth. *King George V*. London: Weideneld & Nicolson, 1983.

Rose, Lionel. *The Massacre of the Innocents: Infanticide in Britain, 1800–1939*. London: Routledge & Kegan Paul, 1986.

Rosen, Ruth. *The Lost Sisterhood: Prostitution in America, 1900–1918*. Baltimore: Johns Hopkins University Press, 1982.

Rosenberg, Charles E. *The Trial of the Assassin Guiteau*. Chicago: University of Chicago Press, 1978.

Ross, Ellen. "Fierce Questions and Taunts: Married Life in Working-Class London, 1870–1914." *Feminist Studies* 8 (1982): 575–602.

Roughead, William. *Bad Companions*. Edinburgh: Green, 1930.

Roughead, William, ed. *Trial of Dr. Pritchard*. London: Hodge, 1906.

Royden, A. Maude, ed. *Downward Paths: An Inquiry into the Causes Which Contribute to the Making of the Prostitute.* London: Bell, 1916.

Rumbelow, Donald. *The Complete Jack the Ripper.* London: W. H. Allen, 1975.

Russell, Bertrand, and Russell, Patricia, eds. *The Amberley Papers.* London: Hogarth, 1937.

Russell, Norman. *The Novelist and Mammon: Literary Responses to the World of Commerce in the Nineteenth Century.* Oxford: Clarendon, 1986.

Ryan, William B. *Infanticide: Its Law, Prevalence, Prevention and History.* London: Churchill, 1862.

Rylands, L. Gordon. *Crime: Its Cause and Remedy.* London: Fisher Unwin, 1889.

Savage, Gail. "The Willful Communication of a Loathsome Disease: Marital Conflict and Venereal Disease in Victorian England." *Victorian Studies* 34 (1990): 35–54

Schur, Edwin M. *Crimes without Victims.* Englewood Cliffs: Prentice-Hall, 1965.

———. *Our Criminal Society.* Englewood Cliffs: Prentice-Hall, 1969.

Scott, Chris. *Jack.* Toronto: Macmillan, 1988.

Scott, J. W. Robertson. *The Life and Death of a Newspaper.* London: Methuen, 1952.

Sears, Donald J. *To Kill Again: The Motivation and Development of Serial Murder.* Wilmington: SR Books, 1991.

Shanley, Mary Lyndon. *Feminism, Marriage and the Law in Victorian England, 1850–1895.* Princeton: Princeton University Press, 1989.

Sharpe, J. A. "The History of Violence in England: Some Observations." *Past and Present* 108 (1985) 206–15.

Sheppard, Francis. *London 1808–1870: The Infernal Wen.* London: Secker & Warburg, 1971.

Shore, W. Teignmouth, ed. *Trial of Thomas Neill Cream.* London: Hodge, 1923.

Short, K. R. M. *The Dynamite War: Irish Bombers in Victorian Britain.* Atlantic Hylands, N.J.: Humanities Press, 1979.

Shorter, Edward. "On Writing the History of Rape." *Signs* 3 (1977–78): 471–82.

Shortt, S. E. D. *Victorian Lunacy: Richard M. Bucke and the Practice of Late Nineteenth-Century Psychiatry.* Cambridge: Cambridge University Press, 1986.

Showalter, Elaine. *The Female Malady: Women, Madness and English Culture, 1830–1980.* New York: Pantheon, 1985.

———. *Sexual Anarchy: Gender and Culture at the Fin de Siècle.* New York: Viking, 1990.

Sigsworth, E. M., and Wyke, T. S. "A Study of Victorian Prostitution and Venereal Disease." In *Suffer and Be Still: Women in the Victorian Age,* Martha Vicinus, ed., pp. 77–99. Bloomington: Indiana University Press, 1972.

Sims, George R. *My Life: Sixty Years' Recollections of Bohemian London.* London: Nash, 1917.

Simpson, Brian. *Cannibalism and the Common Law: The Story of the Tragic Last Voyage of the Mignonette and the Strange Legal Proceedings to Which It Gave Rise.* Chicago: University of Chicago Press, 1984.

Sindall, Robert. "Middle-Class Crime in Nineteenth Century England." *Criminal Justice History* 4 (1983): 23–40.

Smith, Frederick J. *Lectures on Medical Jurisprudence and Toxicology*. London: Churchill, 1900.

Smith, Henry. *A Plea for the Unborn*. London: Watts, 1897.

Smith, Joan. *Misogynies*. London: Faber & Faber, 1989.

Smith, Patterson. "Books on the American Serial Killer." *Bookman's Yearbook*, 1989–90, pp. 9–18.

Smith, Roger. *Trial by Medicine: Insanity and Responsibility in Victorian Trials*. Edinburgh: Edinburgh University Press, 1981.

Smith, Sydney, ed. *Taylor's Principles and Practices of Medical Jurisprudence*. 2 vols. London: Churchill, 1951.

Smith-Rosenberg, Carroll. *Disorderly Conduct: Visions of Gender in Victorian America*. New York: Knopf, 1985.

Soloway, Richard. *Demography and Degeneration: Eugenics and the Declining Birthrate in Twentieth-Century Britain*. Chapel Hill: University of North Carolina Press, 1990.

Spierenburg, Pieter. *The Spectacle of Suffering: Executions and the Evolution of Repression from a Preindustrial Metropolis to the European Experience*. Cambridge: Cambridge University Press, 1984.

Stafford, David A. T. "Spies and Gentlemen: The Birth of the British Spy Novel, 1893–1914." *Victorian Studies* 24 (1981): 489–509.

Stall, Sylvanus. *What a Young Man Ought to Know*. Toronto: Briggs, 1897.

Starrett, Vincent. "The Chicago Career of Dr. Cream—1880." In *Chicago Murders*, Sewell P. Wright, ed., pp. 14–44. New York: Duell, Sloane & Pearce, 1945.

Stevenson, Robert Louis. *Strange Case of Dr. Jekyll and Mr. Hyde*. London: Longmans, 1886.

Stevenson, Thomas. *The Principles and Practices of Medical Jurisprudence*. 2 vols. London: Churchill, 1883.

——. *The Principles and Practices of Medical Jurisprudence*. 2 vols. London: Churchill, 1894.

Stoker, Bram. *Dracula*. London: Constable, 1897.

Stone, Lawrence. "Interpersonal Violence in English Society, 1300–1980." *Past and Present* 101 (1983): 206–15.

——. *Road to Divorce, 1530–1987*. Oxford: Oxford University Press, 1990.

Storch, Robert D. "Police Control of Street Prostitution in Victorian London: A Study in Contexts of Police Action." In *Police and Society*, David H. Bailey, ed., pp. 49–72. Beverly Hills: Sage, 1977.

Storer, Horatio R. *On Criminal Abortion: Its Nature, Its Evidence, and Its Law*. Boston: Little, Brown, 1868.

Stubbs, Patricia. *Women and Fiction: Feminism and the Novel, 1880–1920*. New York: Barnes & Noble, 1979.

Styrap, Jukes de. *The Young Practioner*. London: H. K. Lewis, 1890.

Sweeney, John. *At Scotland Yard*. London: Grant Richards, 1904.

Symons, Julian. *Bloody Murder: From the Detective Story to the Crime Novel*. London: Penguin, 1974.

Tait, Lawson. *Diseases of Women and Abdominal Surgery*. Leicester: Richardson, 1889.

———. *The Uselessness of Vivisection*. London: Victoria Street Society, 1882.

Taylor, Alfred S. *A Manual of Medical Jurisprudence*. New York: Lea, 1897.

Taylor, John W. *On the Diminishing Birth Rate*. London: British Gynaecological Society, 1904.

Thane, Pat. "Late Victorian Women." In *Later Victorian Britain, 1867–1900*, T. R. Gourvish and Alan O'Day, eds., pp. 175–208. London: Macmillan, 1988.

Thiénard, Antonin. *L'assassinat*. Paris: Girard and Brière, 1892.

Thomas, James E. *The English Prison Officer since 1850: A Study in Conflict*. London: Routledge & Kegan Paul, 1972.

Thompson, Laurence. *The Enthusiasts: A Biography of John and Katherine Bruce Glasier*. London: Gollancz, 1971.

Todd, John. *Serpents in the Doves' Nest*. Boston: Lee & Shepard, 1867.

Trudd, Andrea. *Domestic Crime and the Victorian Novel*. New York: St. Martin's, 1989.

Trudgill, Eric. *Madonnas and Magdalens: The Origins and Development of Victorian Sexual Attitudes*. London: Heinemann, 1976.

Trumbach, Randolph. "London's Sodomites: Homosexual Behavior and Western Culture in the Eighteenth Century." *Journal of Social History* 2 (1977): 1–33.

———. *Sodomy Trials: Seven Documents*. New York: Garland, 1986.

Vice Commission of Chicago. *The Social Evil in Chicago*. Chicago: Gunthorpe-Warren, 1911.

Vicinus, Martha. *Independent Women: Work and Community for Single Women, 1850–1920*. Chicago: University of Chicago Press, 1985.

Villey, Raymond. *Histoire du secret médical*. Paris: Seghers, 1986.

Vincent, William. "The Whitechaple Murders." *Police Review*, 6 January 1978, pp. 16–17.

Walford, Edward. *Old and New London*. London: Cassell, 1872–78.

Walker, Nigel. *Crime and Insanity in England*. Edinburgh: Edinburgh University Press, 1968.

Walkowitz, Judith R. "Jack the Ripper and the Myth of Male Violence." *Feminist Studies* 8 (1982): 543–75.

———. *Prostitution and Victorian Society: Women, Class, and the State*. New York: Cambridge University Press, 1980.

Watson, Colin. *Snobbery with Violence: Crime Stories and Their Audience*. New York: St. Martins, 1971.

Watson, Eric R., ed. *Adolph Beck, 1877–1904*. Edinburgh: Hodge, 1925.

Weber, Eugen. *France, Fin-de-siècle*. Cambridge, Mass.: Harvard University Press, 1988.

Weeks, Jeffrey. *Coming Out: Homosexual Politics in Britain from the Nineteenth Century to the Present*. London: Quartet, 1977.

Wells, H. G. *The Island of Dr. Moreau*. London: Heinemann, 1896.

———. *Mankind in the Making*. London: Chapman & Hall, 1903.

Welsh, Alexander. *George Eliot and Blackmail.* Cambridge, Mass.: Harvard University Press, 1985.
Wensley, Frederick Porter. *Detective Days.* London: Cassell, 1931.
West, D. J. *Sexual Crimes and Confrontations: A Study of Victims and Offenders.* Aldershot: Gower, 1987.
White, Arnold. *Efficiency and Empire.* Brighton: Harvester Press, 1973 [1901].
————. *The Problems of a Great City.* London: Remington, 1886.
White, H. P. *A Regional History of the Railways of Great Britain,* vol. 3: *Greater London.* Newton Abbot: David & Charles, 1963.
White, Luise. "Prostitutes, Reformers and Historians." *Criminal Justice History* 6 (1985): 201–281.
Whittington-Egan, Richard. *A Casebook on Jack the Ripper.* London: Wildy, 1975.
Wiener, Martin J. *Reconstructing the Criminal: Culture, Law and Policy in England, 1830–1914.* Cambridge: Cambridge University Press, 1990.
Wilde, Oscar. "Pen, Pencil and Poison." In *The Annotated Oscar Wilde,* H. Montgomery Hyde, ed., pp. 383–97. London: Orbis, 1982.
Williams, Sydney Edward. *Kerr on Fraud and Mistake.* London: Sweet & Maxwell, 1929.
Wilson, Colin, and Pitman, Patricia. *Encyclopedia of Murder.* London: Barker, 1961.
Wilson, Colin, and Seaman, Donald. *The Serial Killers.* London: W. H. Allen, 1990.
Wilson, Patrick. *Murderess.* London: Michael Joseph, 1971.
Winder, W. H. D. "The Development of Blackmail." *Modern Law Review* 5 (1941): 21–49.
Winslow, Forbes. *The Plea of Insanity in Criminal Cases.* London: Renshaw, 1843.
Wohl, Anthony S. *The Eternal Slum: Housing and Social Policy in Victorian London.* Montreal: McGill-Queens, 1977.
Wolfe, Charlotte. *Magnus Hirschfeld: A Portrait of a Pioneer in Sexology.* London: Quartet Books, 1986.
Woodham-Smith, Cecil. *Florence Nightingale, 1820–1910.* London: Constable, 1950.
Zangwill, Israel. *The Big Ben Mystery.* London: Heinemann, 1913 [1903].

INDEX